# Going Pro for $200

## Revisiting the Nikon D1

### Expanded Editon

Shawn M. Tomlinson's
Guide to Photography
Volumes 5

by

shawn m tomlinson

2015

# Going Pro for $200

## *Revisiting the Nikon D1*
### *Expanded Edition*

*Shawn M. Tomlinson's*
*Guide to Photography*
*Volume 5*

ISBN: 978-1-329-63450-3

Cover photo © 2014 by
Gary W. Ziroli

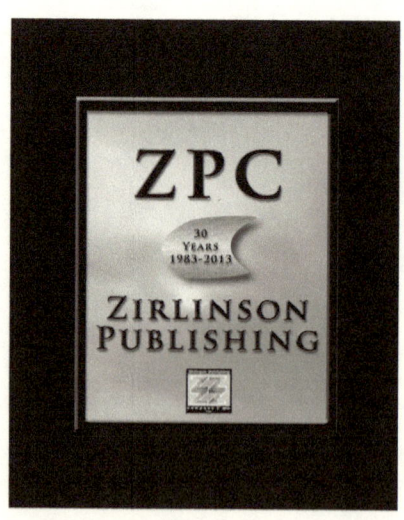

# Contents

# A Note on the Expanded Edition

This is the second edition of this book.

After the first edition appeared as an eBook, I started to prepare the print editions and realized more should be said about the Nikon D1.

Of course, anyone who knows me knows I could fill a book twice this big about virtually any camera I use. Whether all of that would be useful is another story.

Still, I think that if you are looking to buy what amounts to an ancient professional digital single-lens reflex camera such as the Nikon D1 — or its sequels, the Nikon D1x and D1H — it makes sense to have as much information about those cameras as possible.

Very few people want to talk about older cameras — unless they are classic film cameras — but I think there is a lot of life left in these beasts.

I hadn't used the D1 much recently because I shoot mostly with the Nikon D2x and Nikon D800e, but today, I took out the venerable D1 and it still feels so good in my hands.

I also was surprised looking through my files at how many photographs I have shot with the D1 since it came into my possession in the spring of 2014. And, once I got the hang of it, those images look really good.

I know the Nikon D1 will serve you well, as it has me. This book is designed to get you started with it and to enjoy the nostalgia of the early days of DSLRs.

*— Shawn M. Tomlinson, Oct. 19, 2015, Ballston Lake*

# Note

Note: The Nikon D1's Aperture-priority mode is designated as "A" on the DSLR. There is no "Auto" Mode on the D1, and I never use this mode anyway.

Note: The captions for the photos give the location, date and camera data for each image. What it means is:

Nikon D1, 80mm, 1/250, f/9, ISO 200, P, pattern metering
© 2014, 2015 by Shawn M. Tomlinson

**Camera: Nikon D1**
**Focal Length: 80mm**
**Shutter Speed: 1/250**
**Aperture: f/9**
**ISO sensitivity: 200**
**Mode: P (program)**
**Metering: Pattern**

**Other Modes are:**
**S: shutter priority**
**A: aperture priority**
**M: manual**

# Going Pro for $200

## Revisiting the Nikon D1

*Shawn M. Tomlinson's*
*Guide to Photography*
*Volume 5*

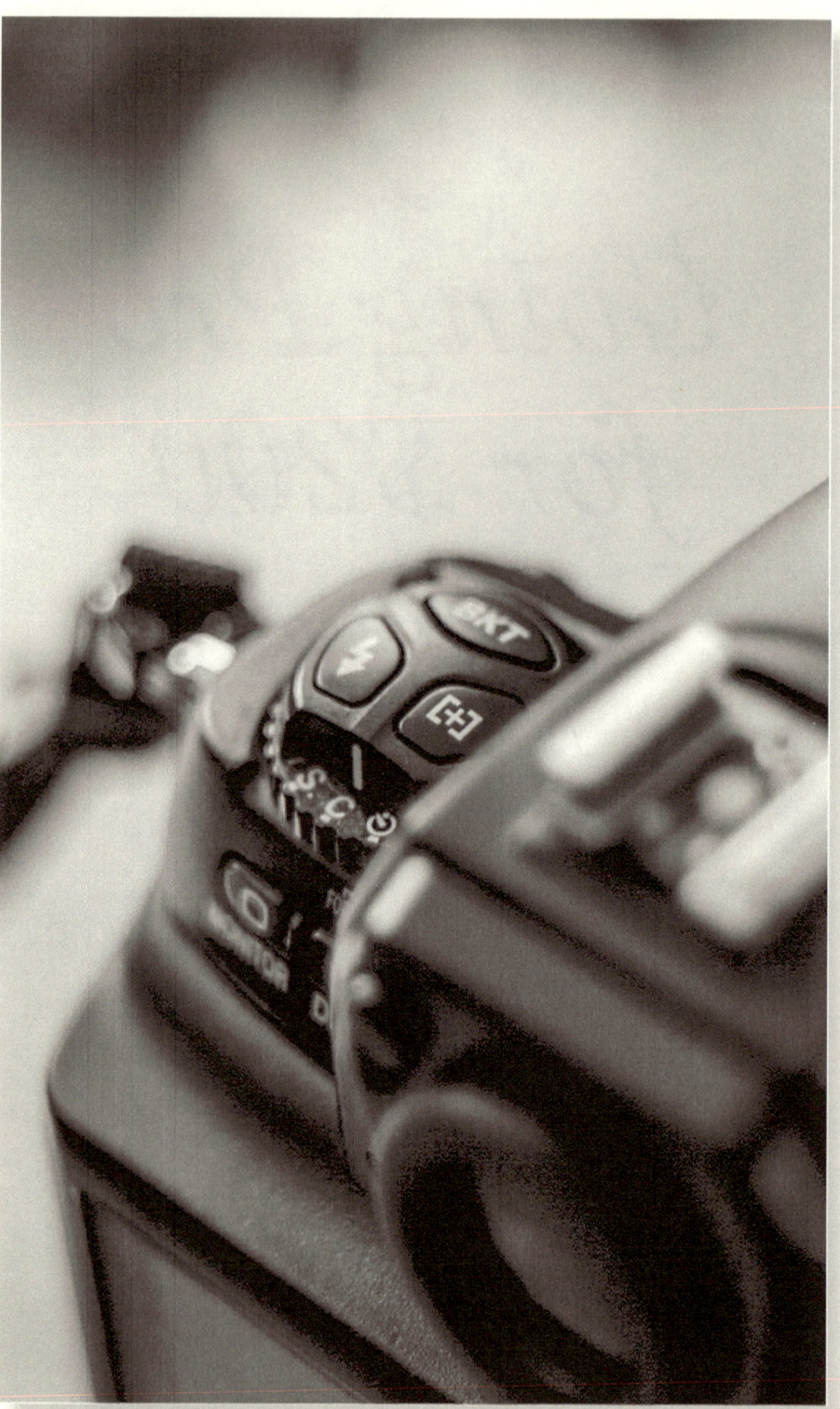

# First Words

You've heard about the wonders of the professional digital single-lens reflex cameras, how they handle, how they feel in your hands.

You've looked at Internet reviews and sample images.

You've *oooed* and *ahhhed* at every curve, button and dial on the pro DSLRs.

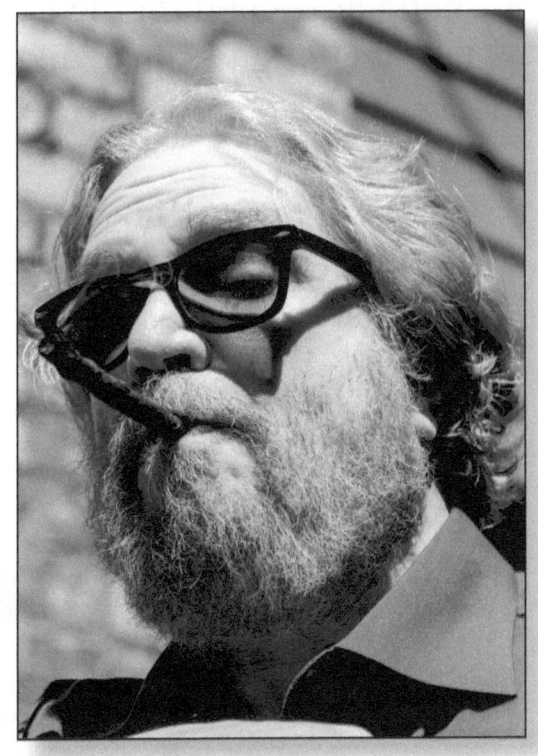

Shawn M. Tomlinson,
Saratoga Springs, NY, July 11, 2015.
© 2015 Gary W. Ziroli

Let's face it: you've drooled.

So have I.

But those prices.

Yikes.

Never did you think as a photographer enthusiast or wedding photographer or weekend photographer that a pro DSLR — a Canon 1Dx, a Nikon D3x or a

Nikon D4s — was within reach.

The price tags on these beauties range from a mere $6,500 for the D4s to $6,800 for the 1Dx and a whopping $8,000 for the D3X.

OK, well, I guess that Nikon D3300 will be nice, too, or that Canon EOS Rebel...

NO!

I will NOT succumb!

I will not walk around carrying a DSLR that says "Rebel" on it.

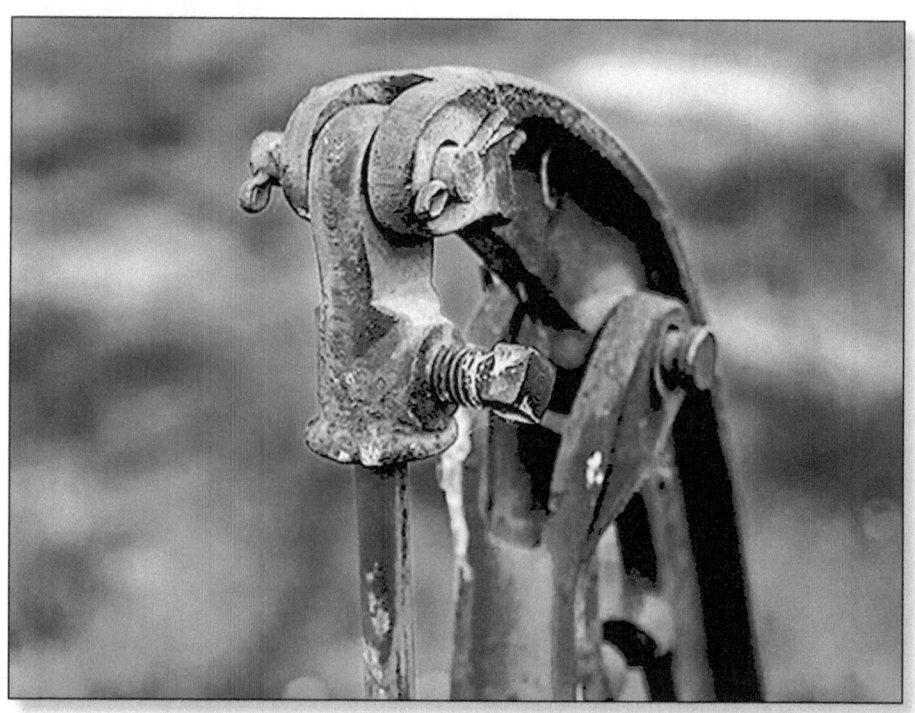

Broadalbin-Mayfield Rural Cemetery, Broadalbin, NY, June 15, 2014
Nikon D1, 52mm, 1/125, f/4.8, ISO 200, Av, pattern metering
© 2014, 2015 by Shawn M. Tomlinson

NEVER!

Don't worry.

You don't have to, either.

In fact, you can put your hands on a professional DSLR body and a lens for around $200 if you really want to know what all the fuss is about.

No, I'm not talking about a Nikon D4s that, ah, "fell off a truck" somewhere.

I'm talking about the very first, ground-up DSLR for the professional market.

The Nikon D1.

Many may scoff, but there are good reasons to acquire this pro DSLR that once cost $6,000 when

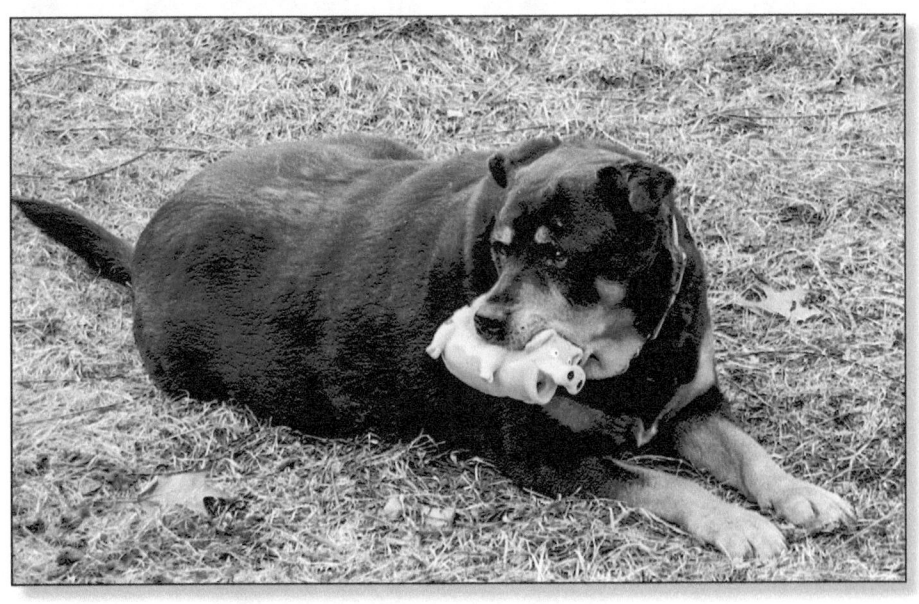

Baby, Ballston Lake, NY, Jan. 1, 2015
Nikon D1, 80mm, 1/125, f/5.6, ISO 400, Av, pattern metering
© 2015 by Shawn M. Tomlinson

it was new in 1999. That's $8,551.01 in 2015 dollars, according to the U.S. Bureau of Labor Statistics.

The first reason is you can get one now for around $100.

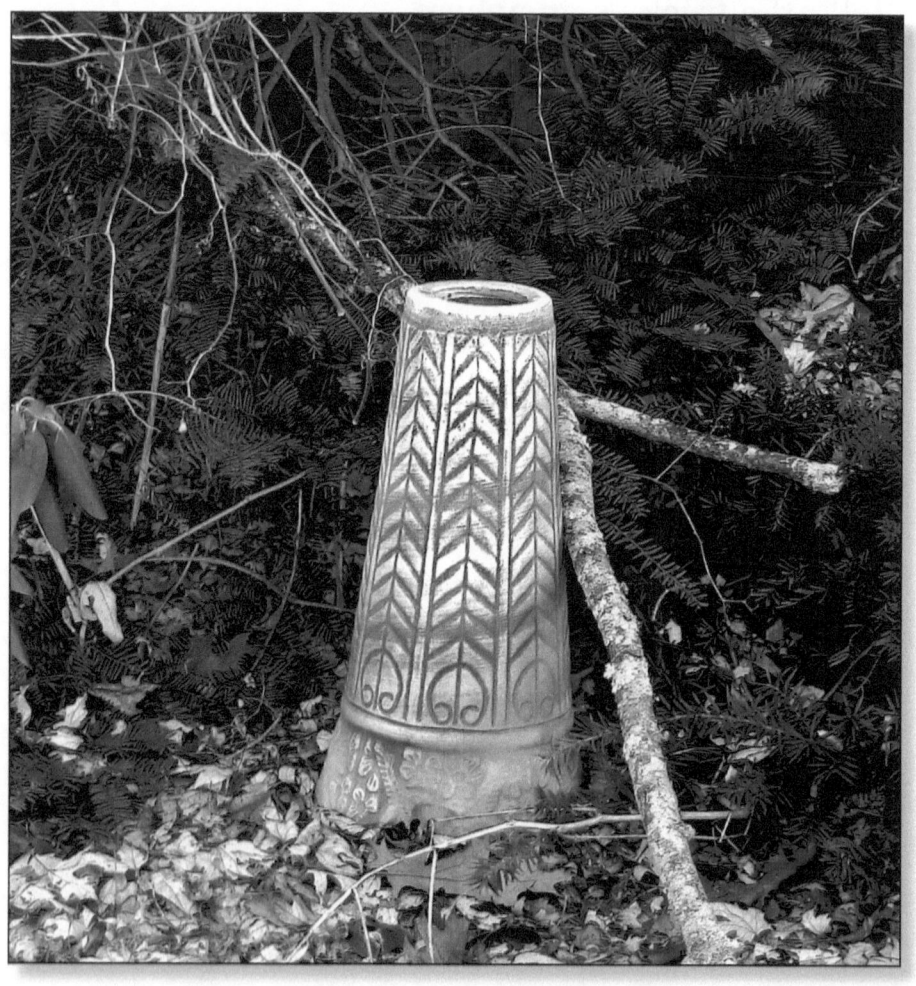

Ballston Lake, NY, April 2, 2014
Nikon D1, 80mm, 1/30, f/5.6, ISO 200, P, pattern
© 2015 Shawn M. Tomlinson

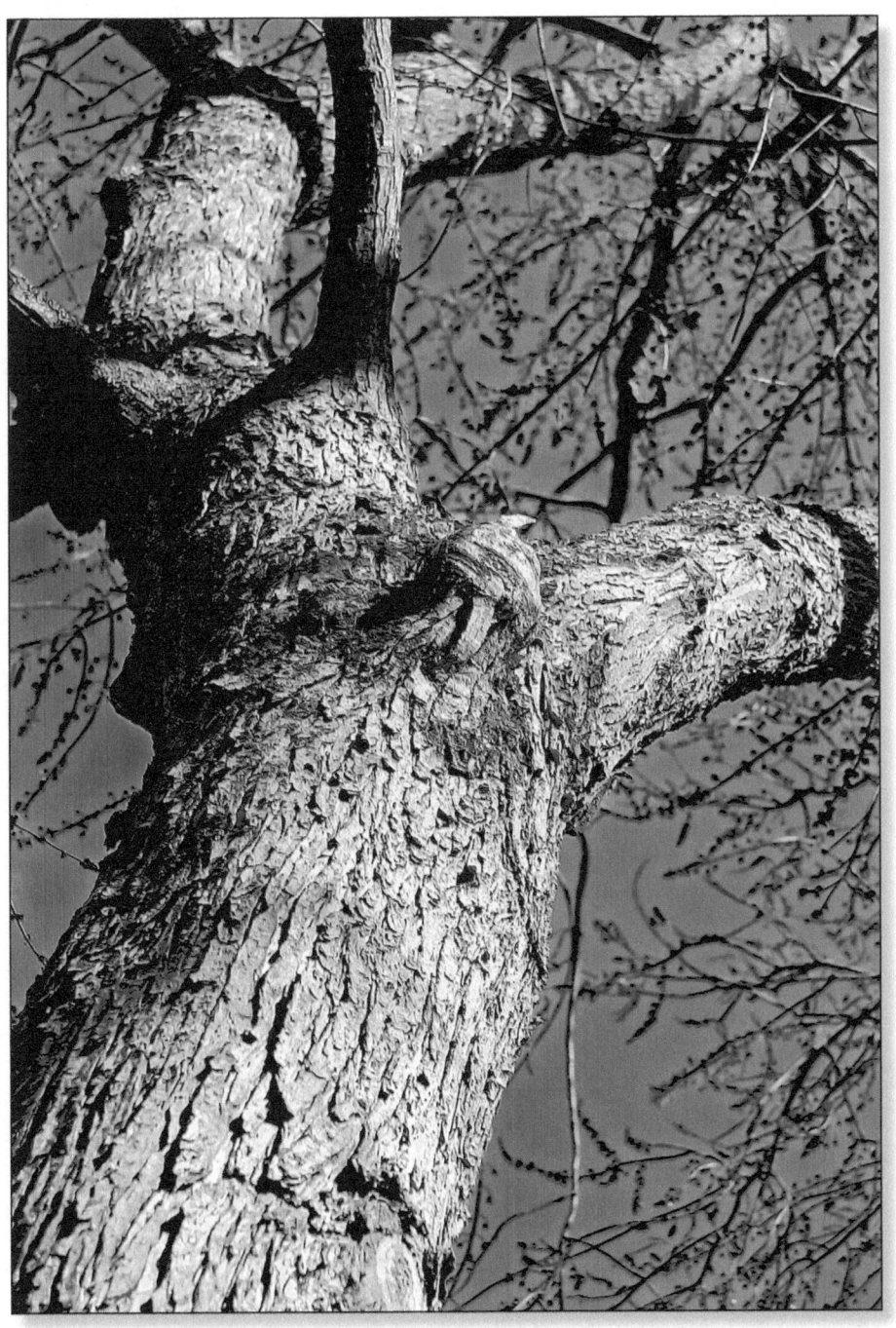

Ballston Lake, NY, April 2, 2014
Nikon D1, 70mm, 1/200, f/7.6, ISO 200, P, pattern
© 2015 Shawn M. Tomlinson

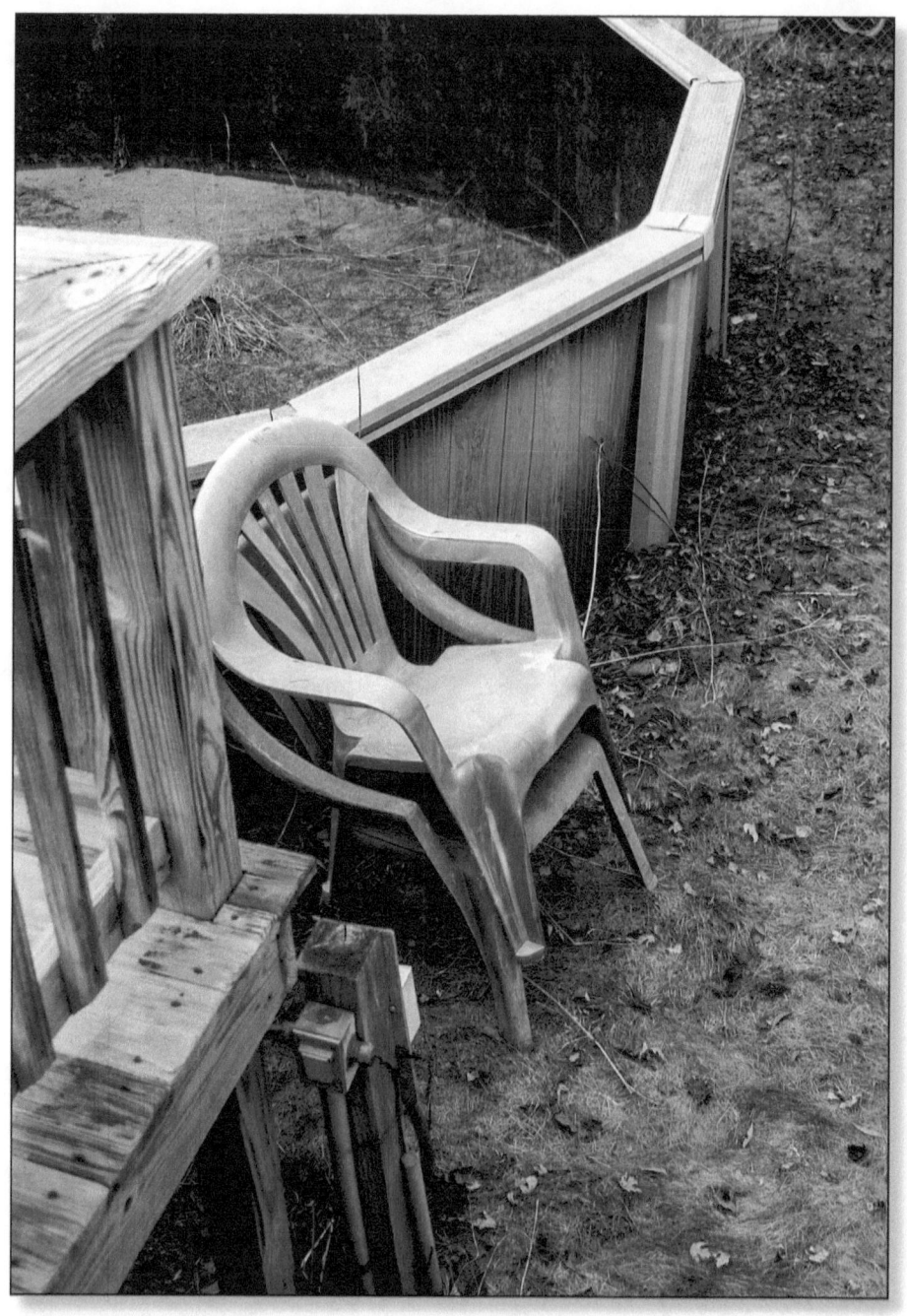

Ballston Lake, NY, Jan. 1, 2015
Nikon D1, 28mm, 1/500, f/3.5, ISO 400, Av pattern metering
© 2015 by Shawn M. Tomlinson

# Part 1
# The Pro 'Feel'

In the film single-lens reflex days, as now in the DSLR days, the professional cameras had a solid, sturdy, beat-hell-out-of-it-all-day-and-it-works-fine build.

They were built, at least by the 1970s, to feel solid, strong and good in your hands.

And they do.

The best feeling, best looking workhorse pro

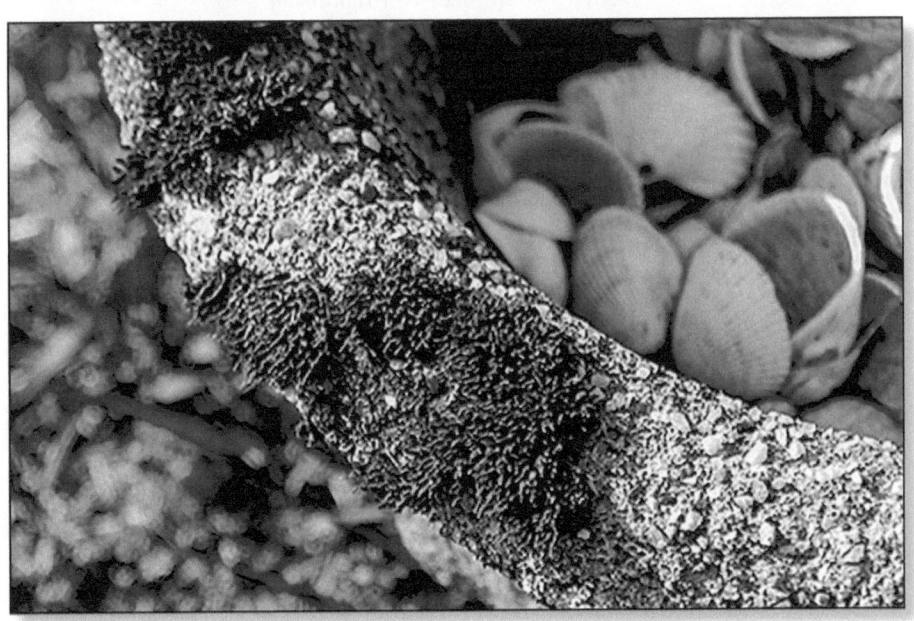

Broadalbin-Mayfield Rural Cemetery, Broadalbin, NY, June 15, 2014
Nikon D1, 82mm, 1/250, f/5.6, ISO 200, Av, pattern metering
© 2014, 2015 by Shawn M. Tomlinson

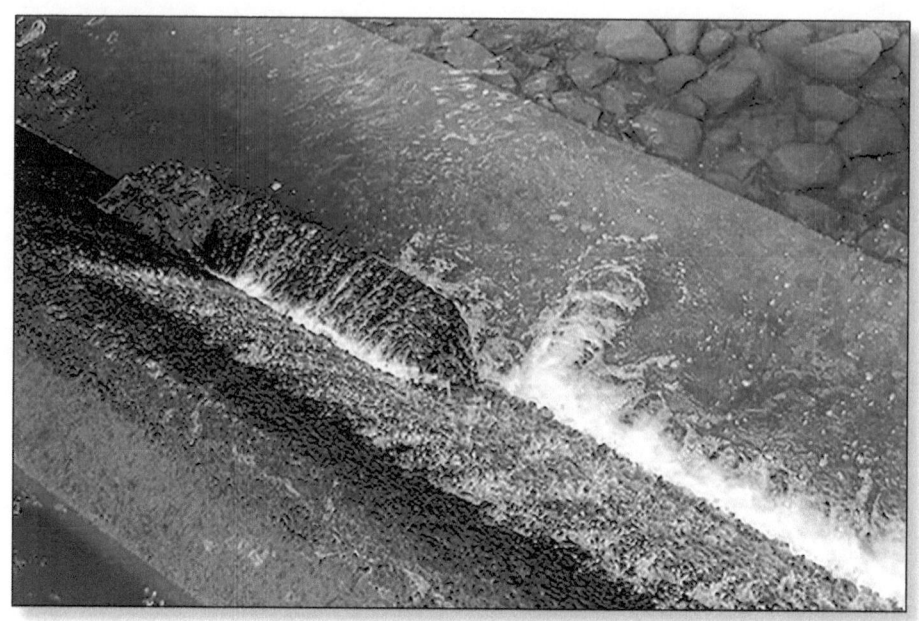

Indian Kill Nature Preserve, Glenville, NY, July 21, 2014
Nikon D1, 28mm, 1/125, f/3.5, ISO 200, Av pattern metering
© 2014, 2015 by Shawn M. Tomlinson

SLR was the Nikon F4s.

Sure, the F5 still gets all the accolades, but it was an uglier, heavier version of the elegant, sleek, redesigned-from-scratch-practically F4s.

This film SLR, the F4S, is the closest thing to a modern DSLR you can hold that takes fantastic images on film.

It looks and feels a lot like a modern pro DSLR.

I like the look and feel of it so much, I often have dreamed about putting the guts of a D1 or D1x or D2x inside the F4s somehow and getting the best of both worlds.

The Nikon F4s was the first pro SLR that had a

film motor winder built in. Previously, all such motor winders were add-on optional features.

A motor winder was an essential accessory for shooting fast because it advanced the film for you.

If you didn't have one, you still had to manually wind the film to the next frame

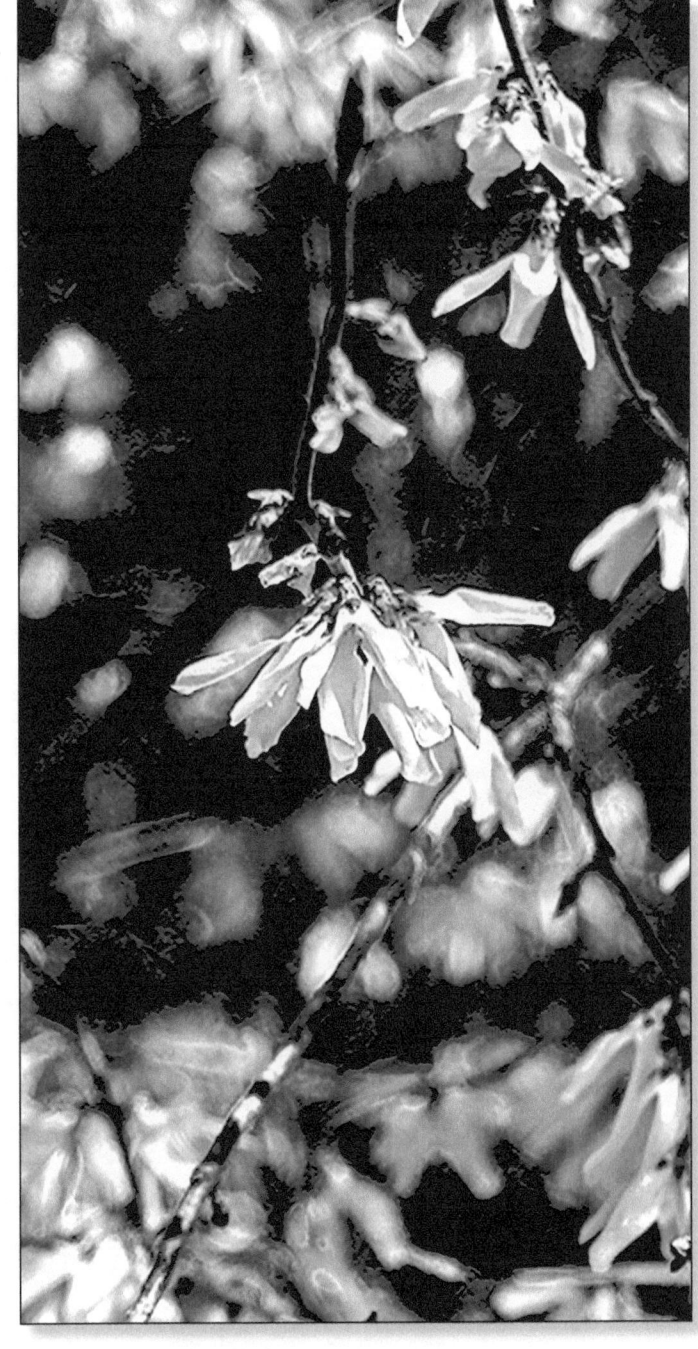

Ballston Lake, NY, May 1, 2014
Nikon D1, 66mm, 1/1500, f/5.3, ISO 200, Av, spot metering
© 2014, 2015 by Shawn M. Tomlinson

every time you shot a photo.

The motor winder added a lot of weight and usually needed a lot of batteries to operate.

The Nikon F4 — without the "s" — had not film advance lever to manually move the film to the next frame.

Every time you shot an image, the camera

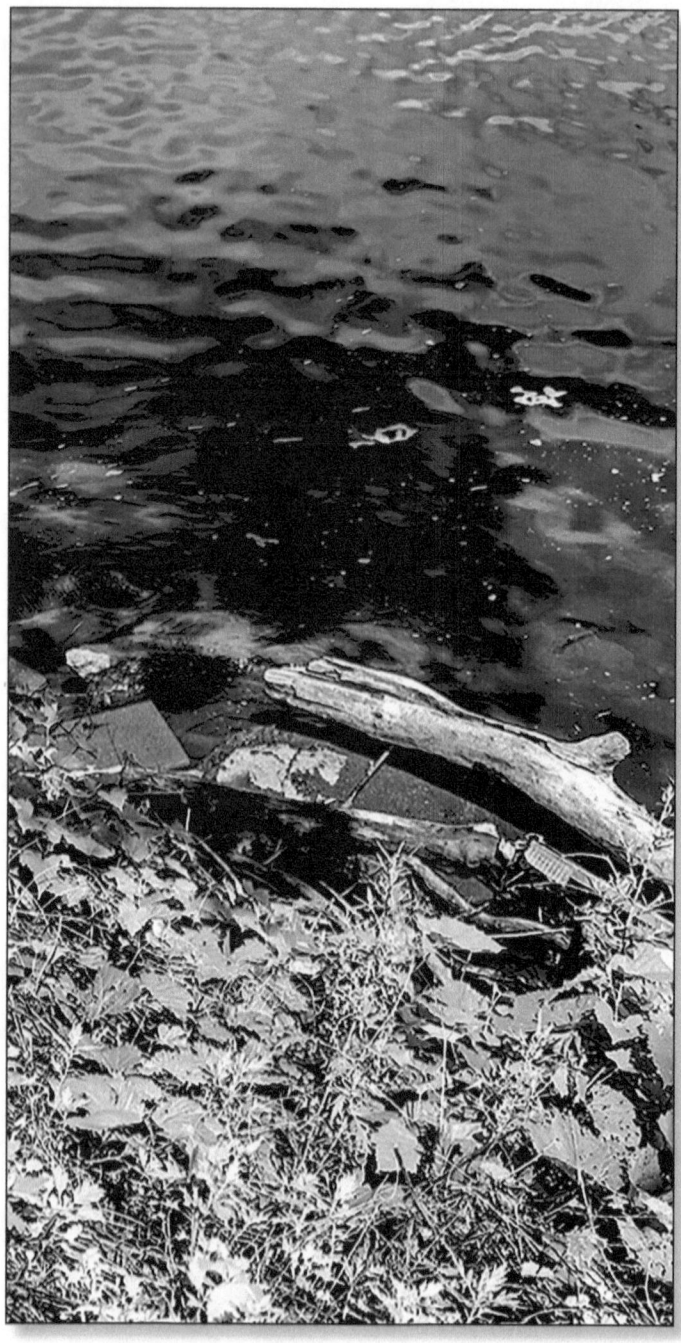

Kiwanis Park, Rotterdam Junction, NY, July 29, 2014
Nikon D1, 35mm, 1/1000, f/3.8, ISO 200, Av, pattern metering
© 2014, 2015 by Shawn M. Tomlinson

moved the film ahead by one or multiple frames, depending upon what you set on the drive dial.

The F4 was about the same size as Nikon F3 and F2, its predecessors.

You could, as I said, add motor winders to the F2 and F3, but they were big and clunky. The one for the F3 is at an odd angle to the F3 camera body, designed, I suppose, to feel better in your hands.

It doesn't, at least in my hands. It feels awkward.

With the winder built into the F4, it made the camera smaller and lighter, but because it ran on AA batteries, it needed frequent battery changes and it needed the batteries to take photos, unlike its

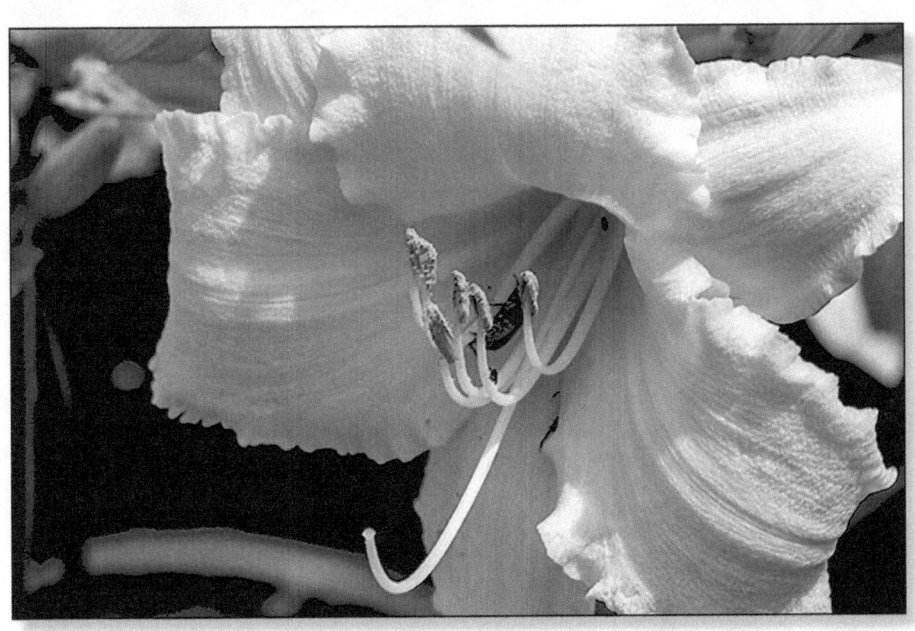

Saratoga Springs, NY, July 8, 2014
Nikon D1, 80mm, 1/250, f/9, ISO 200, P, pattern metering
© 2014, 2015 by Shawn M. Tomlinson

predecessors. The F2 and F3 only needed batteries for the light meter, so many photographers didn't trust the Nikon F4.

Hence, the battery grip was introduced by Nikon — which then called the camera the F4s with the grip attached — and the model for future SLRs and

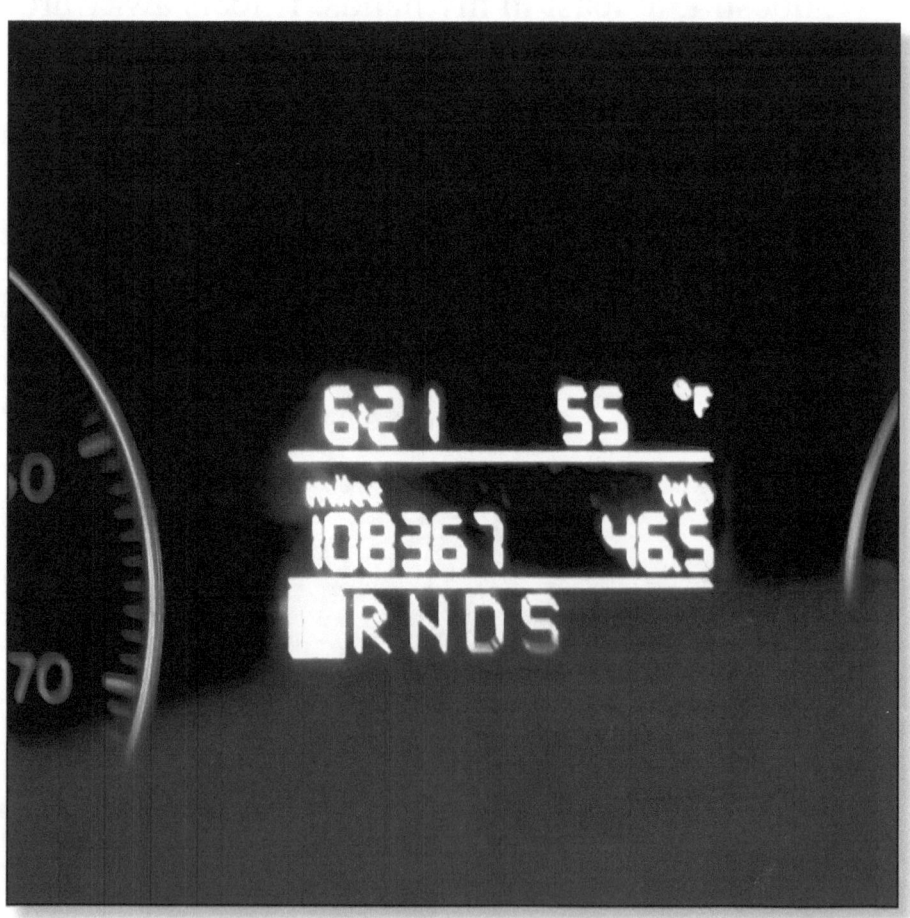

Glenville, NY, April 2, 2014
Nikon D1, 75mm, 1/10, f/5.6, ISO 200, P, pattern
© 2015 Shawn M. Tomlinson

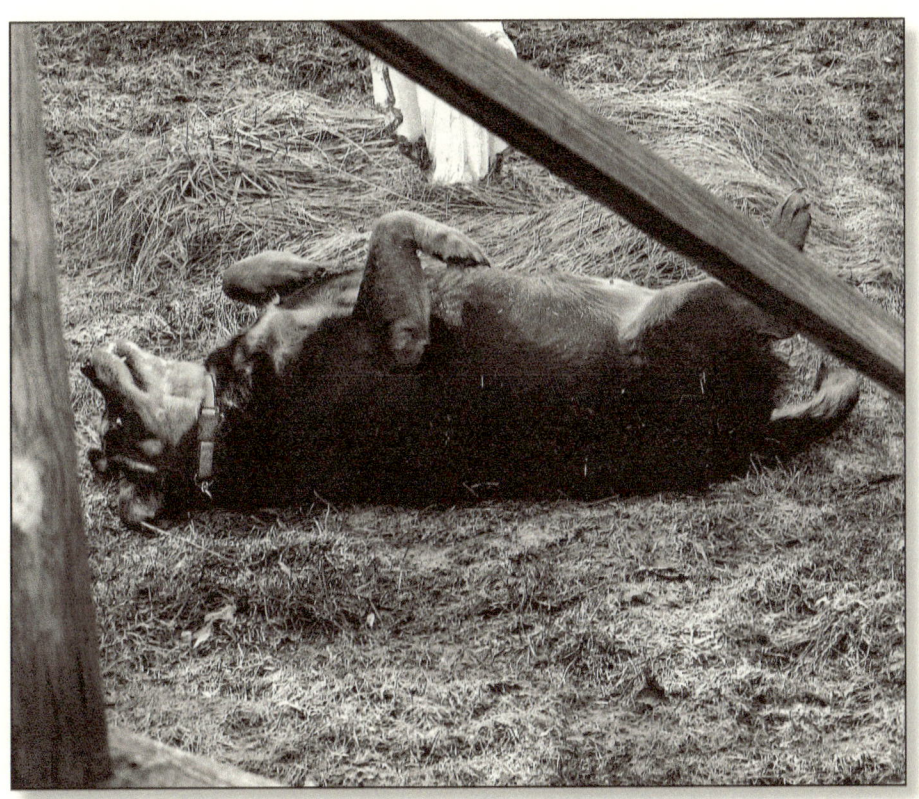

Baby, Ballston Lake, NY, April 3, 2014
Nikon D1, 80mm, 1/350, f/10, ISO 200, P, pattern
© 2015 Shawn M. Tomlinson

DSLRs was made.

The other thing the F4s introduced was fully integrated autofocus.

There were autofocus SLRs prior to the Nikon F4s, but they were a little — or sometimes a lot — clunky.

You could get a Nikon F3 and a few autofocus lenses for it, but when the engineers at Nikon looked at a replacement for the aging F3, they vir-

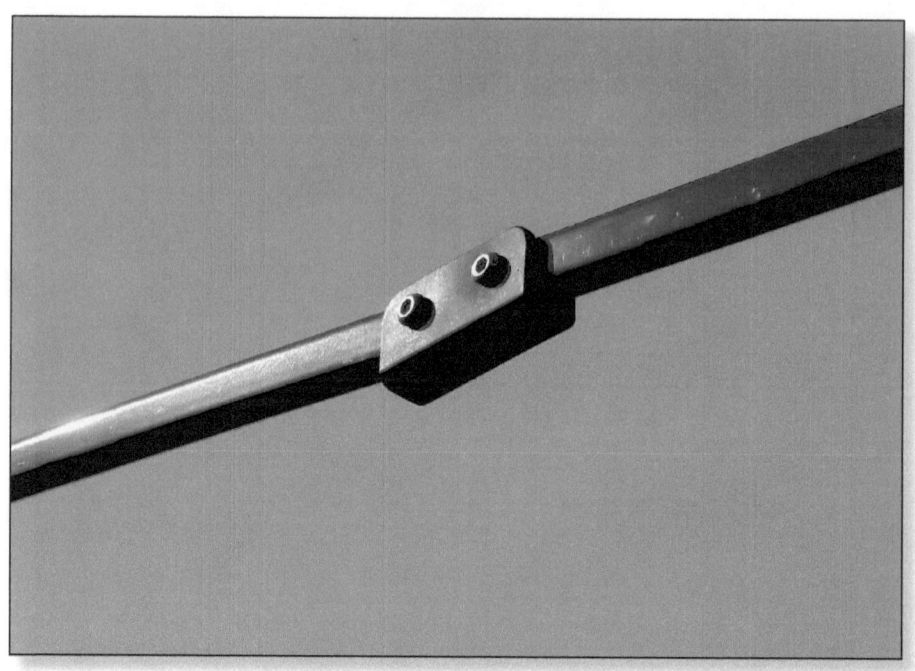

Ballston Lake, NY, April 3, 2014
Nikon D1, 80mm, 1/800, f/15, ISO 200, P, pattern
© 2015 Shawn M. Tomlinson

tually started over. They made the film winding thing and autofocus integral to the design.

This was such a major change in concept and design for a pro DSLR that some pros didn't like it. However, the Nikon F4s marks the dividing line between the old-style nearly all-mechanical pro SLR — the F3 — and the modern world.

If, as I mentioned, you hold an F4s in your hands and shoot with it, you will be quite comfortable with it, even if you've only ever used a DSLR.

It is that modern.

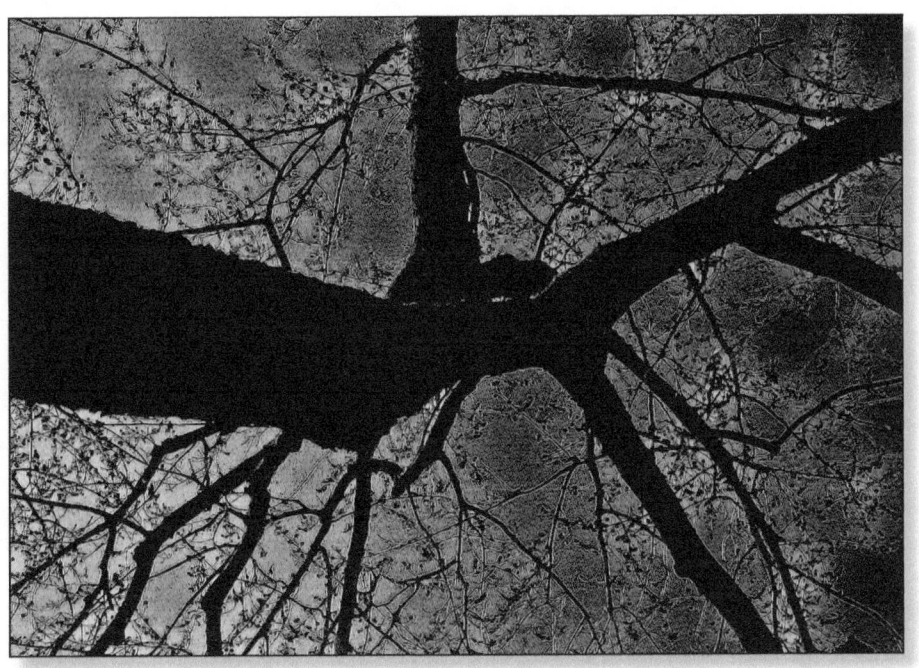

Ballston Lake, NY, April 6, 2014
Nikon D1, 5omm, 1/1500, f/20, ISO 200, P, pattern
© 2015 Shawn M. Tomlinson

Yet it was introduced in 1988.

The sleekness of the Nikon F4s did not appeal to all the pros, and Nikon generally listens to this class of photographers.

And, as good as the F4s was/is, though, the photography world did not freeze frame on it for all time.

Instead, Nikon went to the F5 and then starting working with Rochester's now-fallen giant, Kodak, to combine its camera bodies with Kodak's digital sensors.

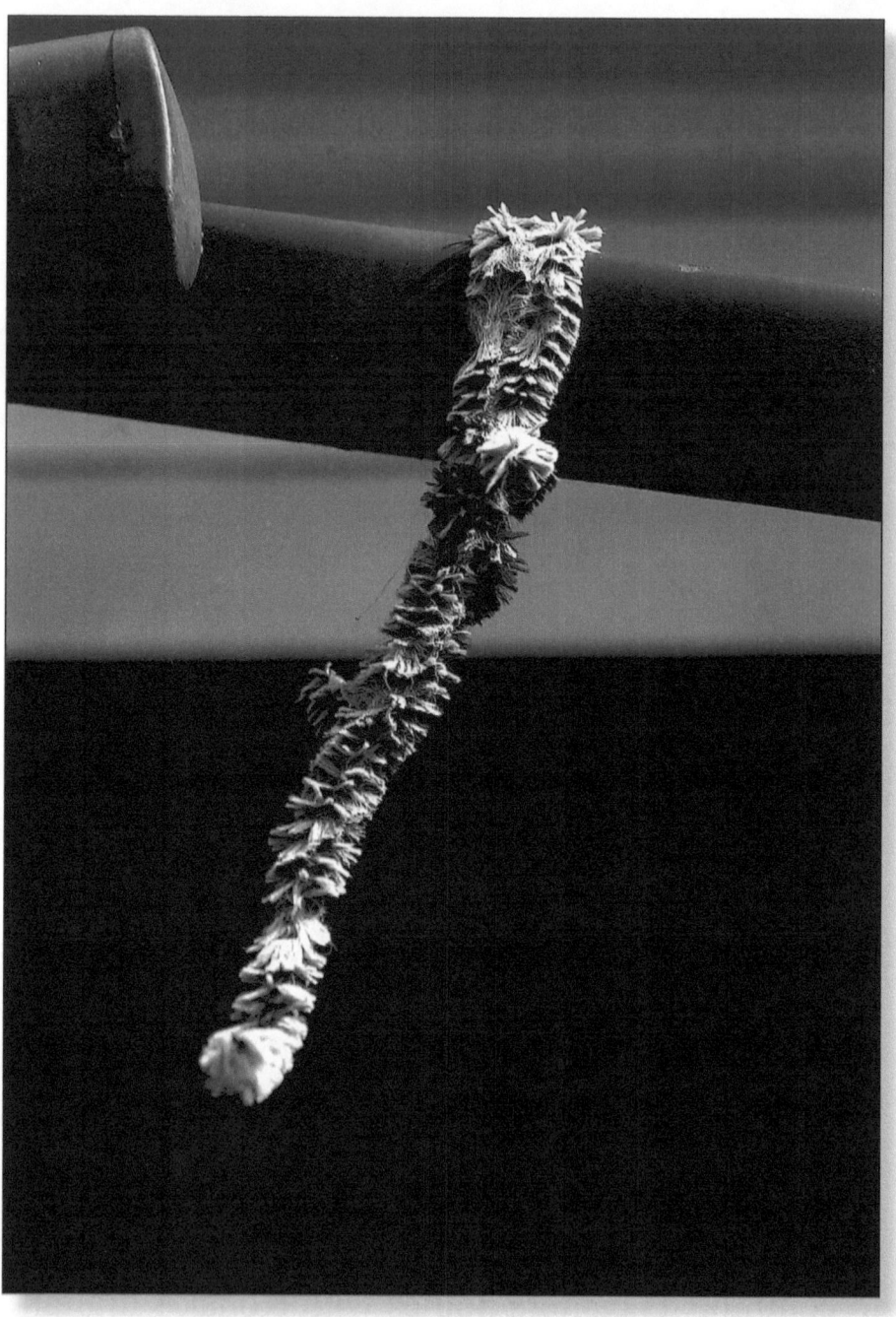

Ballston Lake, NY, April 3, 2014
Nikon D1, 66mm, 1/320, f/10, ISO 200, P, pattern
© 2015 Shawn M. Tomlinson

Technically, Kodak started using its digital sensor add-ons with the Nikon N90s — a camera very close in design to the F4s, but not quite as sturdy — and the Nikon F3.

The Kodak DCS module on a Nikon F3 more than doubled the camera's size, making it a bit awk-

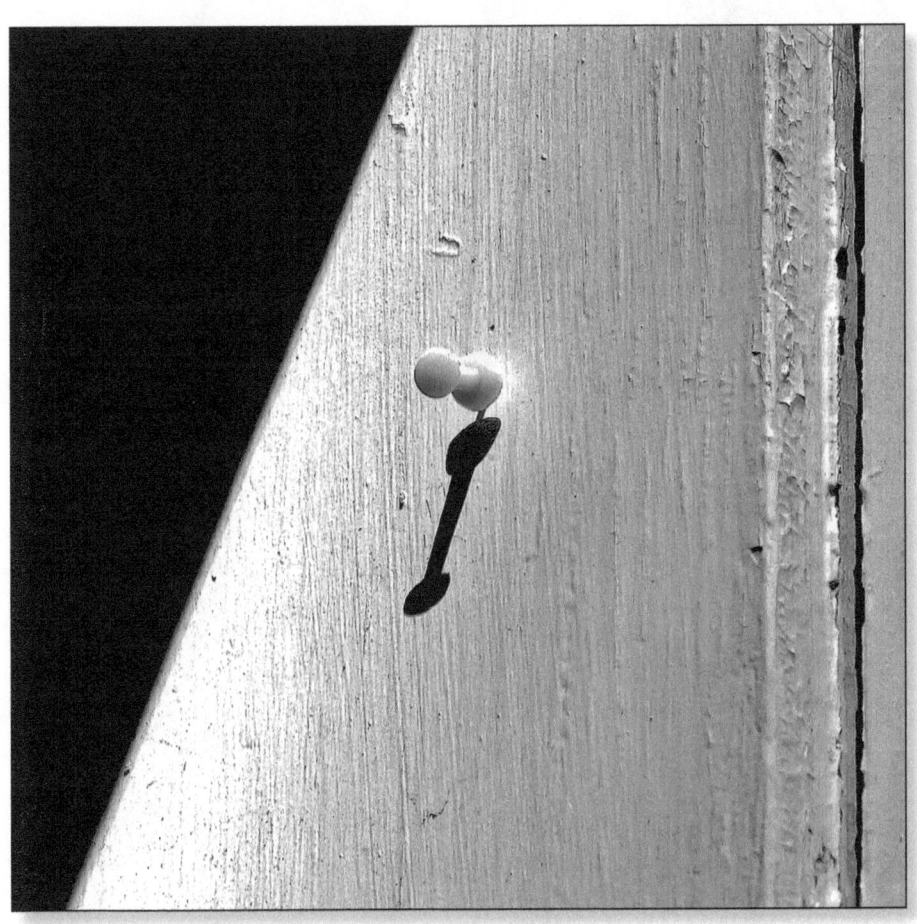

Ballston Lake, NY, April 6, 2014
Nikon D1, 80mm, 1/750, f/14, ISO 200, P, pattern
© 2015 Shawn M. Tomlinson

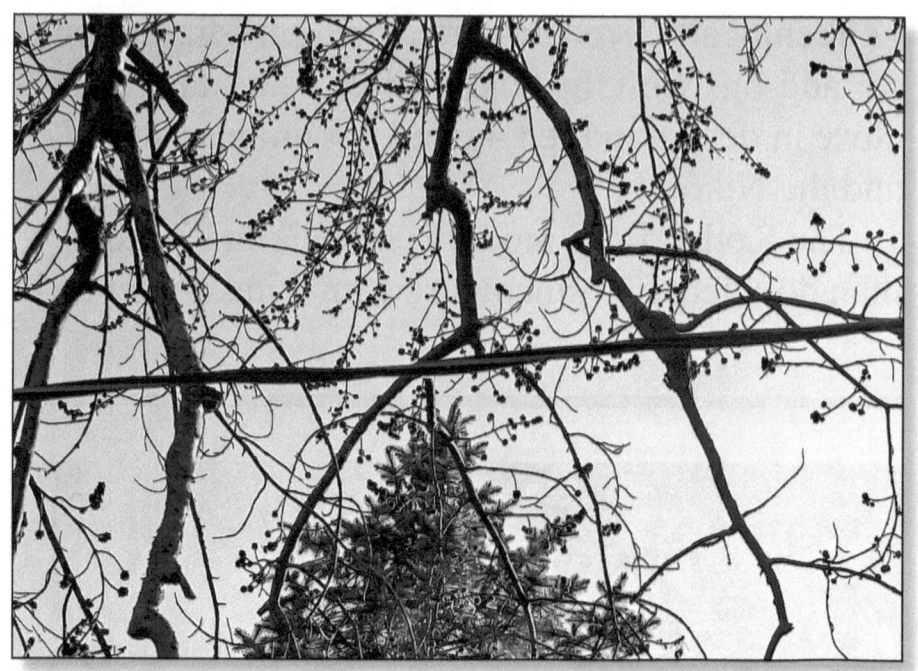

Ballston Lake, NY, April 2, 2014
Nikon D1, 66mm, 1/250, f/7.6, ISO 200, P, pattern
© 2015 Shawn M. Tomlinson

ward, but it was a start.

After working with Kodak off and on for a few years, the folks at Nikon decided, "screw this" and designed their first wholly original DSLR.

It was the D1, the prelude to the 21st century and the turning point — at least from an historical perspective — from film to digital.

OK, it probably owes more of its design to the Nikon F5, but there is a certain elegance to it that is reminiscent of the F4s.

The differences between pro cameras and everything really is who they are built for.

Entry-level cameras are marketed to people just making the transition from point-and-shoot cameras or their smartphone cameras to the first tentative steps into serious photography.

The camera makers always realized that to capture this audience, they need to make these en-

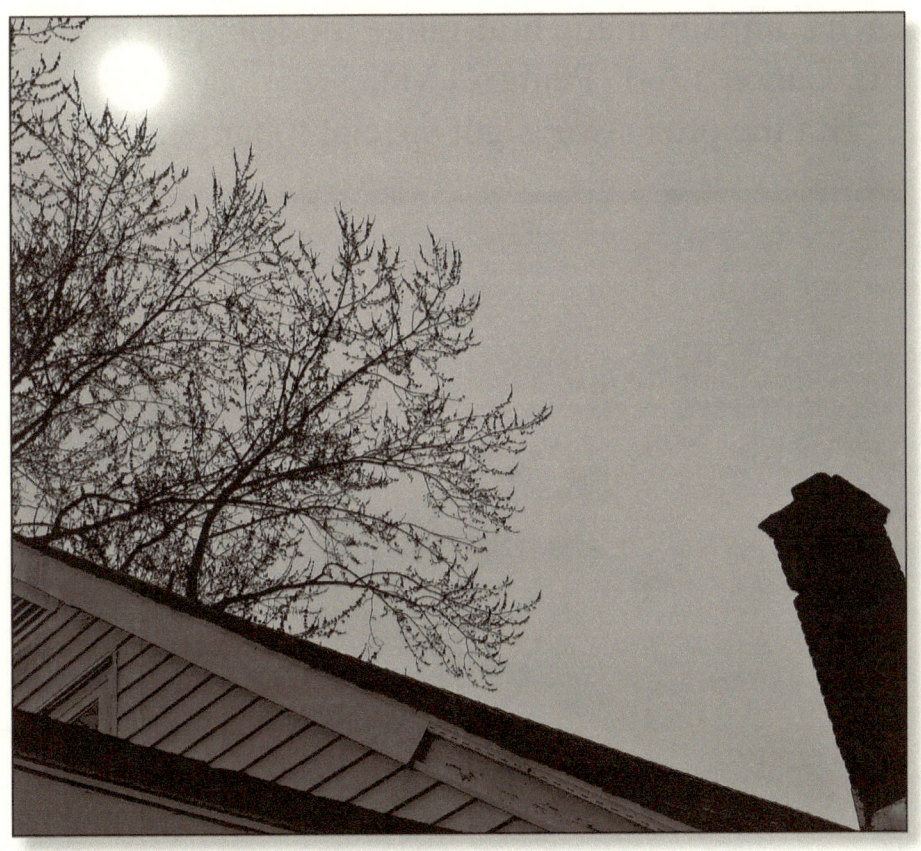

Ballston Lake, NY, April 7, 2014
Nikon D1, 28mm, 1/500, f/11, ISO 200, P, pattern
© 2015 Shawn M. Tomlinson

try-level cameras as cheap as possible while retaining the quality associated with the brand name.

Every camera manufacturer took this idea a little too far at least once each in the film era.

Nikon's biggest load of crap was the EM.

Canon's was the T50.

Pentax joined in with several, but notably, the ZX-50.

For those already familiar with SLR cameras, each company made mid-range models: Nikon's FE, Canon's A-1, Pentax's MX.

But the pros always got special treatment.

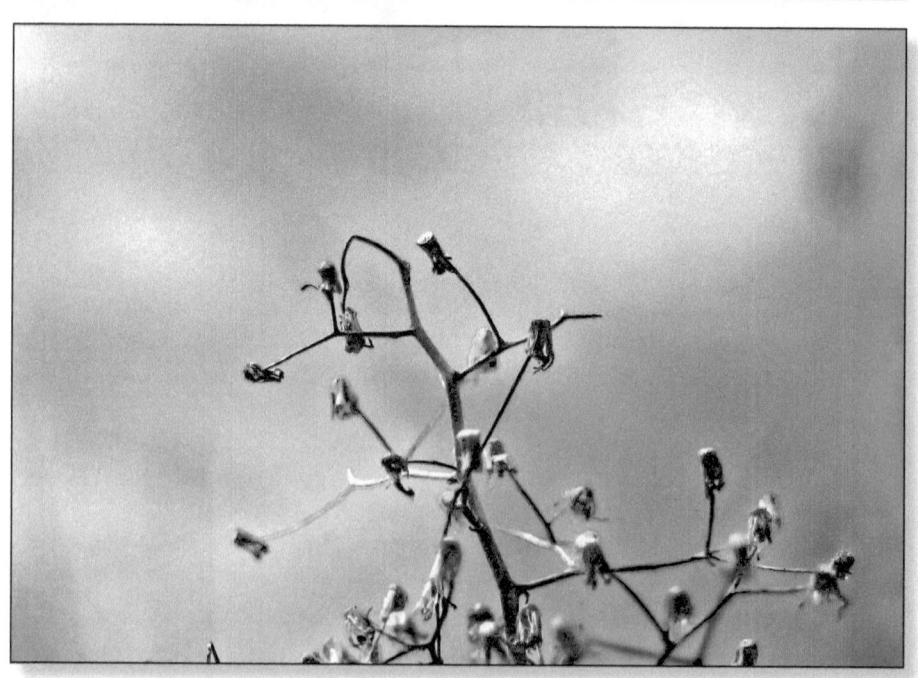

Ballston Lake, NY, April 11, 2014
Nikon D1, 80mm, 1/12800, f/5.6, ISO 1600, A, spot
© 2015 Shawn M. Tomlinson

This was and is the primary market for SLRs/DSLRs as the starting point from which the entry-level and mid-range cameras later are derived.

The latest innovations are in the pro models first, certainly, but it's more than that.

Professional photographers, especially those covering news and sports, tend to bang up their gear a lot.

Not on purpose, of course, but in the course of "getting the shot."

Pros can't be worried about handling their cameras delicately or they would be too concerned with

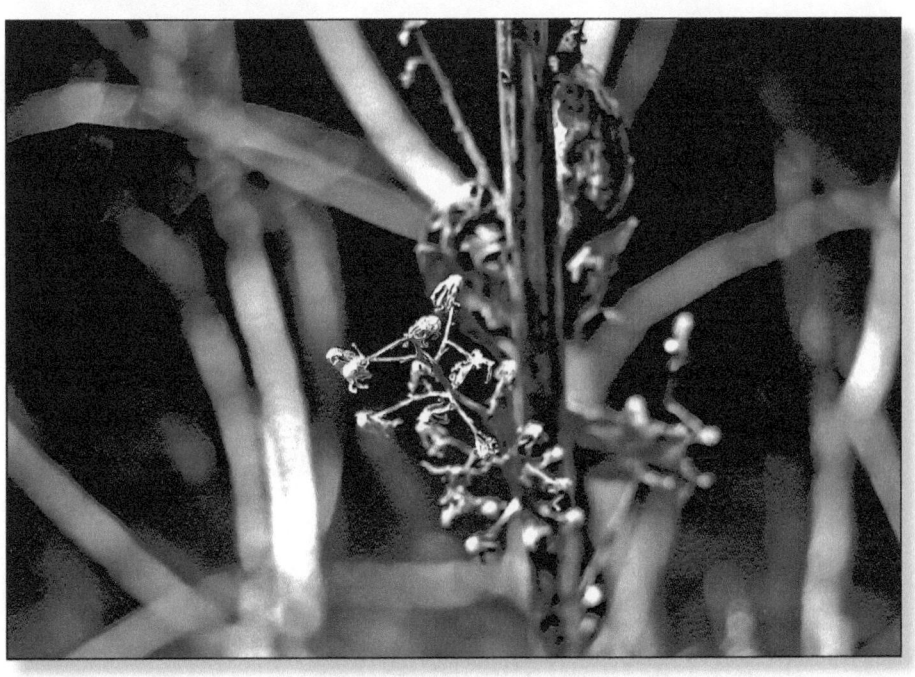

Ballston Lake, NY, April 11, 2014
Nikon D1, 80mm, 1/1250, f/5.6, ISO 1600, A, spot
© 2015 Shawn M. Tomlinson

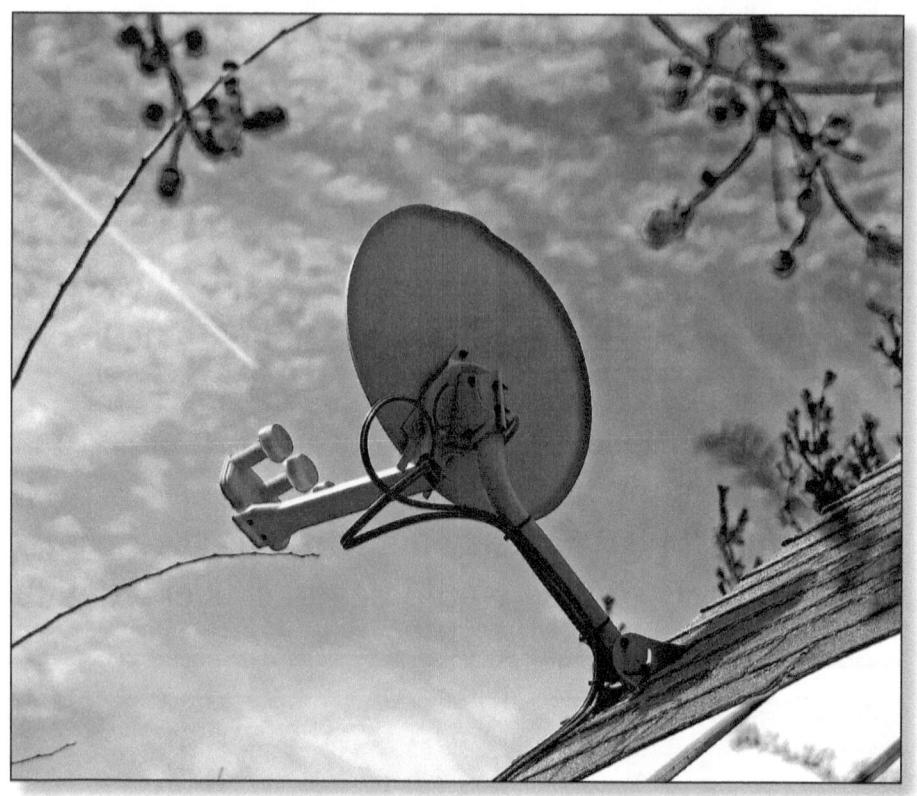

Ballston Lake, NY, April 11, 2014
Nikon D1, 80mm, 1/3200, f/5.6, ISO 1600, A, spot
© 2015 Shawn M. Tomlinson

that and not concerned enough with that important photograph.

So, from early on, pro cameras had to withstand the type of unintentional abuse that cheaper cameras did not.

This means that the inner frame of pro cameras is very tough metal.

It means the outer plastic is very strong.

It means hitting a pro DSLR on something while

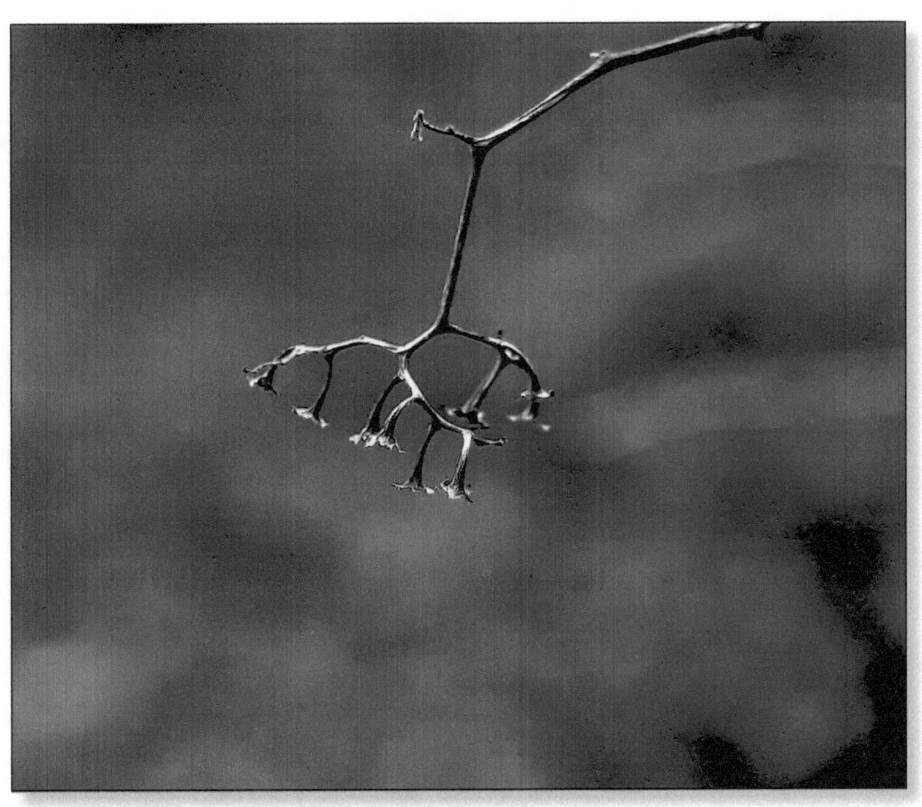

Ballston Lake, NY, April 11, 2014
Nikon D1, 80mm, 1/1600, f/5.6, ISO 1600, A, spot
© 2015 Shawn M. Tomlinson

racing down the basketball court won't stop the shoot.

Picking up any pro DSLR, holding it in your hands and shooting with it is a very different experience than other DSLRs.

You can feel the strength, the sturdiness.

It gives you confidence and lets you know you aren't likely to be betrayed by a failing camera in the middle of an important assignment.

All DSLRs can pro-duce fantastic images, so it's import-ant to have the one in your hands that "feels" right, that gives you the best control over your images, and the one that serves you best as a camera.

Not everyone likes the feel of pro DSLRs, mainly

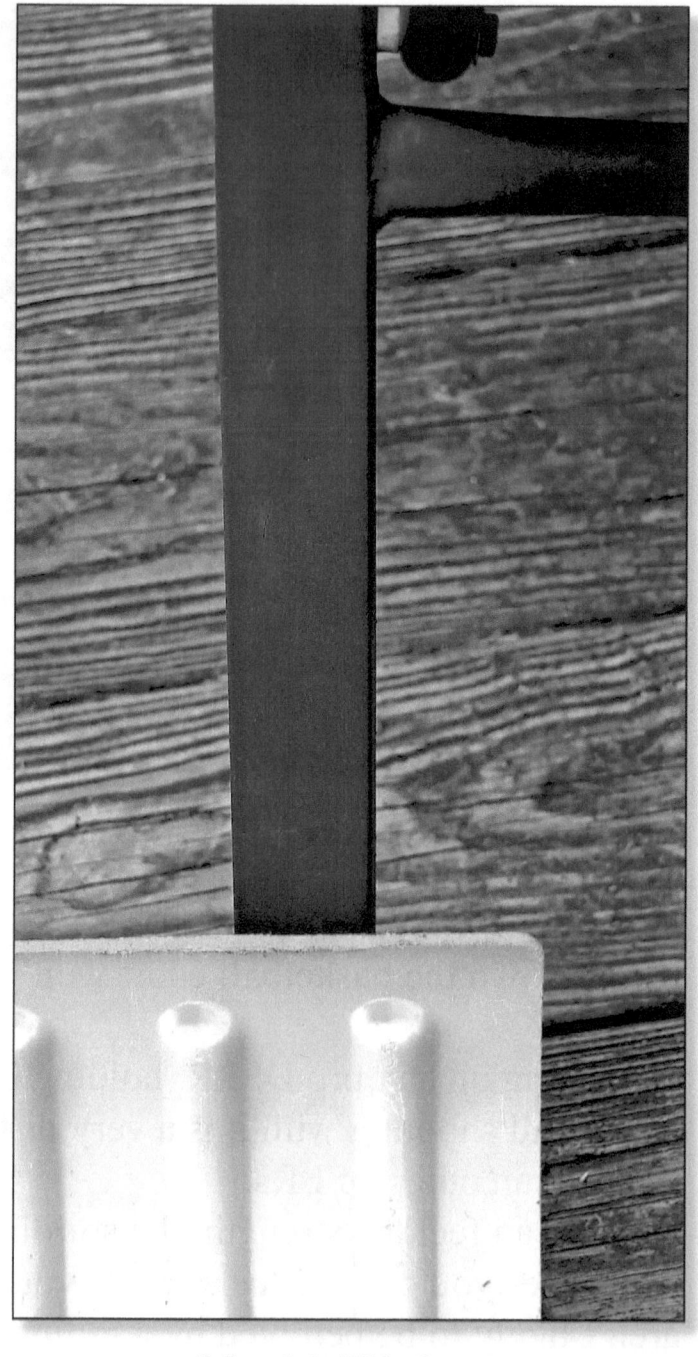

Ballston Lake, NY, April 7, 2014
Nikon D1, 80mm, 1/125, f/6, ISO 200, P, pattern
© 2015 Shawn M. Tomlinson

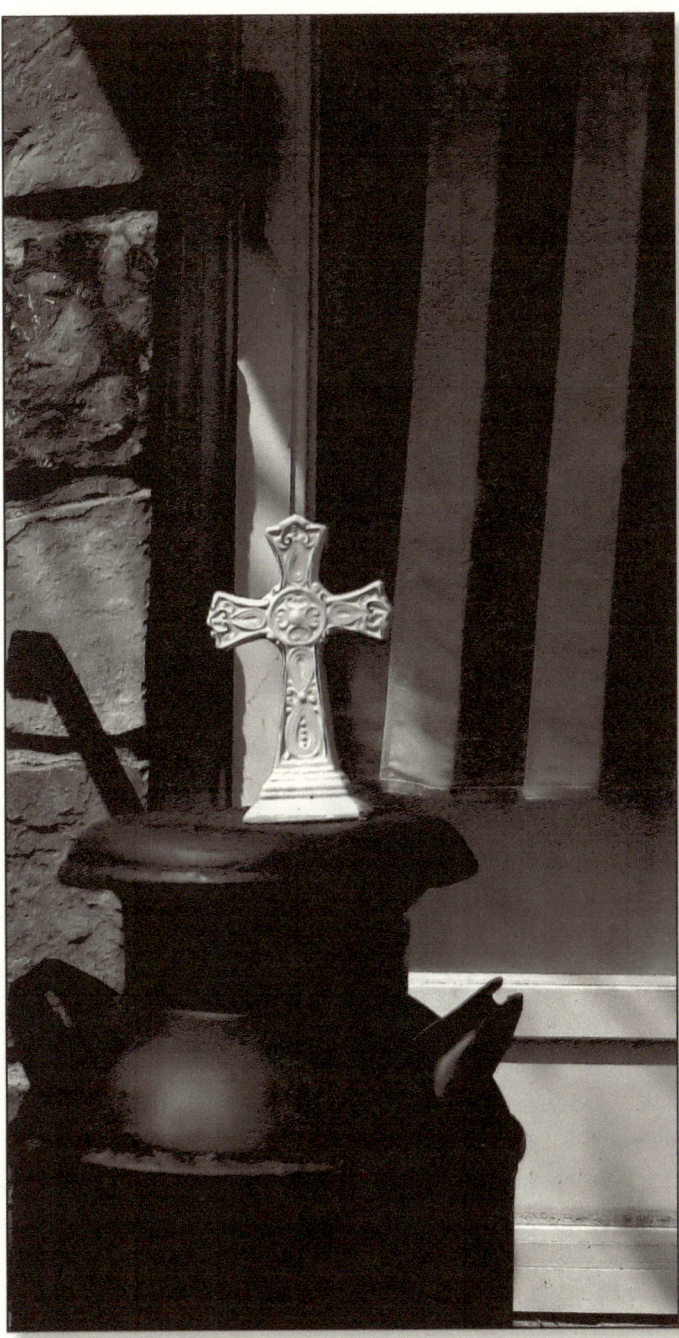

because
they are
significant-
ly heavier
than oth-
er DSLR
cameras.

Those
who do
just love
that re-
sounding
and re-
assuring
sound the
pro shut-
ter release
makes.

Here
it is im-
portant to
consider
just what
you want
to pho-
tograph
before
jumping

Ballston Lake, NY, April 11, 2014
Nikon D1, 80mm, 1/8000, f/5.6, ISO 1600, A, spot
© 2015 Shawn M. Tomlinson

into a pro DSLR such as the D1.

It is less important with a D1 than a D4s because a D1 costs a small fraction of a D4s, but it still is important.

For example, I shoot with — and have shot with — many DSLRs, from low- to high-end, and none

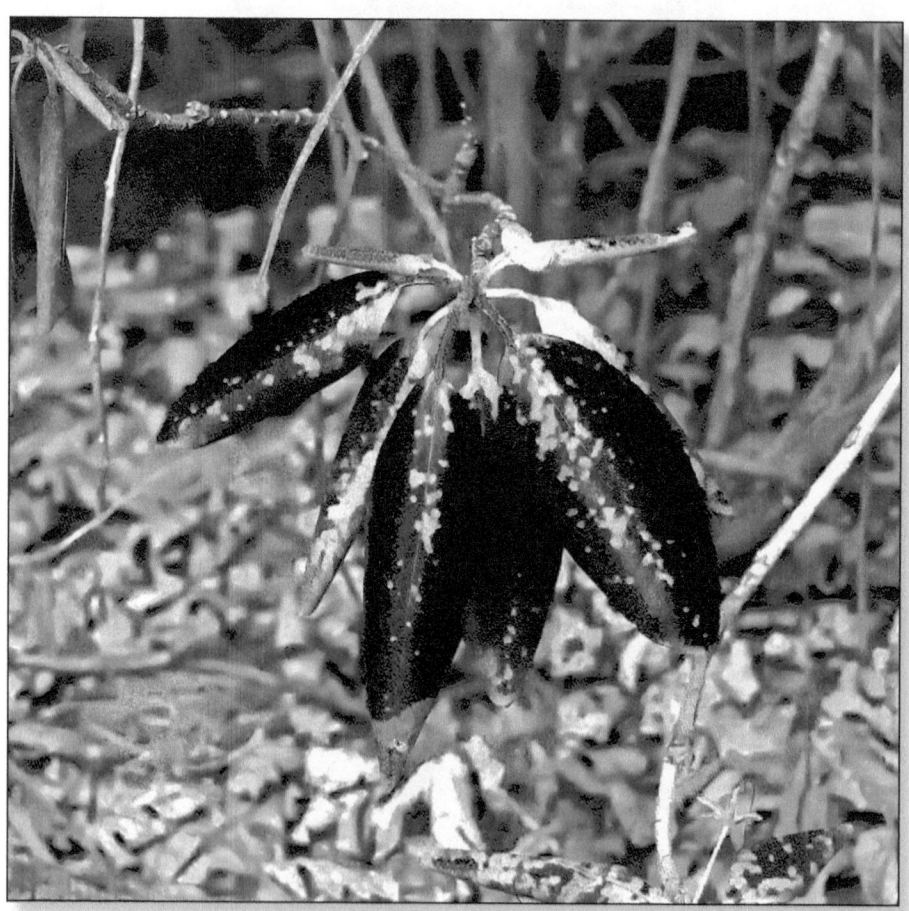

Ballston Lake, NY, April 11, 2014
Nikon D1, 80mm, 1/1600, f/5.6, ISO 1600, A, spot
© 2015 Shawn M. Tomlinson

of them new. These include, by resolution:
    Nikon D1 (pro; 2.65 megapixels)
    Nikon D1x (pro; 5.9 megapixels)
    Nikon D70 (entry-level; 6.1 megapixels)
    Pentax *ist DS (entry level; 6.1 megapixels)
    Canon EOS 10D (entry-level; 6.1 megapixels)

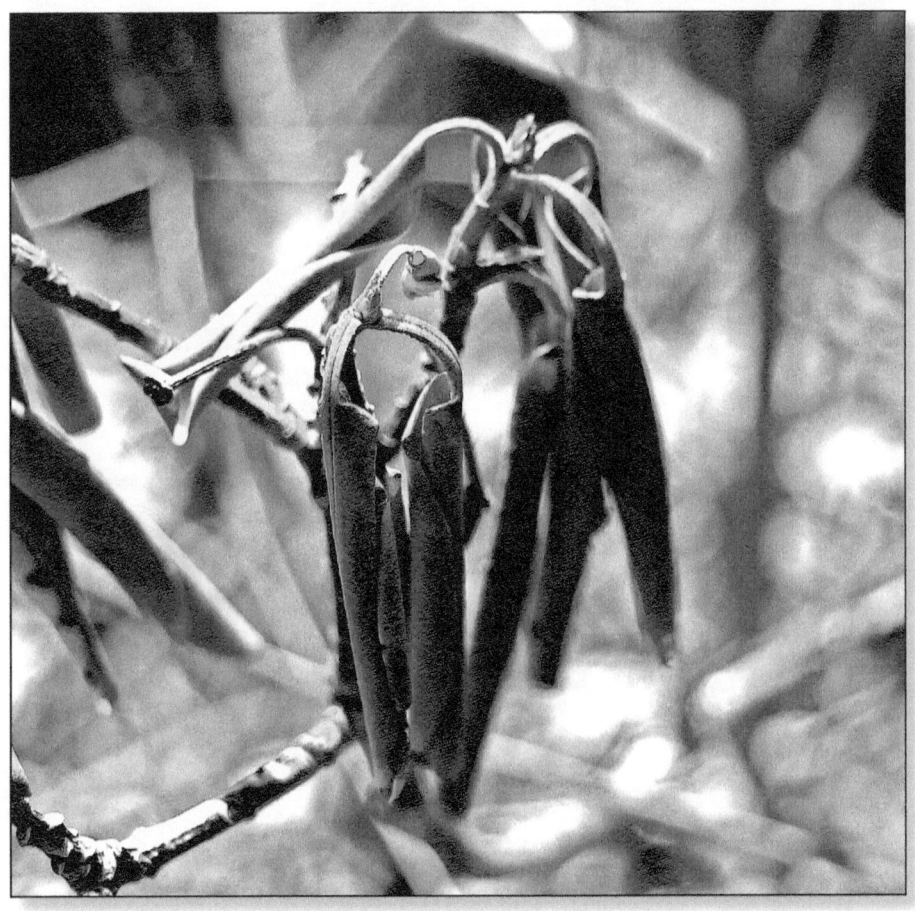

Ballston Lake, NY, April 11, 2014
Nikon D1, 80mm, 1/1250, f/5.6, ISO 1600, A, spot
© 2015 Shawn M. Tomlinson

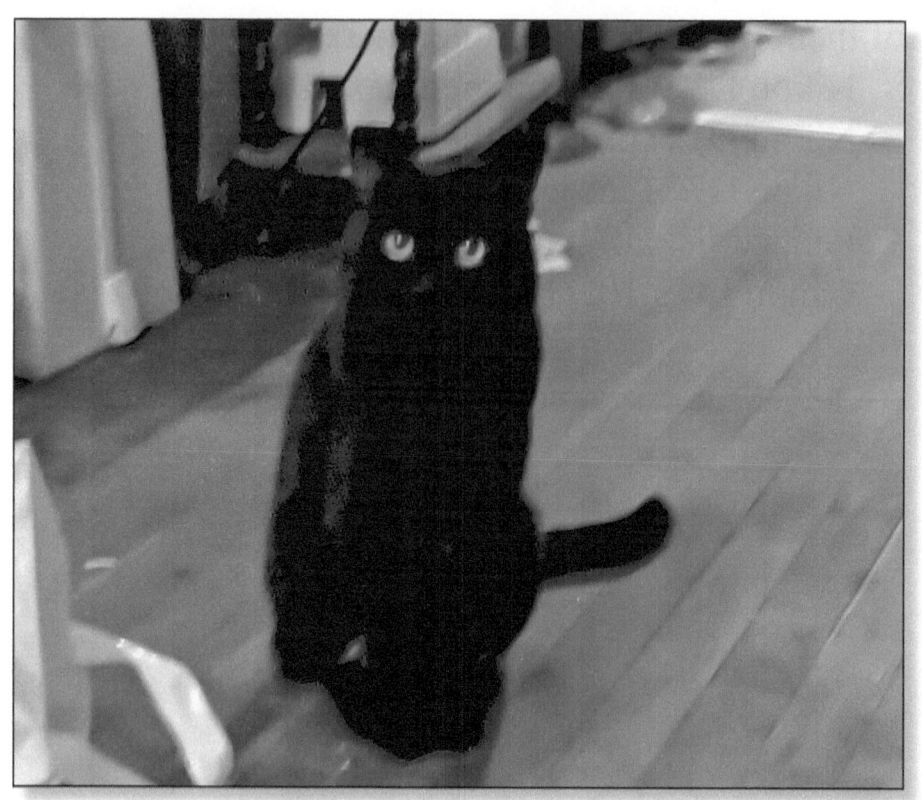

H.P. Lovecraft, Ballston Lake, NY, April 12, 2014
Nikon D1, 31mm, 1/2, f/5.6, ISO 1600, A, spot
© 2015 Shawn M. Tomlinson

Canon EOS 20D (semi-pro; 8.2 megapixels)
Canon EOS 1Ds (pro; 11.1 megapixels)
Sony A100 (entry-level; 10.2 megapixels)
Nikon D80 (semi-pro; 10.2 megapixels)
Nikon D300 (semi-pro; 12.2 megapixels)
Nikon D2x (pro; 12 megapixels)
Pentax K20D (semi-pro; 14.2 megapixels)
Pentax K-5 (semi-pro; 16 megapixels)
Nikon D7000 (semi-pro; 16.2 megapixels)

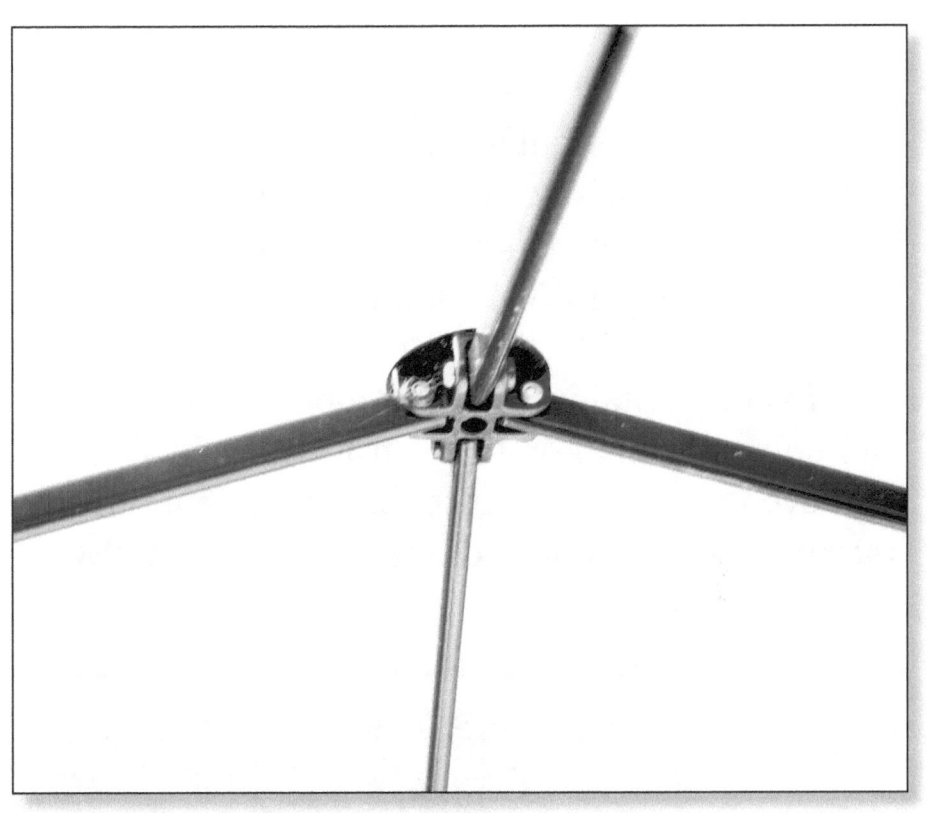

Ballston Lake, NY, April 16, 2014
Nikon D1, 70mm, 1/125, f/5.3, ISO 200, P, spot
© 2015 Shawn M. Tomlinson

Nikon D3200 (entry-level; 24 megapixels)
Nikon D800e (semi-pro; 36.2 megapixels)

I choose the DSLR according to what I am shooting that day, or sometimes, just on a whim.

So, if I am shooting something that requires extreme sharpness and detail in the images, I shoot with the Nikon D800e and the best lens I've ever used, the Nikon AF-S 105mm f/2.8 VR Micro.

But if I want a softer feel to my photos, those DSLRs in the 6- to 10-megapixel range work better.

When would I want a softer feel?

Well, I shoot a lot of flowers, particularly roses, and I found that the Nikon D70 with a less-than-ideal Tamron D LD 70-300mm f/4-5.6 lens produces just the look I like.

If I want digital images that look a bit like older film photos, the Nikon D1 is just the thing. To soften it even a bit further, I use that aforementioned Tamron 70-300mm lens or the "kit" Nikon G 18-55mm f/3.5-5.6 lens.

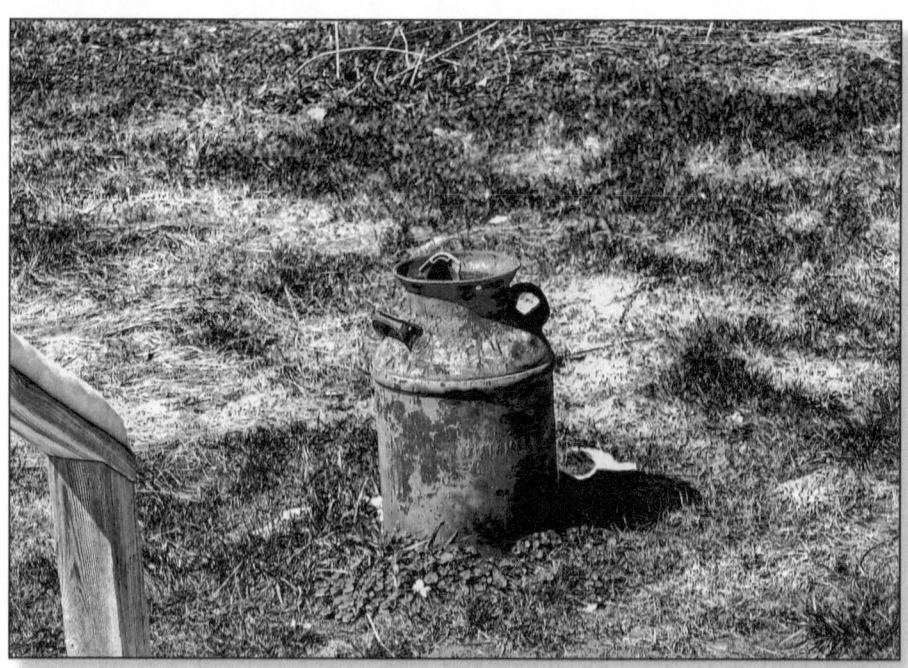

Ballston Lake, NY, April 16, 2014
Nikon D1, 75mm, 1/160, f/7.6, ISO 200, P, spot
© 2015 Shawn M. Tomlinson

The point is that, once you really know your DSLRs — the ones you own — you can pick the one that works best for each shoot.

I probably would not use the Nikon D1 on a crucially important shoot.

It is an old camera by now.

It does not produce the level of sharpness and clarity a modern DSLR does.

It doesn't have the details in the shadows and highlights I need.

But that is not why I bought it.

I bought it because it was the least expensive

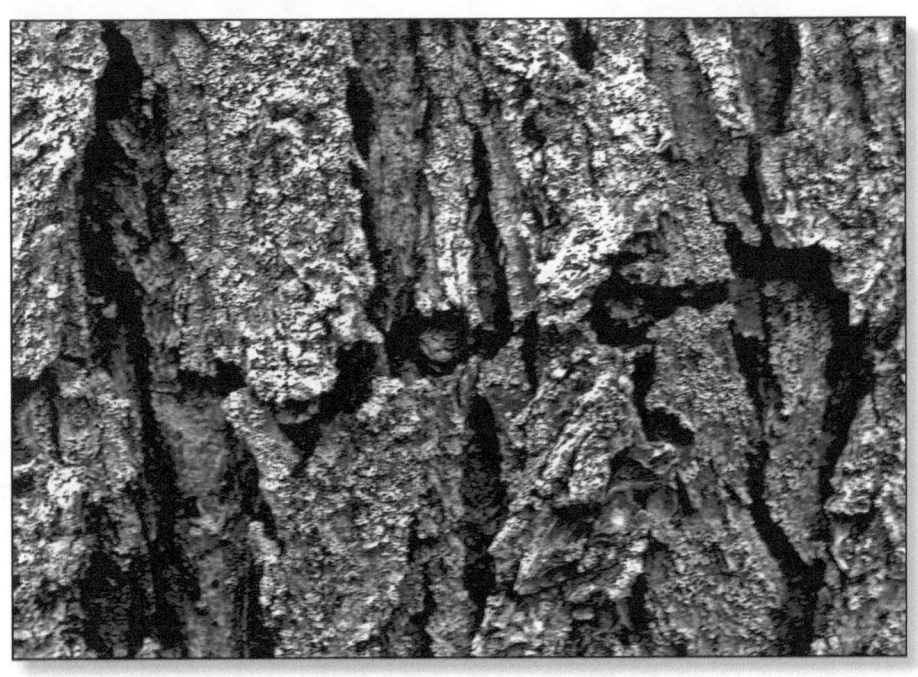

Ballston Lake, NY, April 18, 2014
Nikon D1, 72mm, 1/45, f/5.6, ISO 200, P, spot
© 2015 Shawn M. Tomlinson

way to try and use a pro DSLR.

It has not disappointed me.

Sure, there are times when smaller, semi-pro or "enthusiast" cameras make things easier.

Backpacking up a mountain, for example, where every ounce counts, is not the best place for a pro

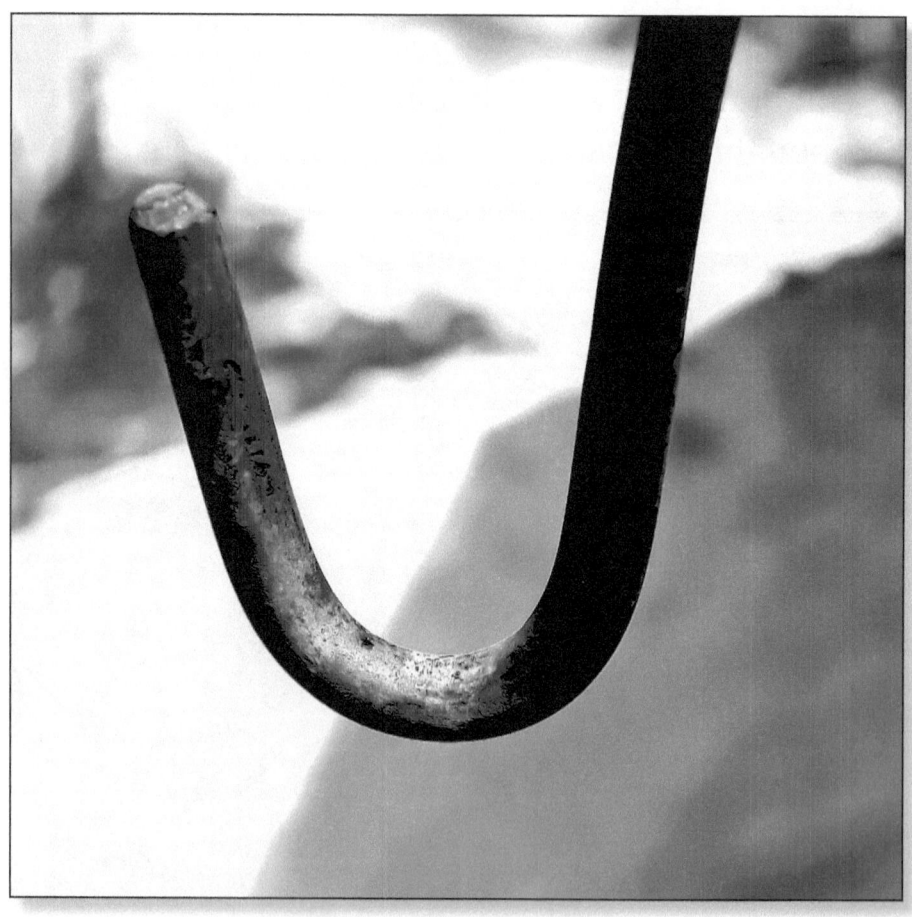

Ballston Lake, NY, April 16, 2014
Nikon D1, 75mm, 1/125, f/7.6, ISO 200, P, spot
© 2015 Shawn M. Tomlinson

DSLR.

And, for the most part, pro DSLRs weren't designed for that anyway.

They were designed for speed and for durability.

That very fact means that buying an older one, even as old as the Nikon D1, raises the odds your new old pro camera still will be working, doing its job as it always did it.

And, since no one is going to use a D1 for a crucial photographic assignment more than a decade-and-a-half after it was made, it's going to be cheap.

More importantly, it's going to be fun.

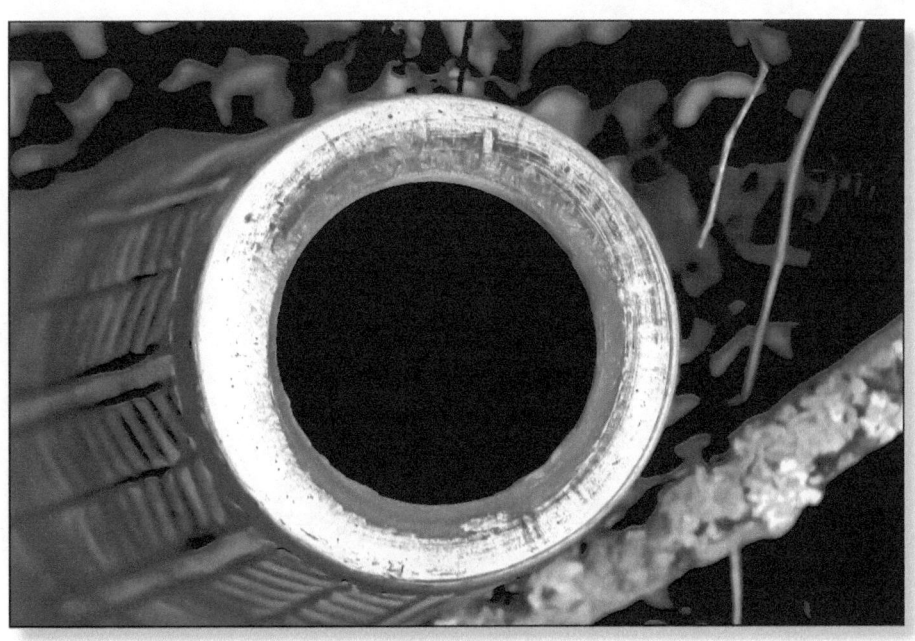

Ballston Lake, NY, April 18, 2014
Nikon D1, 82mm, 1/80, f/5.6, ISO 200, P, spot
© 2015 Shawn M. Tomlinson

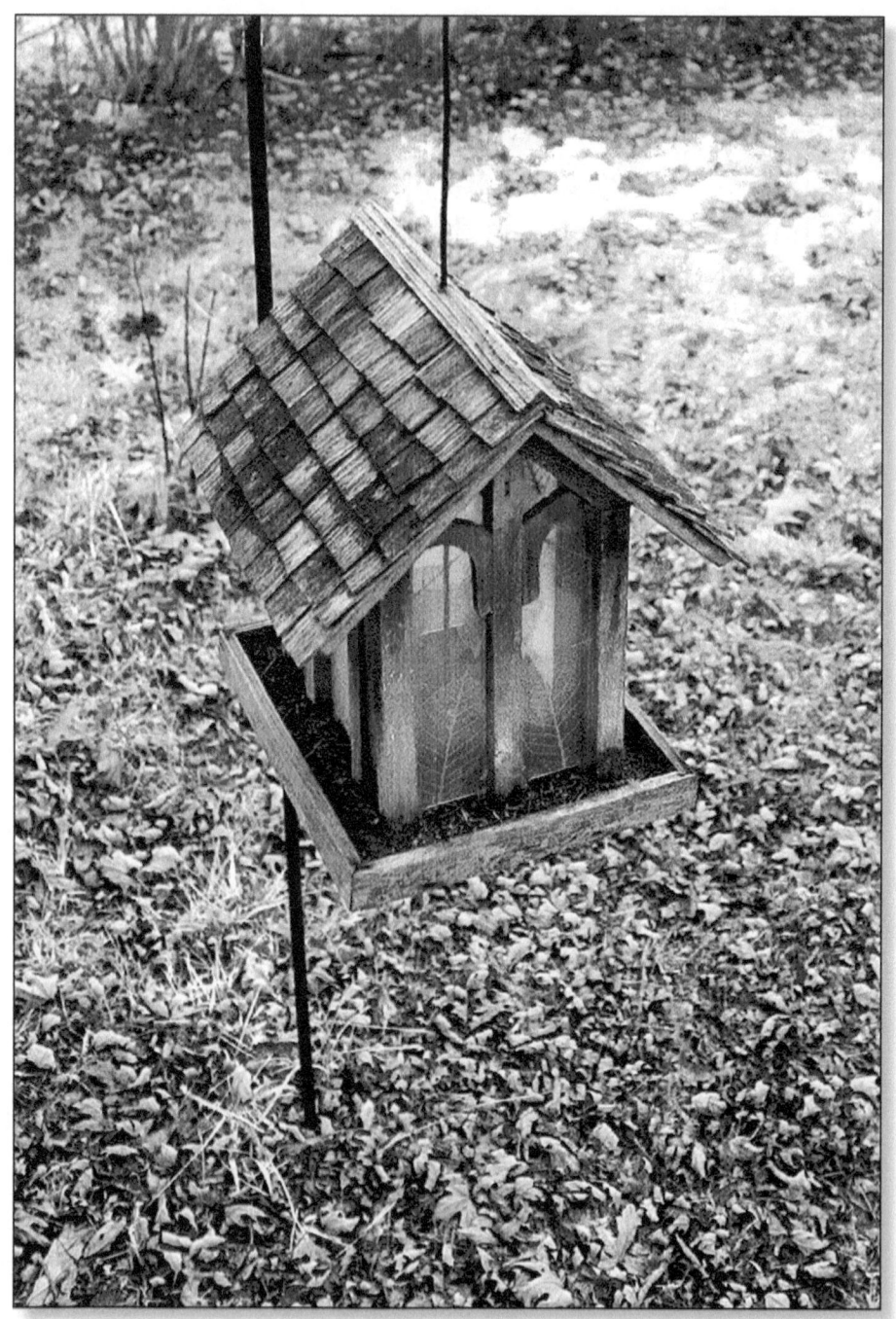

Ballston Lake, NY, Jan. 2, 2015
Nikon D1, 18mm, 1/200, f/3.5, ISO 800, M, pattern metering
© 2015, 2015 by Shawn M. Tomlinson

# Part 2

# The Pros and Cons of Pro DSLRs

Certainly if you're going to spend more than $6,000 for a new pro DSLR, there aren't many cons.

If you want to try a pro DSLR for little money, that means buying an older one, in this case the Nikon D1, so there are some cons, but pros as well.

Here are the basics:

## Pros

- Well-built camera
- Sturdy
- CompactFlash (CF) card (sturdier than SecureDigital [SD] cards)
- Several file formats (RAW, TIFF, JPEG)
- Good color rendition
- Smaller RAW files
- Built-in battery grip
- Viewfinder blind
- Depth-of-field preview
- Vertical shutter release

- Fast, accurate focusing
- Accepts all Nikon lenses from the mid-1970s onward
- Rapid continual shooting
- VERY cheap

# Cons

- Low resolution (by today's standards)
- Heavy
- Convoluted menu system
- Short battery life
- Long buffering time

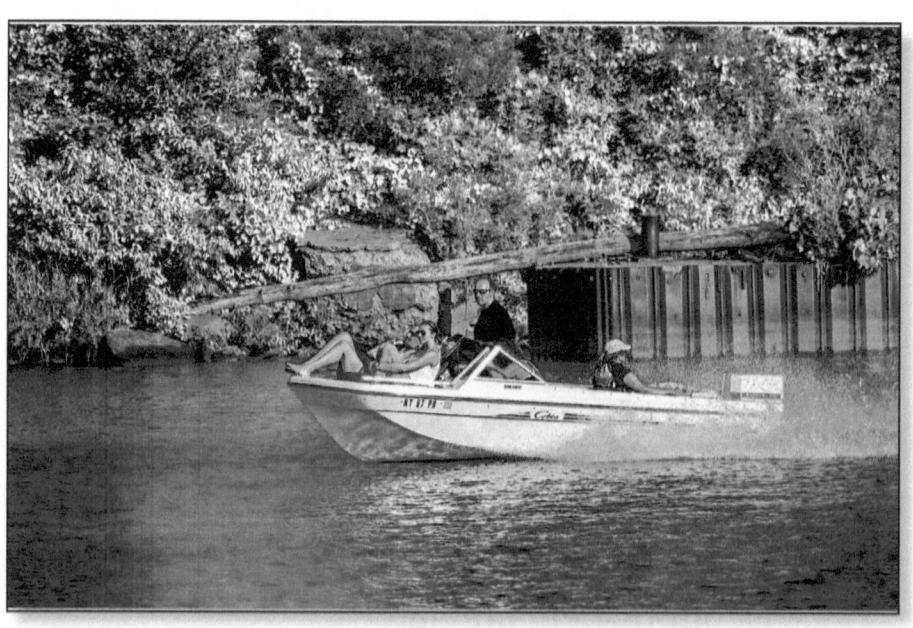

Freeman's Bridge, Schenectady, NY, July 6, 2014
Nikon D1, 300mm (prime), 1/2000, f/4.5, ISO 200, P, center-weighted metering
© 2014, 2015 by Shawn M. Tomlinson

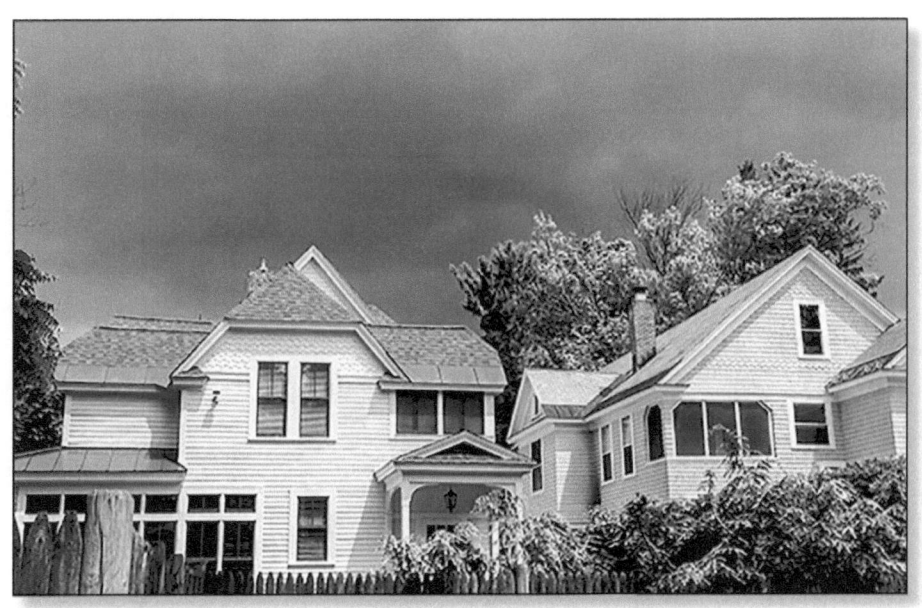

Saratoga Springs, NY, July 8, 2014
Nikon D1, 28mm, 1/320, f/9, ISO 200, P, pattern metering
© 2014, 2015 by Shawn M. Tomlinson

- Small monitor
- Bright area washout
- Memory card size limitation (2gb CF card maximum)
- No fill flash (no pro DSLRs have these, even today)
- Batteries hard to find, expensive.
- Charger very expensive and hard to find
- Sensor cleaning requires an AC adapter to lock up the mirror.

The pros far outweigh the cons of the Nikon D1, but that does not diminish the significance of the cons.

They will get in your way if you are used to a modern DSLR.

The low resolution, which probably is what keeps most peo- ple from wanting or trying a D1 and keeps the price low, really isn't a problem unless you want big printed en- largements.

Keep in mind

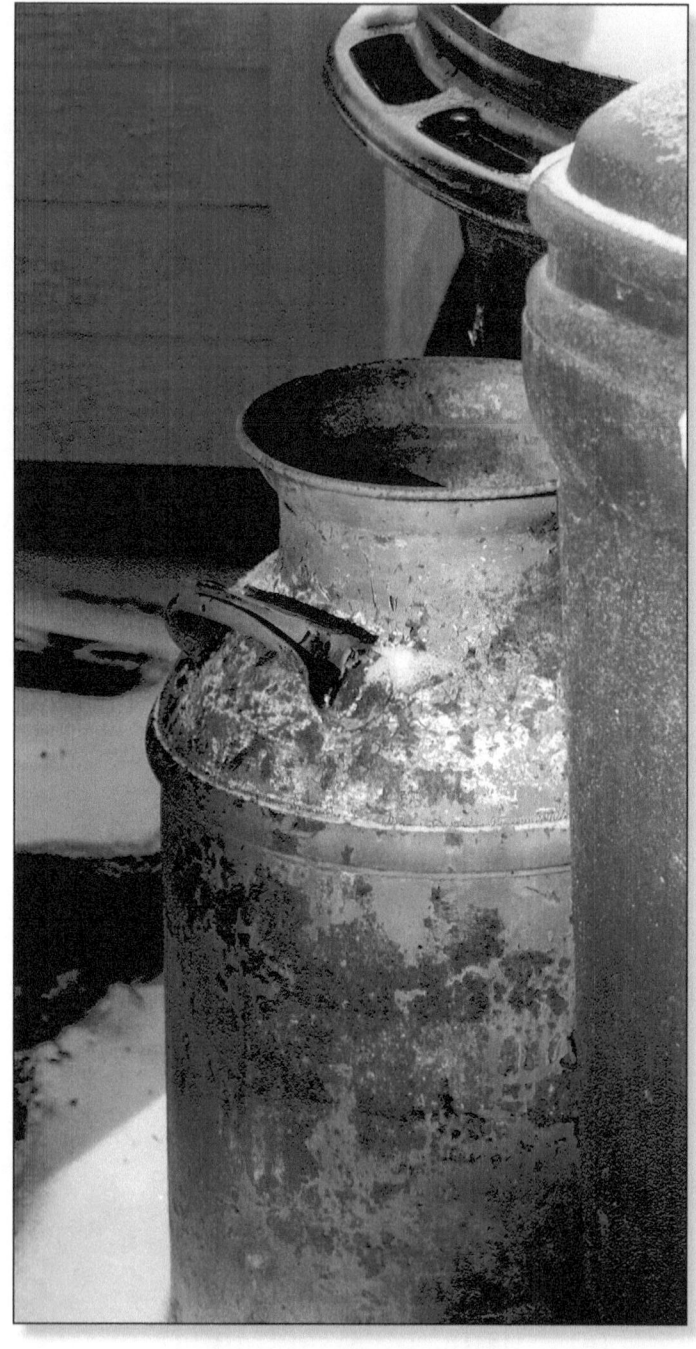

Ballston Lake, NY, May 1, 2014
Nikon D1, 46mm, 1/800, f/5.6, ISO 200, Av, pattern metering
© 2014, 2015 by Shawn M. Tomlinson

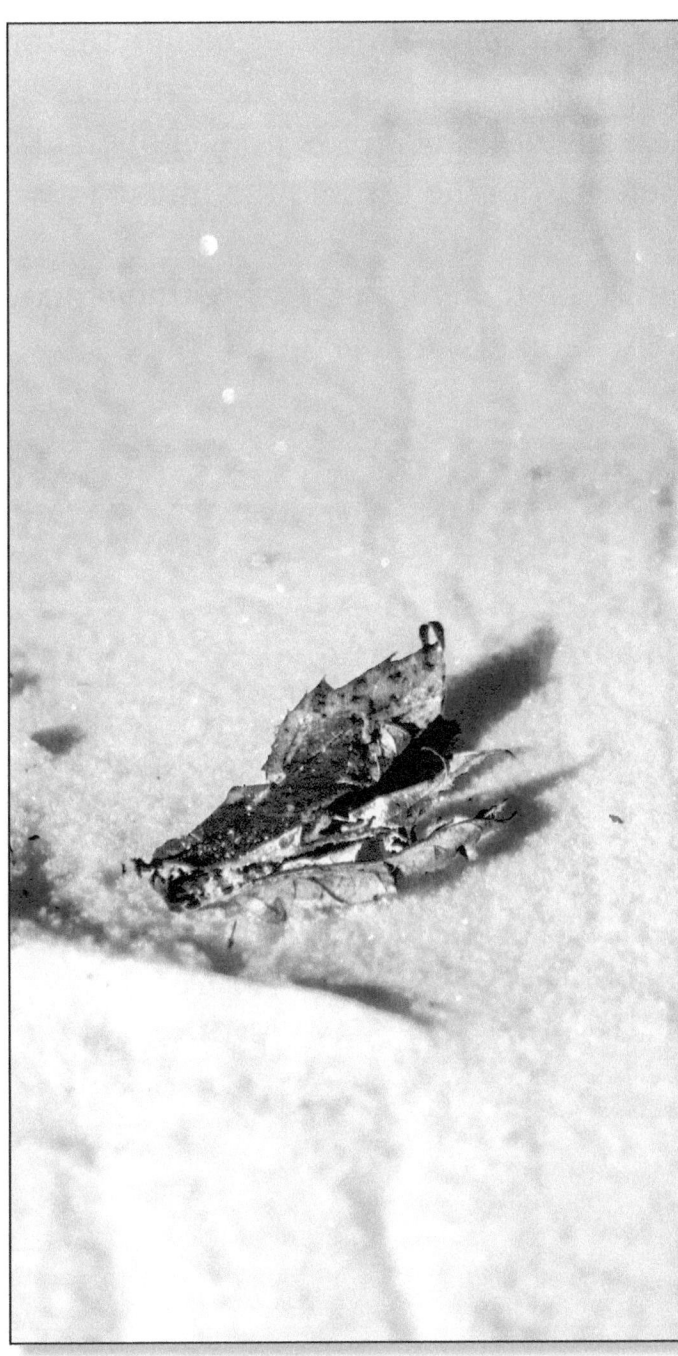

that, even though the D1's resolution is a little less than 3 megapixels, its images are far superior to other 3-megapixel cameras because of the professional technology used to build it.

In other words, if you compare a RAW image shot with the D1 at full resolution

Ballston Lake, NY, May 1, 2014
Nikon D1, 82mm, 1/750, f/5.6, ISO 200, Av, pattern metering
© 2014, 2015 by Shawn M. Tomlinson

to a JPEG from a point-and-shoot Casio camera, for example, you will notice significant differences.

Primarily this means the color is noticeably and significantly better from the D1 and the image is sharper.

When I shoot with the Nikon D1 (2.65 megapixels), D70 (6.1 megapixels) and D7000 (16.2

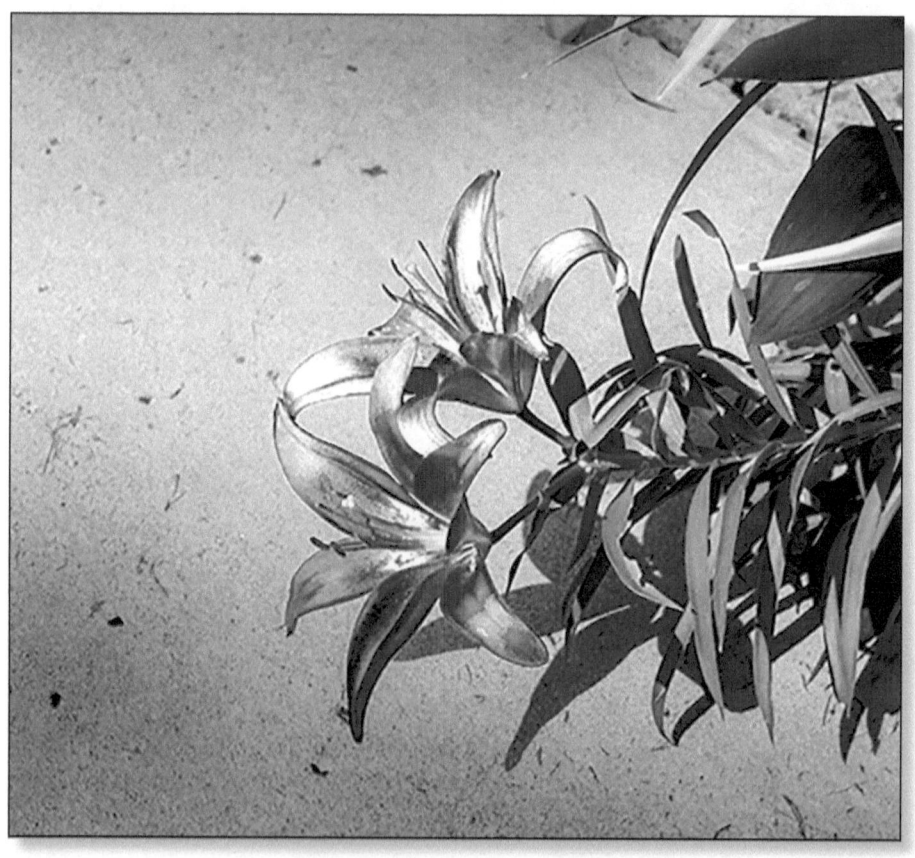

Saratoga Springs, NY, July 1, 2014
Nikon D1, 70mm, 1/640, f/5.3, ISO 200, Av, pattern metering
© 2014, 2015 by Shawn M. Tomlinson

megapixels), there's no question of which one produces better images, especially in the subtle sharpness in the D7000.

However, unless you blow up the images to 100 percent, it is difficult to tell the difference in color, especially between the D1 and D70.

In fact, the lower resolution of the D1 can be an advantage for some subjects.

As I said earlier, I found that when I'm shooting macro images of flowers that the slight soft-

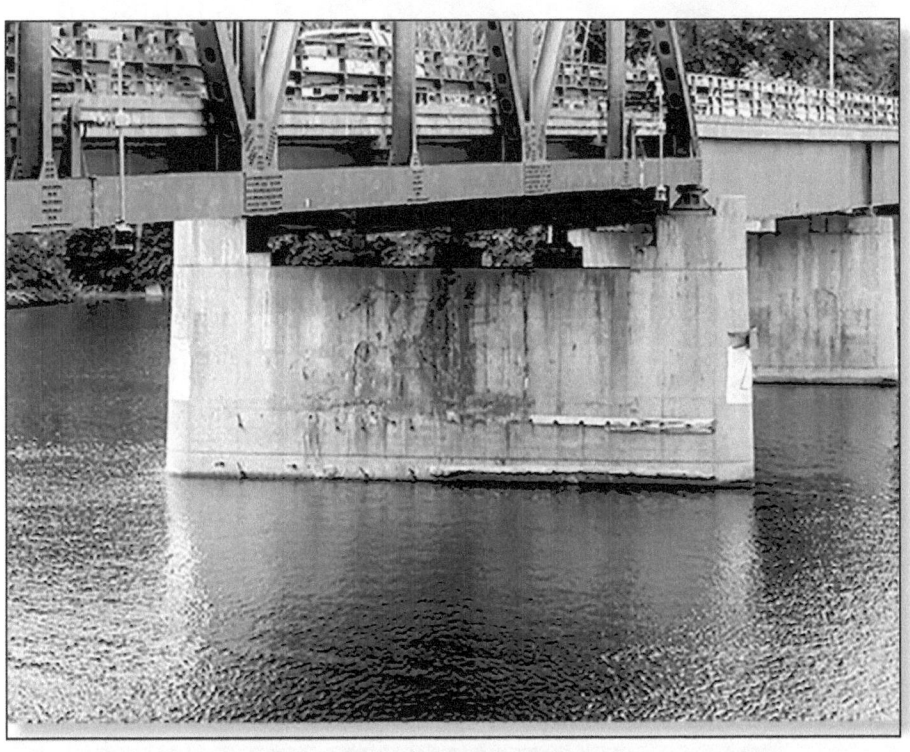

Aqueduct, Rexford, NY, July 16, 2014
Nikon D1, 70mm, 1/160, f/5.3, ISO 200, Av, pattern metering
© 2014, 2015 by Shawn M. Tomlinson

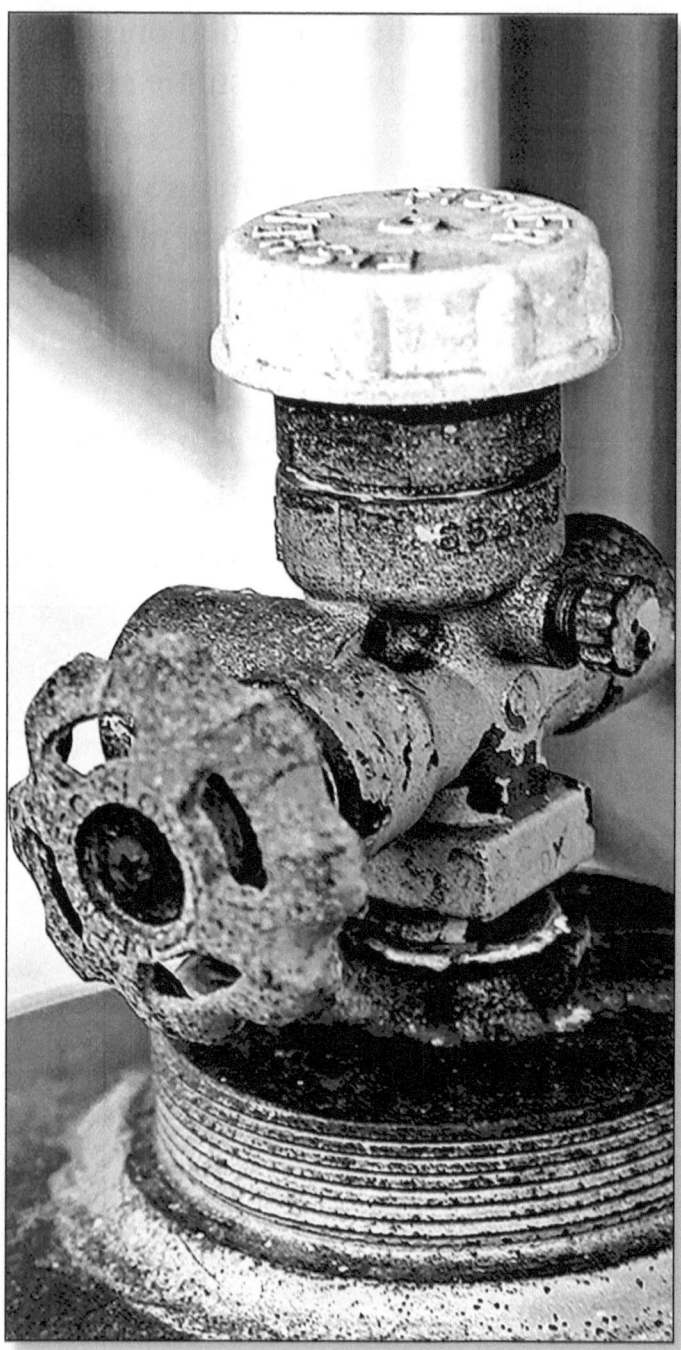

ness of the D1 — due to fewer megapixels — actually produces brilliant images.

The resolution rarely has gotten in my way.

The two things that I do find annoy-ing — but accept as the com-promise for being able to afford and use a pro DSLR — are the convoluted menu sys-

Broadalbin, NY, May 2, 2014
Nikon D1, 82mm, 1/90, f/5.6, ISO 200, Av, pattern metering
© 2014, 2015 by Shawn M. Tomlinson

tem and the long buffering time.

The menus on the D1 are annoying because they are all codes.

You either have to have the manual with you when you shoot or you have to memorize the codes you need.

This problem was solved with the upgraded successors to the D1,

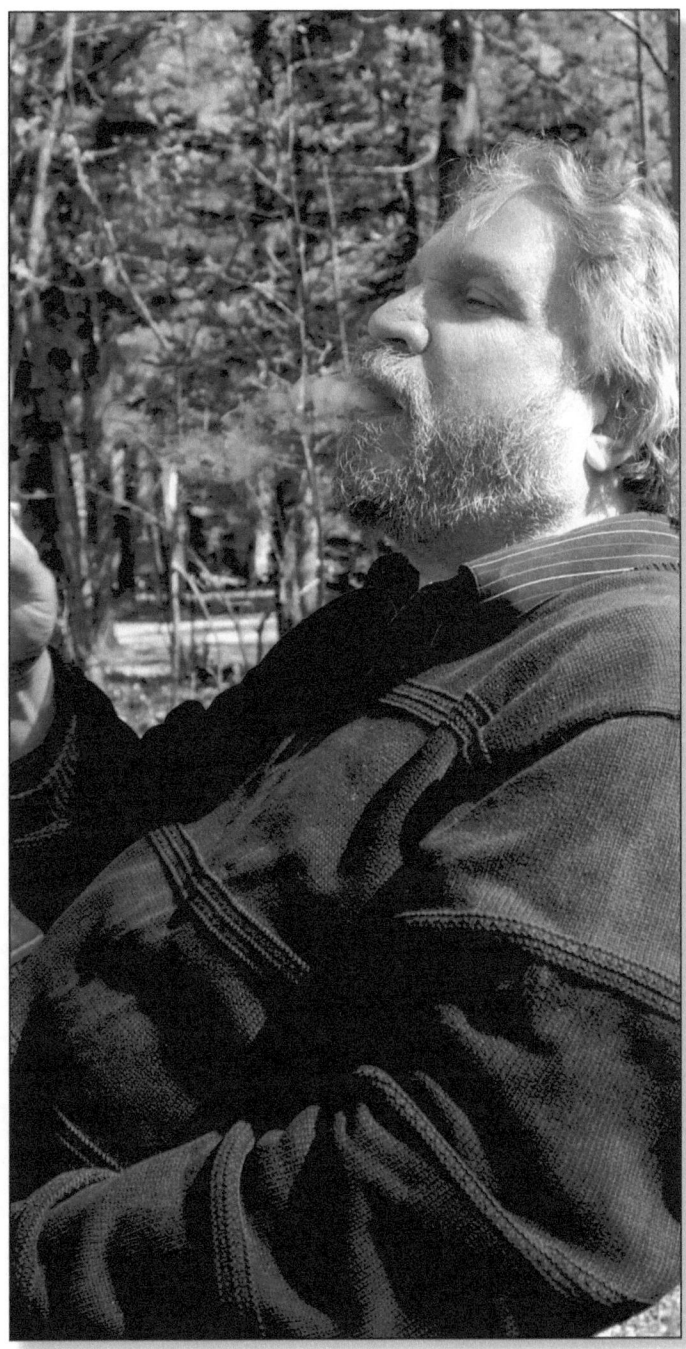

Shawn M. Tomlinson, Caroga Lake, NY, May 20, 2014
Nikon D1, 28mm, 1/320, f/5.6, ISO 400, Av, pattern metering
© 2014, 2015 by Richard H. Nilsen

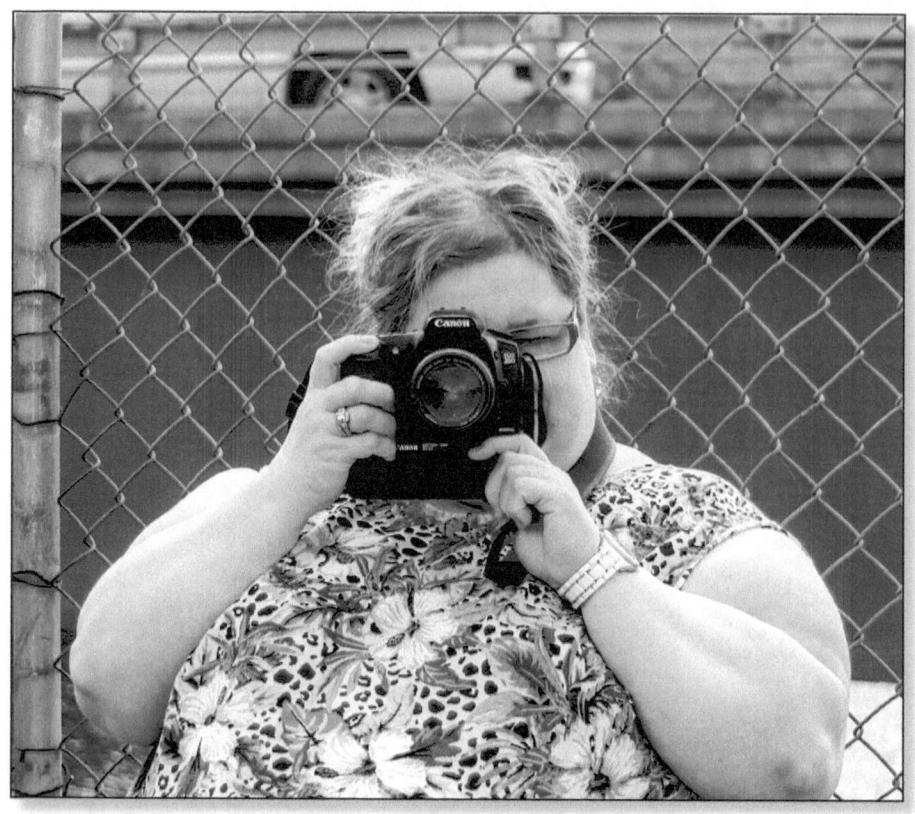

Carole A. Tomlinson, Aqueduct, Rexford, NY, July 16, 2014
Nikon D1, 70mm, 1/350, f/5.3, ISO 200, aperture priority, pattern metering
© 2014, 2015 by Shawn M. Tomlinson

the D1X and D1H.

Still, I really don't need to change many things on the menu, so until I need to, I don't really think about it.

The buffering time, however, does get a bit in my way, or, well, did until I figured out a work-around.

What I mean by buffering time is the time it takes after you press the shutter release button until

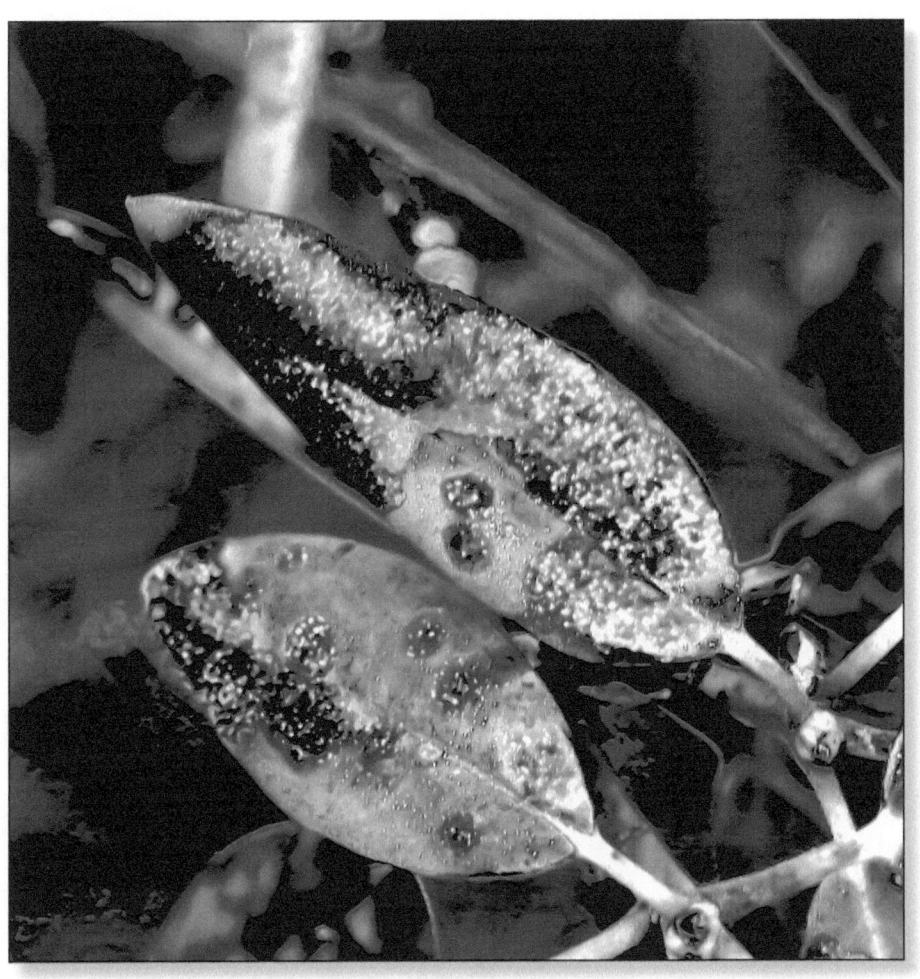

Ballston Lake, NY, April 18, 2014
Nikon D1, 82mm, 1/50, f/5.6, ISO 200, P, spot
© 2015 Shawn M. Tomlinson

the D1 writes the image to the CF card and the thus the time it takes before you can shoot the next photo.

Being as old as it is, and really the first practical DSLR upon which most of today's are based upon, the engineers who designed and built it did not know yet what would and wouldn't get in the way.

They also were limited by the technology of the last part of the 20th century.

So, if you shoot with the D1 in "S" or single shot mode, it takes a while for the image to write to the

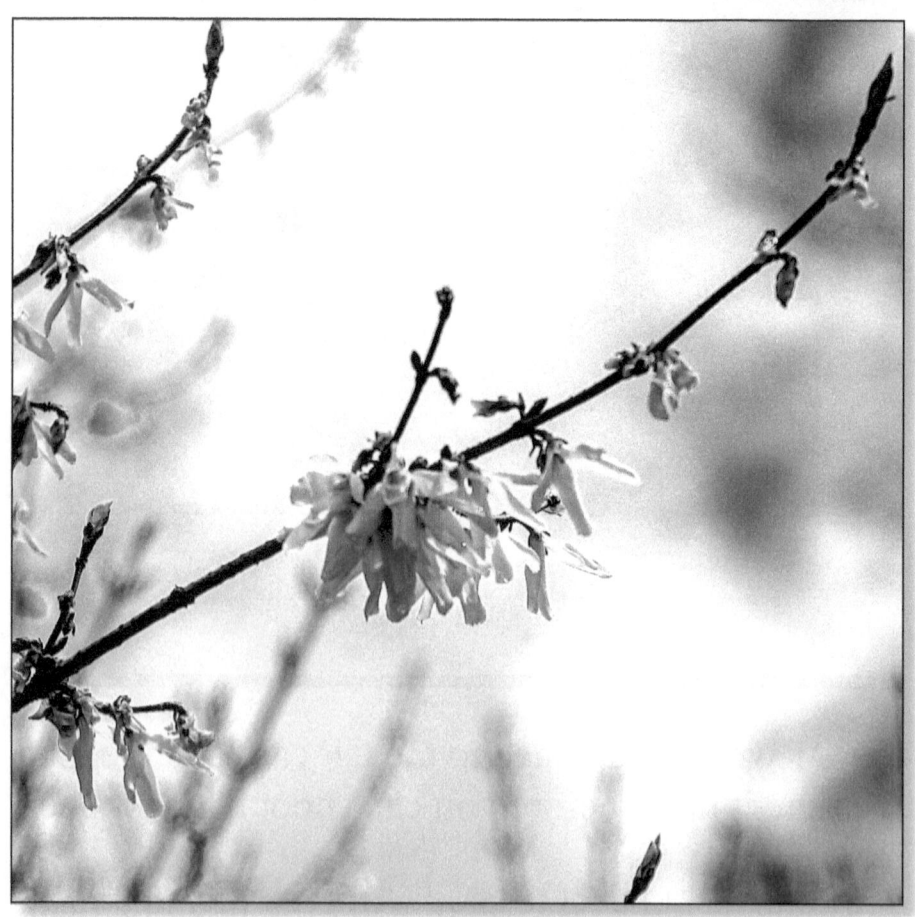

Ballston Lake, NY, May 1, 2014
Nikon D1, 82mm, 1/2500, f/5.6, ISO 200, A, spot
© 2015 Shawn M. Tomlinson

card.

While it's doing this, you can't take a photo, so if you like to shoot a lot and fast, you simply can't in the "S" mode.

The way I got around this is by thinking about how I typically shoot.

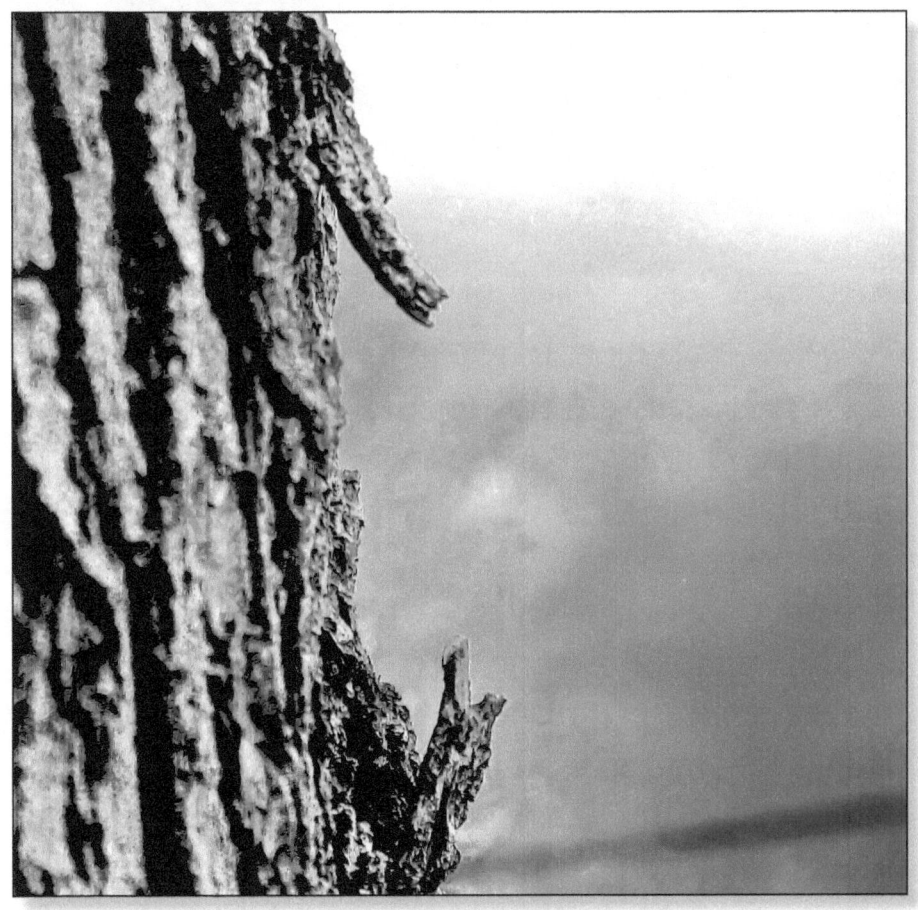

Ballston Lake, NY, April 18, 2014
Nikon D1, 72mm, 1/250, f/9, ISO 200, P, spot
© 2015 Shawn M. Tomlinson

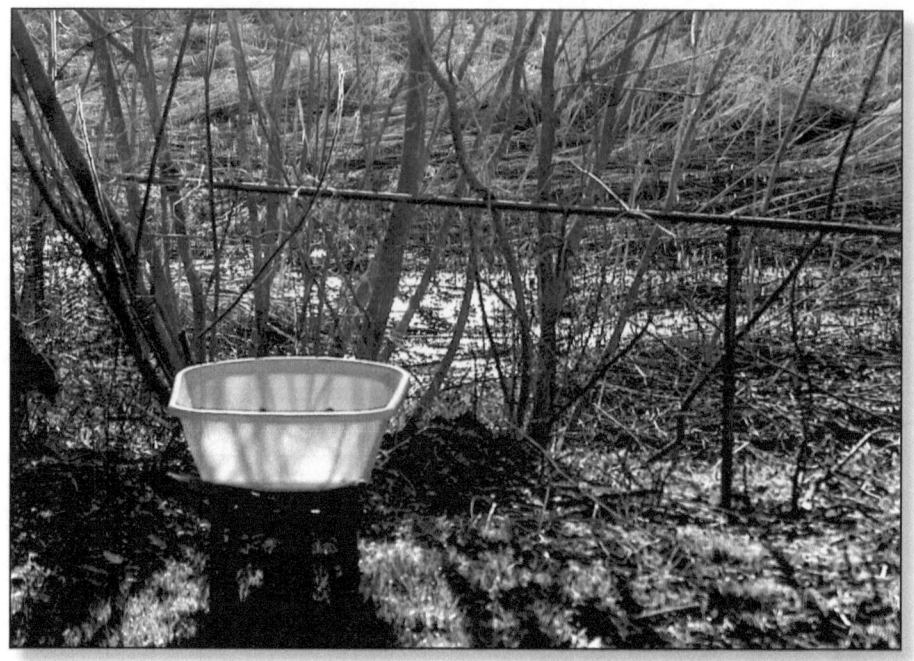

Ballston Lake, NY, May 1, 2014
Nikon D1, 82mm, 1/500, f/5.6, ISO 200, A, pattern
© 2015 Shawn M. Tomlinson

I usually take several images quickly back-to-back, then I don't take any for a few minutes, and then repeat.

So, by setting the D1 to "C" or continual mode, the camera works with me.

This mode allows me to shoot up to five or six images before it stops to buffer, so I can make my usual shots and when I get to the lull period when I'm not shooting, the D1 uses that time to write the images to the card.

Now that I've got the hang of it, this works well.

So, yes, the Nikon D1 is not as easy to use as a Canon EOS Rebel or a Nikon D3300, but, hey, it's a professional DSLR.

It wasn't designed to be easy, just to be great. And it still is.

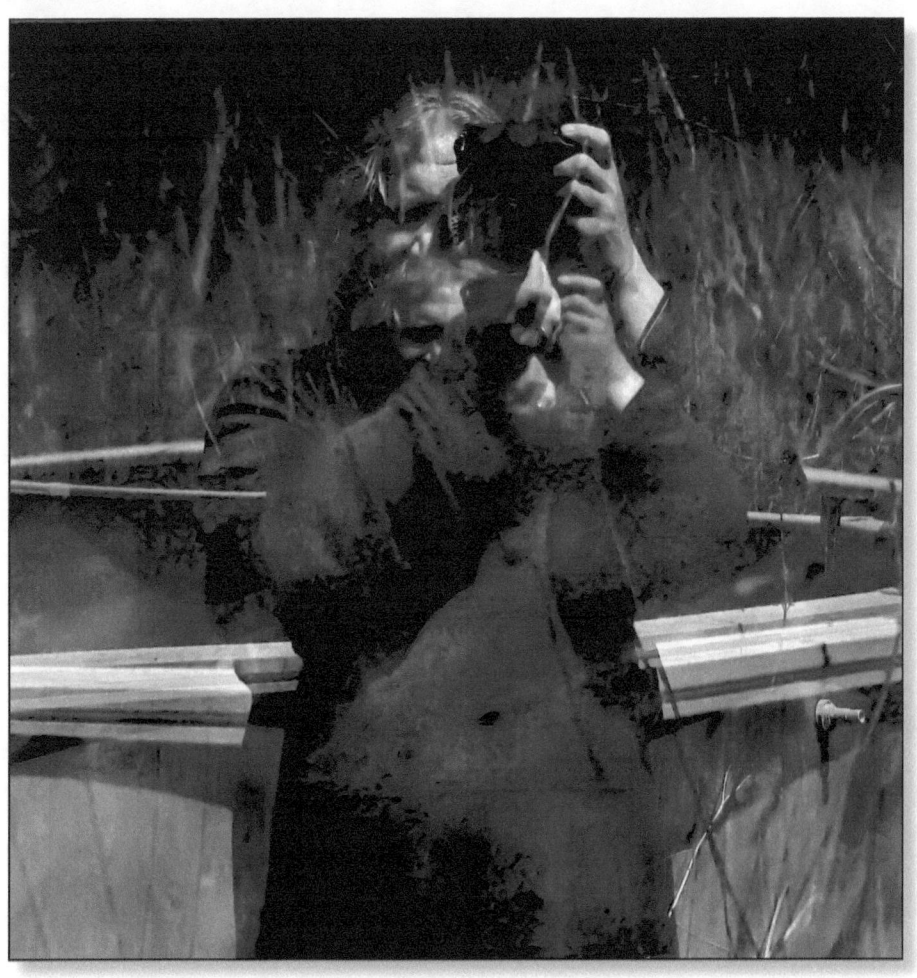

Shawn Tomlinson, Ballston Lake, NY, May 1, 2014
Nikon D1, 48mm, 1/500, f/4.5, ISO 200, A, spot
© 2015 Shawn M. Tomlinson

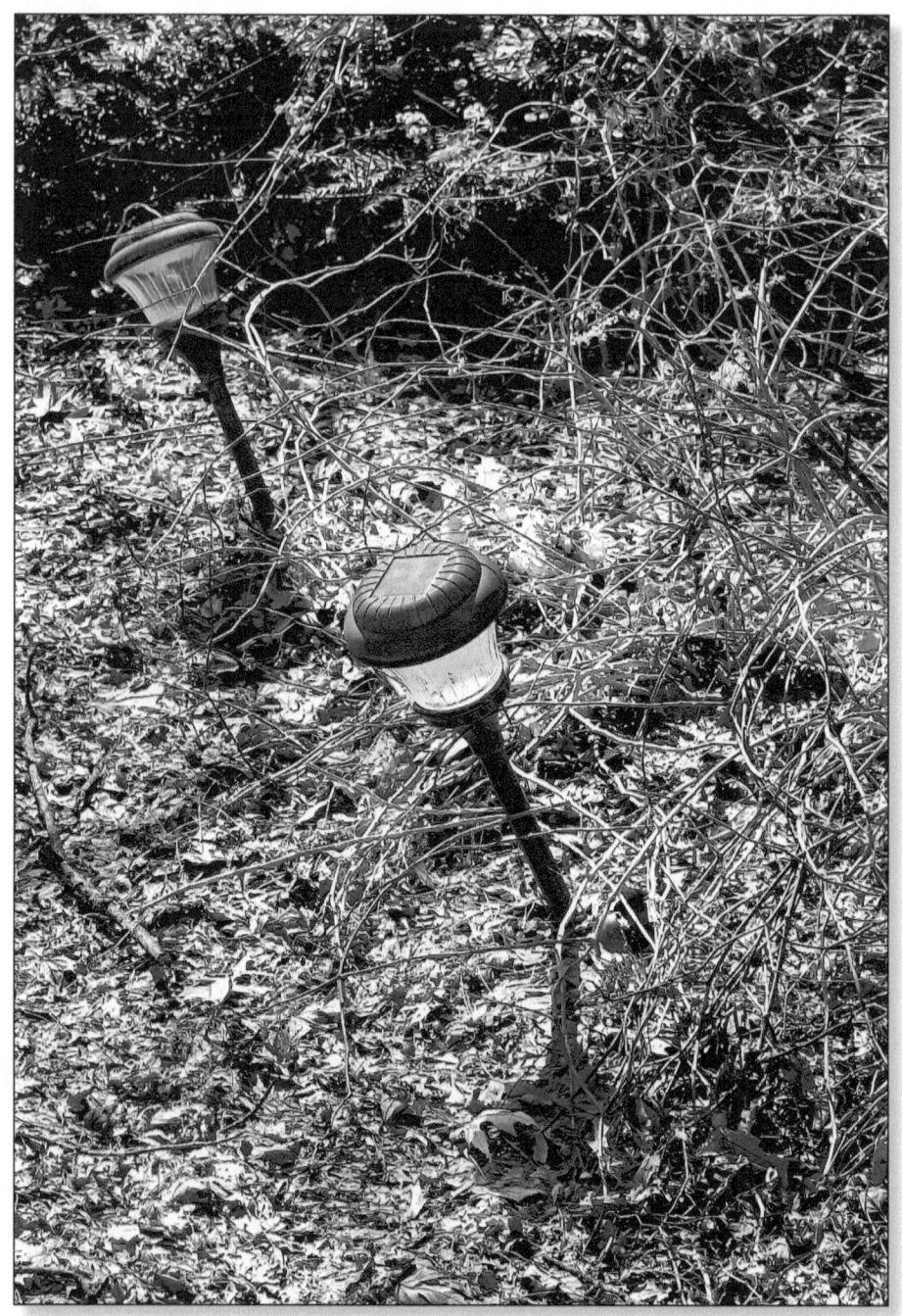

Ballston Lake, NY, April 2, 2014
Nikon D1, 70mm, 1/125, f/11, ISO 200, P, pattern metering
© 2014, 2015 by Shawn M. Tomlinson

# Part 3
# *The Pro Advantage*

A while back, I was forced into the opportunity of revisiting the Nikon D1 because my Nikon D7000 — my main, use-it-every-bloody-day DSLR at the time — died during a shoot.

I was devastated.

I was using the D7000 as my primary camera and it is a fantastic DSLR.

Because I shoot every day, I couldn't let this get in my way.

At the time, I had several other working DSLRs:

• Nikon D70 (entry-level; 6.1 megapixels)
• Pentax *ist DS (entry level; 6.1 megapixels)
• Canon EOS 20D (semi-pro; 8.2 megapixels)
• Pentax K20D (semi-pro; 14.2 megapixels)

Now, from this list, it may appear that the Pentax K20D and its 14.2-megapixel resolution would be the obvious, closest replacement for the 16.2 megapixel Nikon D7000.

The thing is, that wasn't what I ended up shooting with while awaiting a replacement for the D7000.

The reason I moved away from Pentax after 32 years with its cameras is that it does not produce the vivid colors — in my opinion — that the Nikons do, and it doesn't focus nearly as quickly, especially in non-ideal lighting conditions.

The Nikon D1 focuses fast. Very

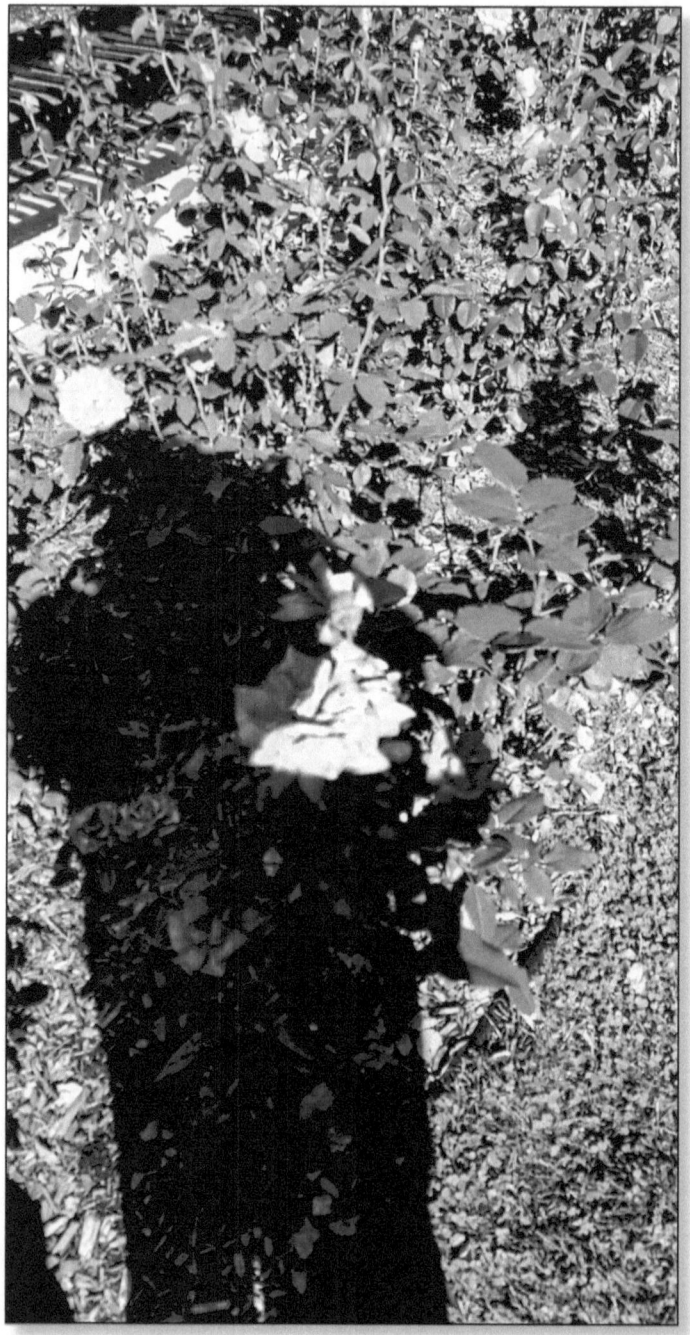

Rose Garden, Central Park, Schenectady, NY, Aug. 17, 2014
Nikon D1, 18mm, 1/400, f/5.6, ISO 200, Av, pattern metering
© 2014, 2015 by Shawn M. Tomlinson

fast.

It's a *pro* DSLR.

So, I took my favorite lens, a prime Nikon AF D 28mm f/2.8, and got out there shooting.

I'd never used a prime lens on the D1 before and the sharpness improvement really showed.

It almost always does, no matter what DSLR you use, with a prime lens.

This lens makes my entry-level D70 sharper, too.

I hadn't shot with the D1 in a while, not since I had been using the D7000.

It was like shooting with a new camera.

Holding the D1 in my hands was and always is a

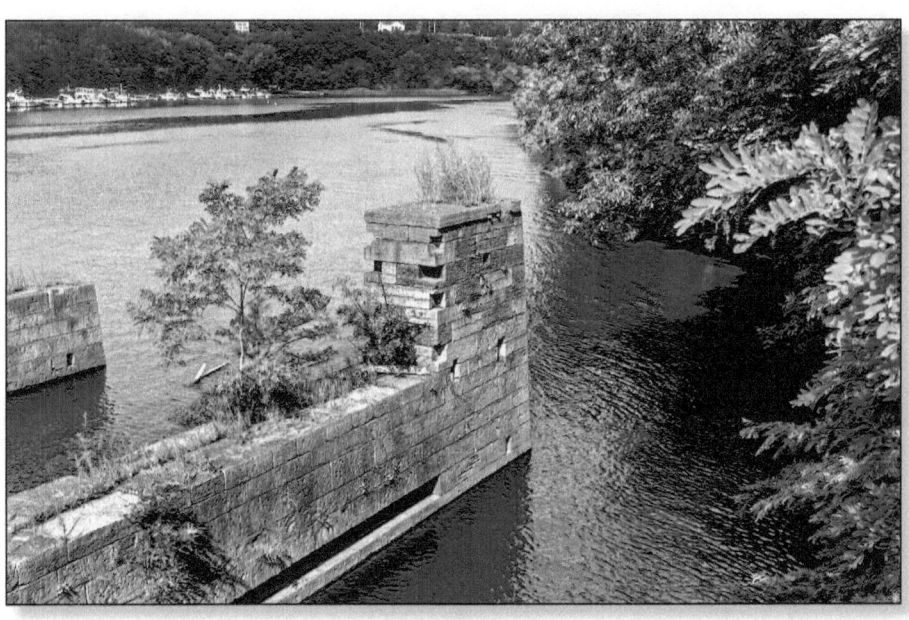

Aqueduct, Rexford, NY, July 16, 2014
Nikon D1, 28mm, 1/1250, f/3.5, ISO 200, Av, pattern metering
© 2014, 2015 by Shawn M. Tomlinson

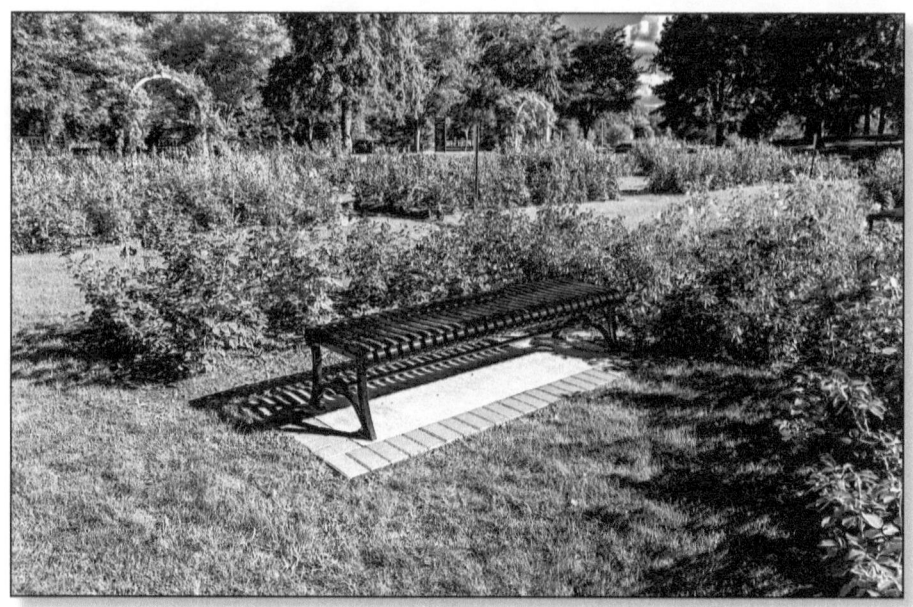

Rose Garden, Central Park, Schenectady, NY, Aug. 17, 2014
Nikon D1, 18mm, 1/500, f/5.6, ISO 200, Av, pattern metering
© 2014, 2015 by Shawn M. Tomlinson

joy.

I like the tough build and weight of it. I like the resounding sound it makes when I press the shutter release.

And the images?

Yes, OK, 2.65-megapixel resolution is not quite as sharp as 16.2, but the images are very good, especially the color.

The key, of course, as I reiterate in everything I write about digital photography, is following the two **ABSOLUTE RULES** for serious shooting:

1) **ALWAYS** shoot in **RAW**.
2) **ALWAYS** shoot at the **LOWEST POSSI-**

**BLE ISO** sensitivity setting.

It isn't the easiest thing to figure out how to set the D1 to RAW — it takes two separate actions to do it in the esoteric menus — but it is worth the headache.

When I first had the D1, I could not figure out — even with the manual — how to set it to RAW.

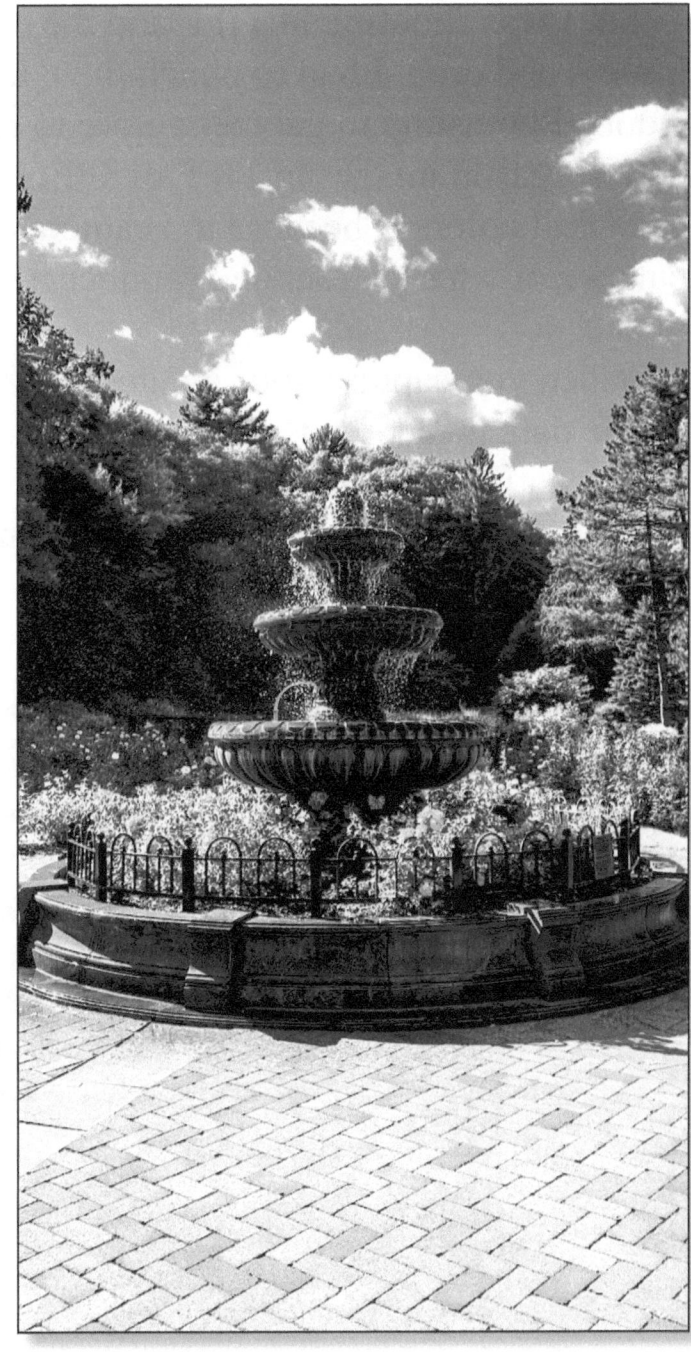

Rose Garden, Central Park, Schenectady, NY, Aug. 17, 2014
Nikon D1, 18mm, 1/500, f/5.6, ISO 200, Av, pattern metering
© 2014, 2015 by Shawn M. Tomlinson

So, I was shooting in TIFF and the colors were lifeless and drab. I had to punch them up a lot in Adobe Photoshop to get them close to reality.

The reason images in TIFF or JPEG in DSLRs have dull colors is because the cameras determine a balance of what you set and produce a compromise image.

When you capture your images in RAW format, all the data is recorded, which gives you much greater latitude in fine-tuning them.

The color straight from the camera in RAW always is better than in JPEG or TIFF.

This is more difficult than it needs to be, but still

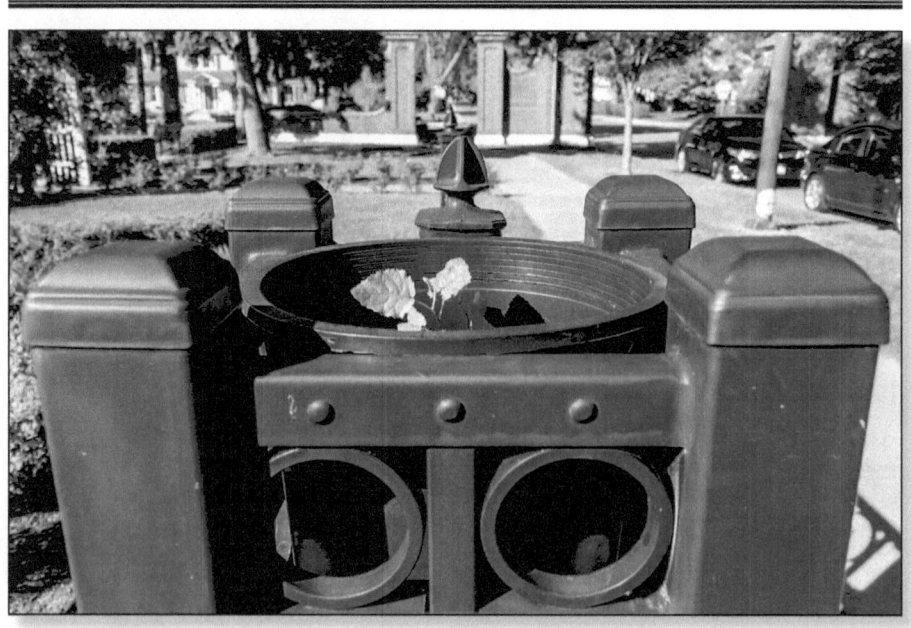

Rose Garden, Central Park, Schenectady, NY, Aug. 17, 2014
Nikon D1, 18mm, 1/500, f/5.6, ISO 200, Av, pattern metering
© 2014, 2015 by Shawn M. Tomlinson

doable.

Here's how to set the D1 to record RAW images:

1) Press the "CSM" (custom function) button on the rear panel at the bottom of the camera.

2) While pressing the "CSM" button, turn the rear Command dial to select custom function "28" shown on the rear small LCD near the bottom next

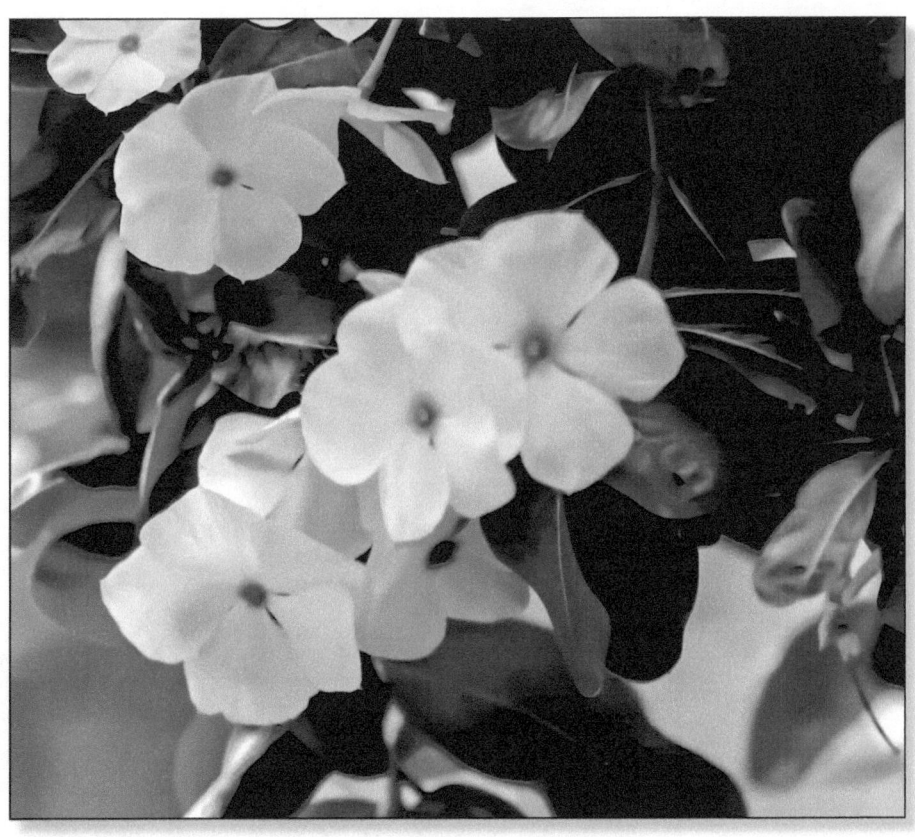

Saratoga Springs, NY, Aug. 5, 2014
Nikon D1, 300mm, 1/1250, f/5.6, ISO 200, S, pattern metering
© 2014, 2015 by Shawn M. Tomlinson

to the buttons.

3) Use the front Sub-Command dial to change it from "0" to "1."

No, you're not done.

4) Press the "QUAL" (quality) button on that same panel at the lower back.

5) While holding it, turn the Command dial (rear) until the small LCD at the back posts the

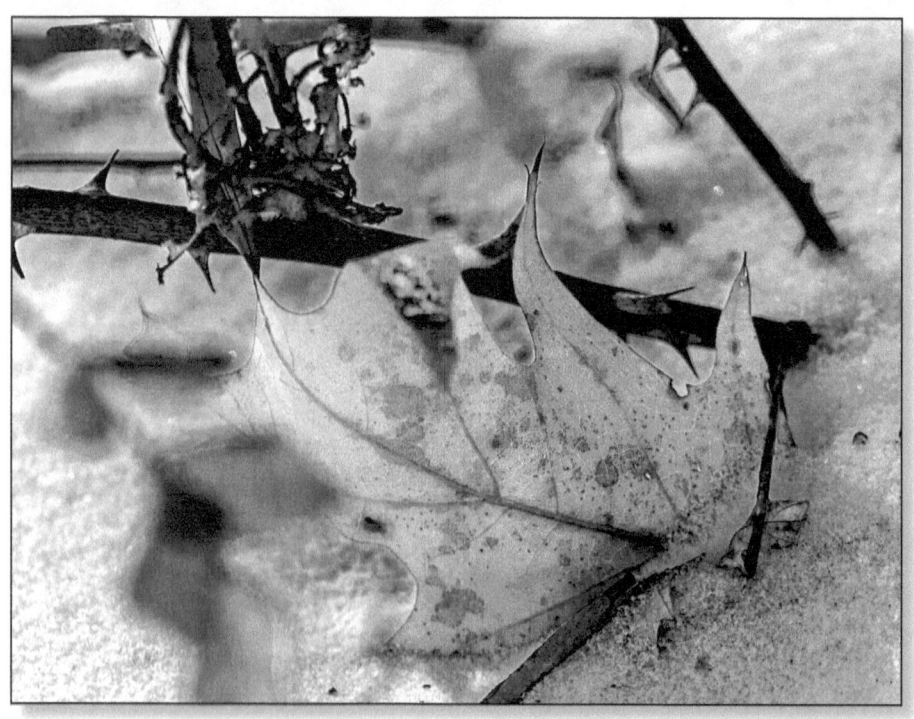

Ballston Lake, NY, Jan. 8, 2015
Nikon D1, 270mm, 1/320, f/5.3, ISO 800, M, pattern metering
© 2015 by Shawn M. Tomlinson

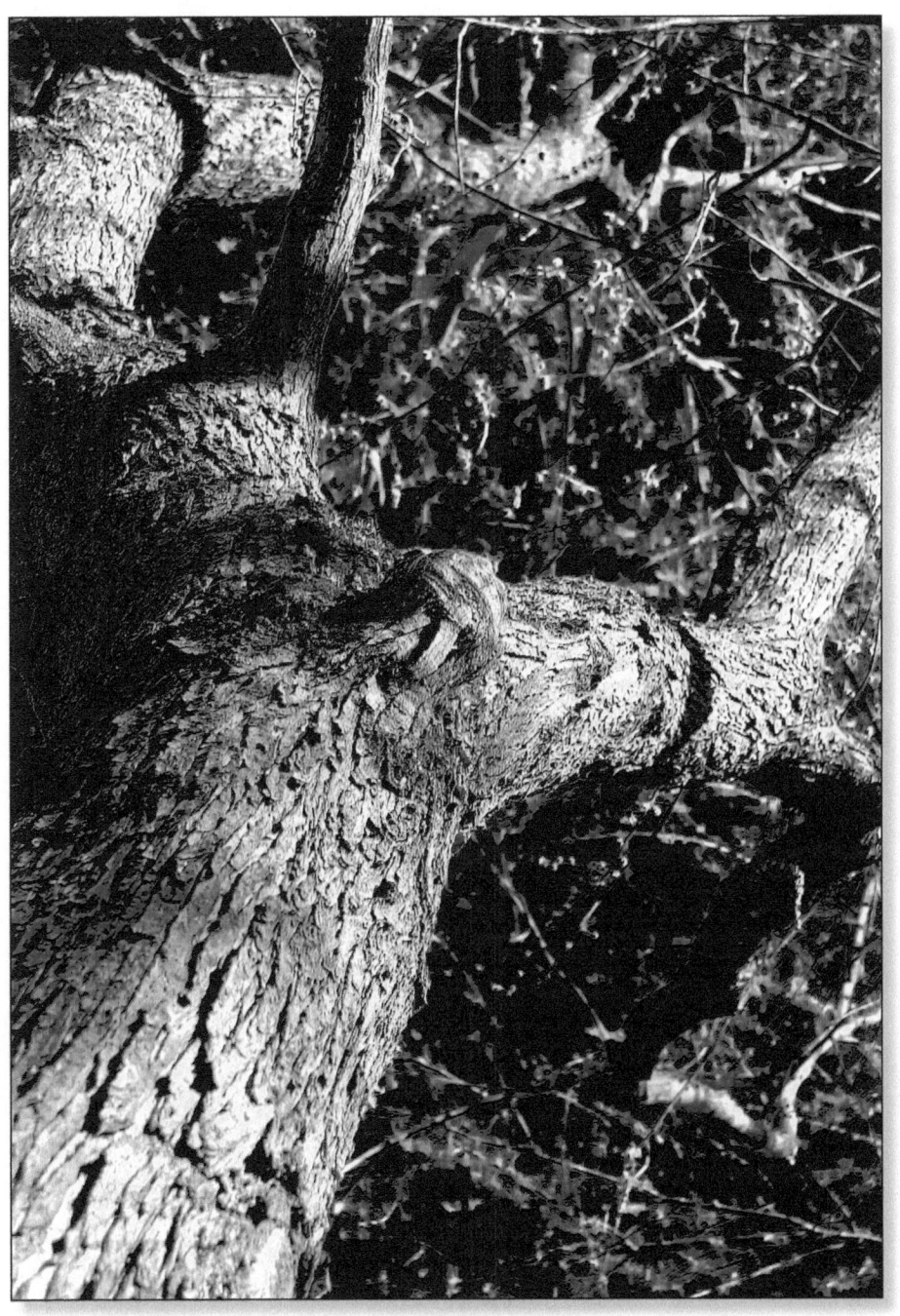

Ballston Lake, NY, April 2, 2014
Nikon D1, 70mm, 1/180, f/6.7, ISO 200, P, pattern metering
© 2014, 2015 by Shawn M. Tomlinson

cryptic "2.7r" message.

Not exactly intuitive.

Still, as I said, it is worth it because once you start shooting in RAW, you will be astonished at the color you will get from the ancient Nikon D1.

Not long after the D7000 died, KEH.com re-

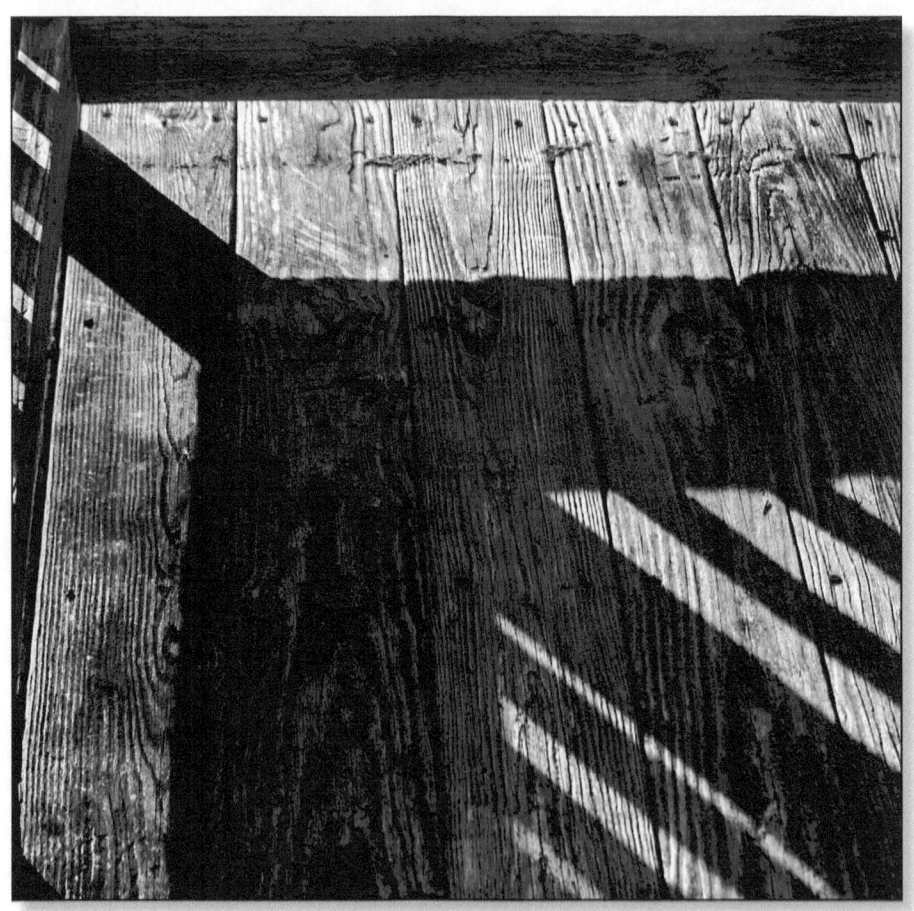

Ballston Lake, NY, May 1, 2014
Nikon D1, 60mm, 1/500, f/5.6, ISO 200, A, pattern
© 2015 Shawn M. Tomlinson

placed it with a special delivery on the Sunday before Christmas, one more reason this is my favorite photographic equipment dealer.

And since the initial publication of this book, my DSLR arsenal has grown considerably.

I also made another mindset change that, if you do it, too, it will make even the ancient Nikon D1

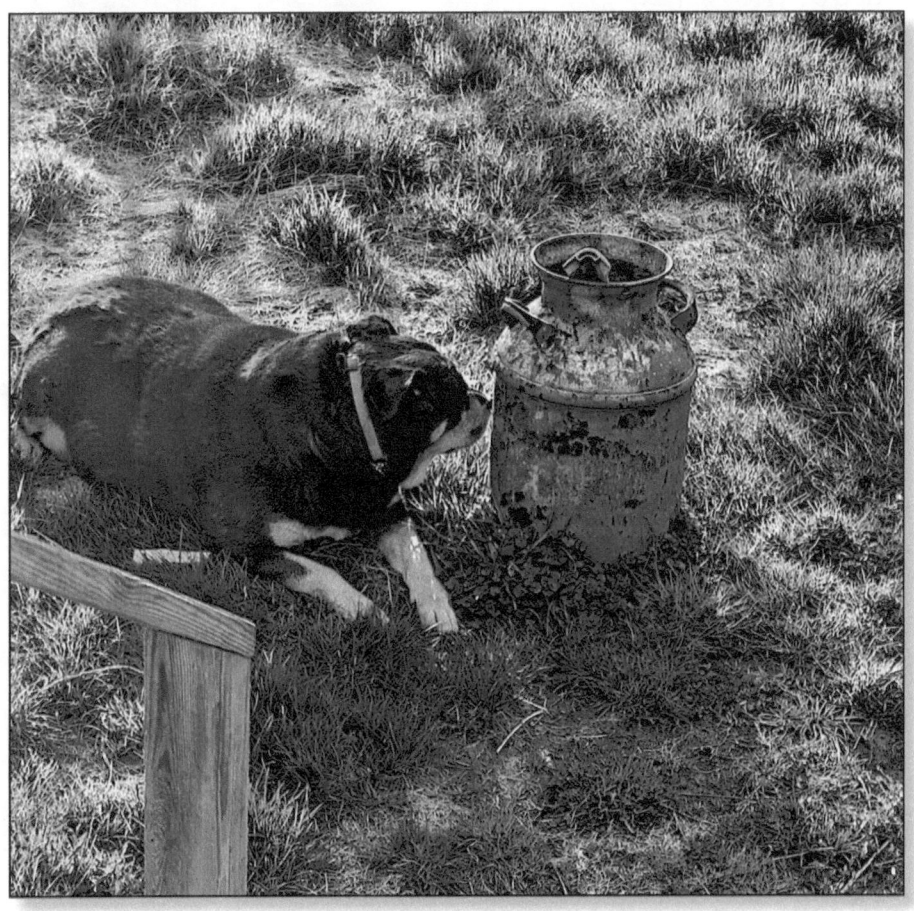

Baby, Ballston Lake, NY, May 1, 2014
Nikon D1, 48mm, 1/250, f/5.6, ISO 200, A, pattern
© 2015 Shawn M. Tomlinson

into a sig-
nificantly
better cam-
era.

First, as
a fun thing,
I acquired
a Sony
A100, the
first DSLR
from that
company.

It was
produced
in 2006
using much
of the
technolo-
gy Sony
acquired
when it
bought it
from Mi-
nolta.

This last
bit was sig-
nificant for
me because

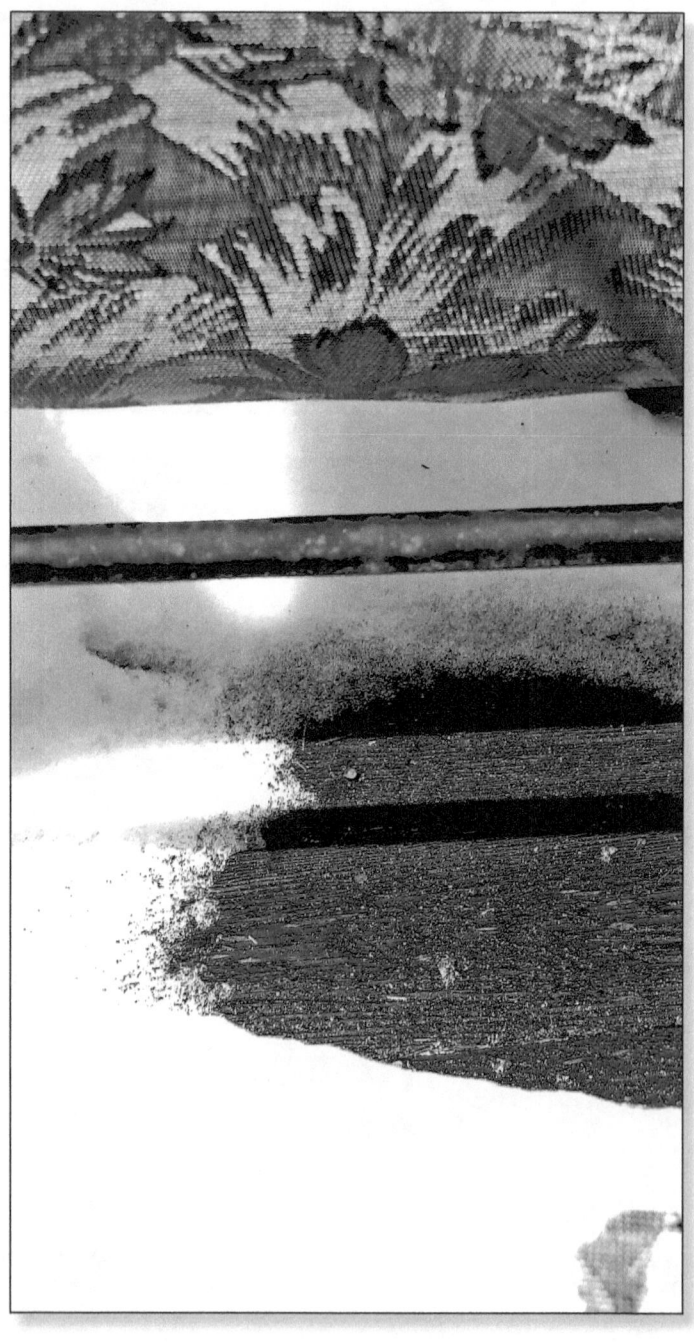

Ballston Lake, NY, April 16, 2014
Nikon D1, 70mm, 1/125, f/7.6, ISO 200, P, spot
© 2015 Shawn M. Tomlinson

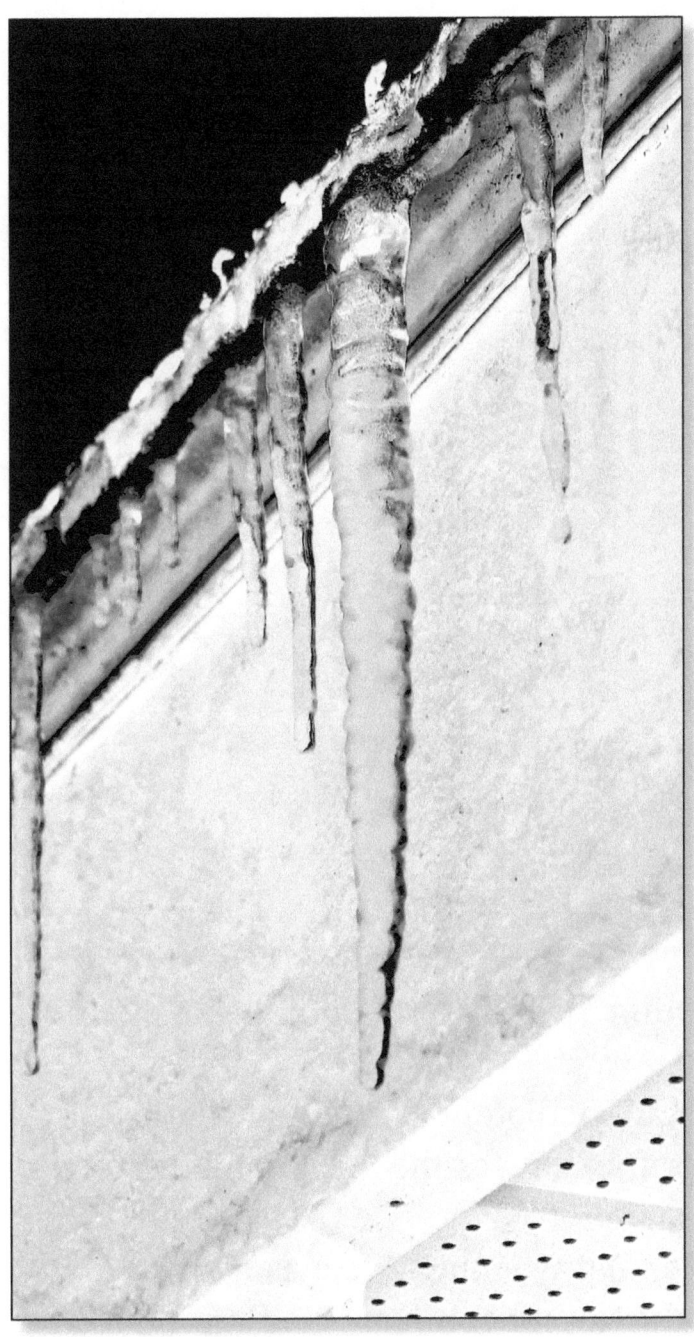

it meant that older autofocus Minolta Maxxum lenses would work on the Sony A100.

These lenses are a lot cheaper — and yet very good, some of them — than buying modern Sony lenses.

When I bought the A100, I already had a Velveeta (Quan-

Ballston Lake, NY, April 16, 2014
Nikon D1, 80mm, 1/160, f/8, ISO 200, P, spot
© 2015 Shawn M. Tomlinson

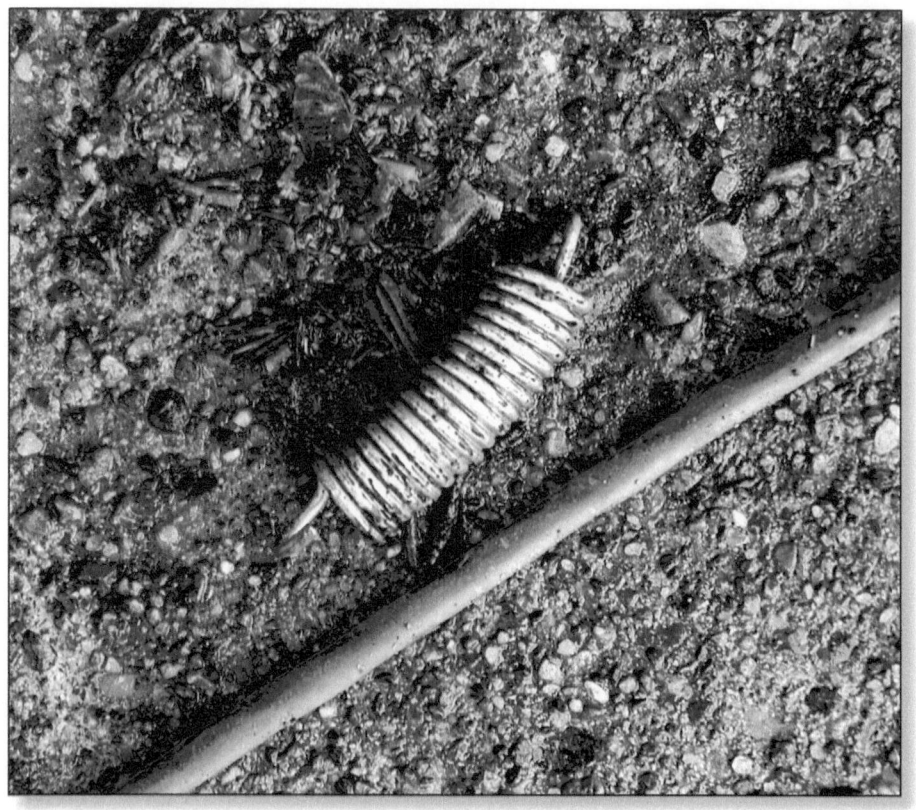

Broadalbin, NY, May 2, 2014
Nikon D1, 82mm, 1/60, f/5.6, ISO 200, A, pattern
© 2015 Shawn M. Tomlinson

taray) 75-300mm Tech-10, so I could start shooting right away.

However, I immediately ordered a Minolta 50mm f/1.7 prime lens for the A100, and the world changed.

As an aside, that Quantaray lens is the best I've seen from that low-end company, and it produced surprisingly good images for me.

That 50mm lens, however, was a revelation.

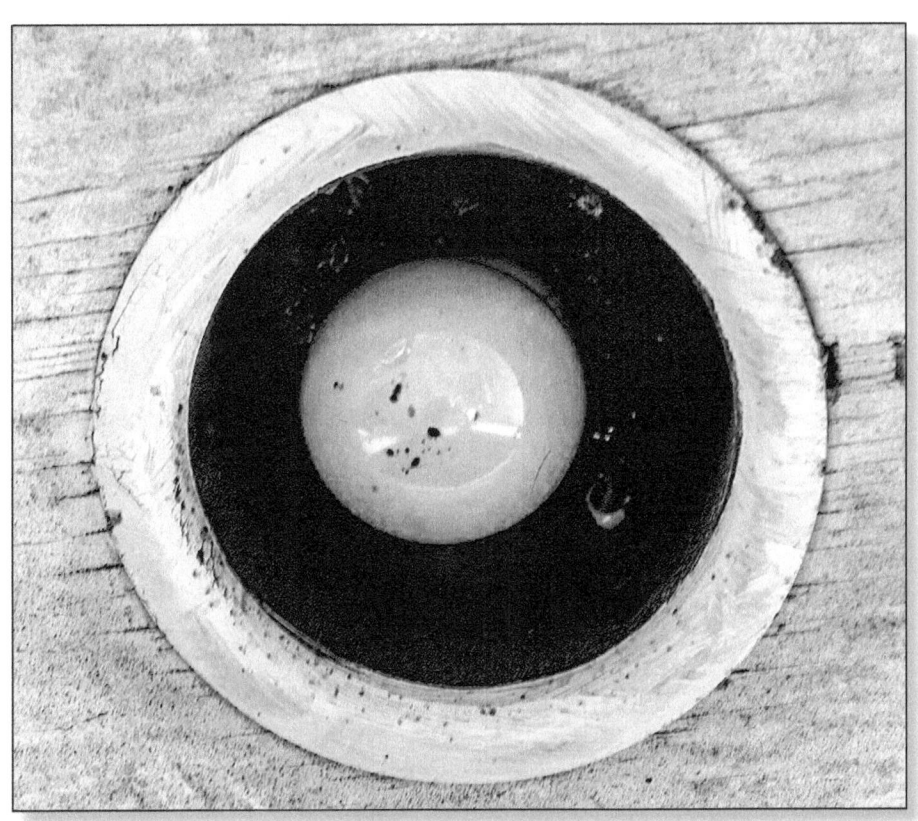

And don't worry, this all connects to the Nikon D1.

Pardon the excursion.

The Sony A100 is kind of a clunky, entry-level DSLR, but it does produce great images. That is especially true when I put a prime lens on it.

The astonishingly sharp images of the prime lens on the Sony A100 led immediately to the purchase of a Canon EF II 50mm f/1.8 prime lens for my

Canon EOS 20D.

The same thing happened.

The images suddenly were much sharper.

I couldn't shell out the money for a Nikon prime right then, but my friend and photographic colleague, Gary Ziroli, had purchased a Nikon AF D 28mm f/2.8 that he wasn't using much, so he

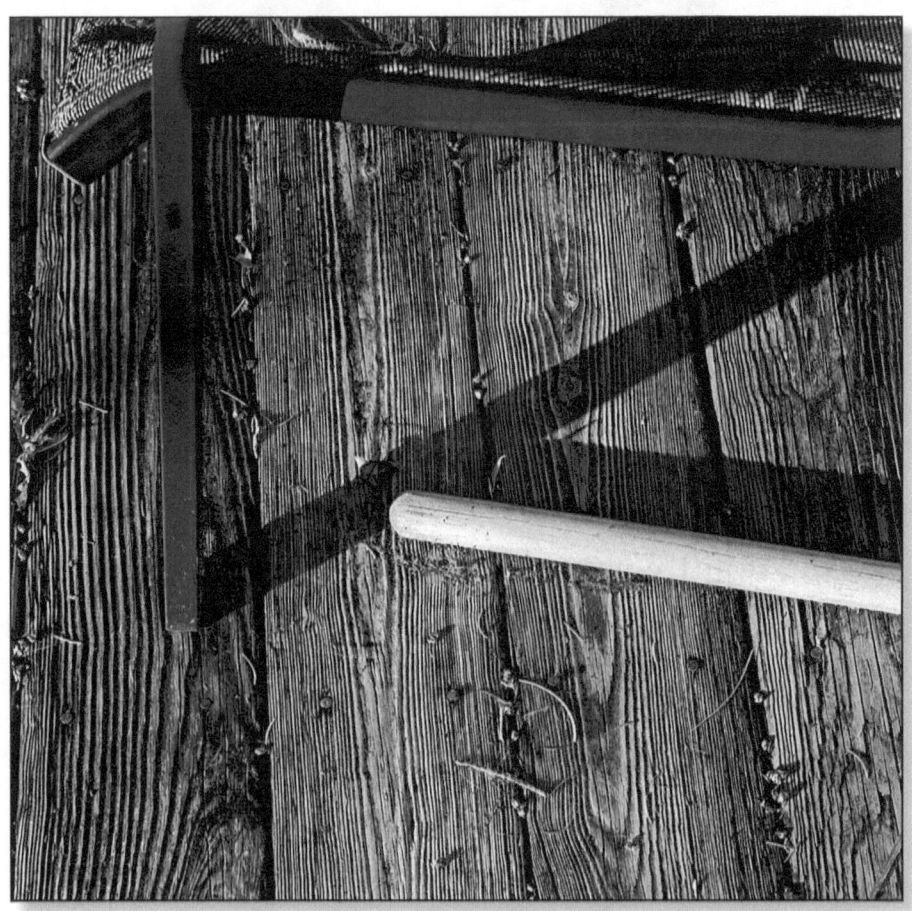

Ballston Lake, NY, May 1, 2014
Nikon D1, 48mm, 1/320, f/5.6, ISO 200, A, pattern
© 2015 Shawn M. Tomlinson

loaned it to me.

In the meantime, I had bought a Nikon D2x because the price had dropped $100.

Later, I added the sensational Nikon D800e.

My sudden obsession with prime lenses — which actually took me full-circle because, of course, I started with 50mm primes in the 1970s

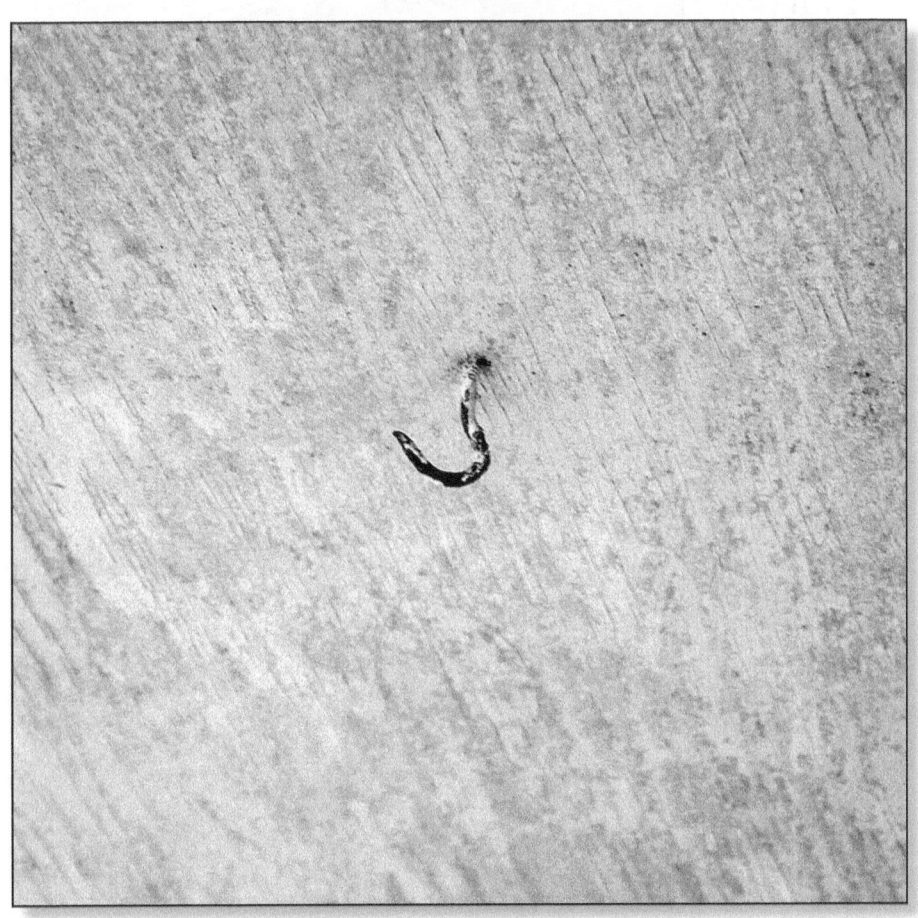

Broadalbin, NY, May 2, 2014
Nikon D1, 82mm, 1/80, f/5.6, ISO 200, A, pattern
© 2015 Shawn M. Tomlinson

— led me to the Nikon AF D 50mm f/1.8 lens, which cost less than $100.

I immediately tried that lens on all my Nikon DSLRs, including the D1. It quickly became my, ahem, prime choice in lenses.

Because prime lenses are so much sharper than zoom

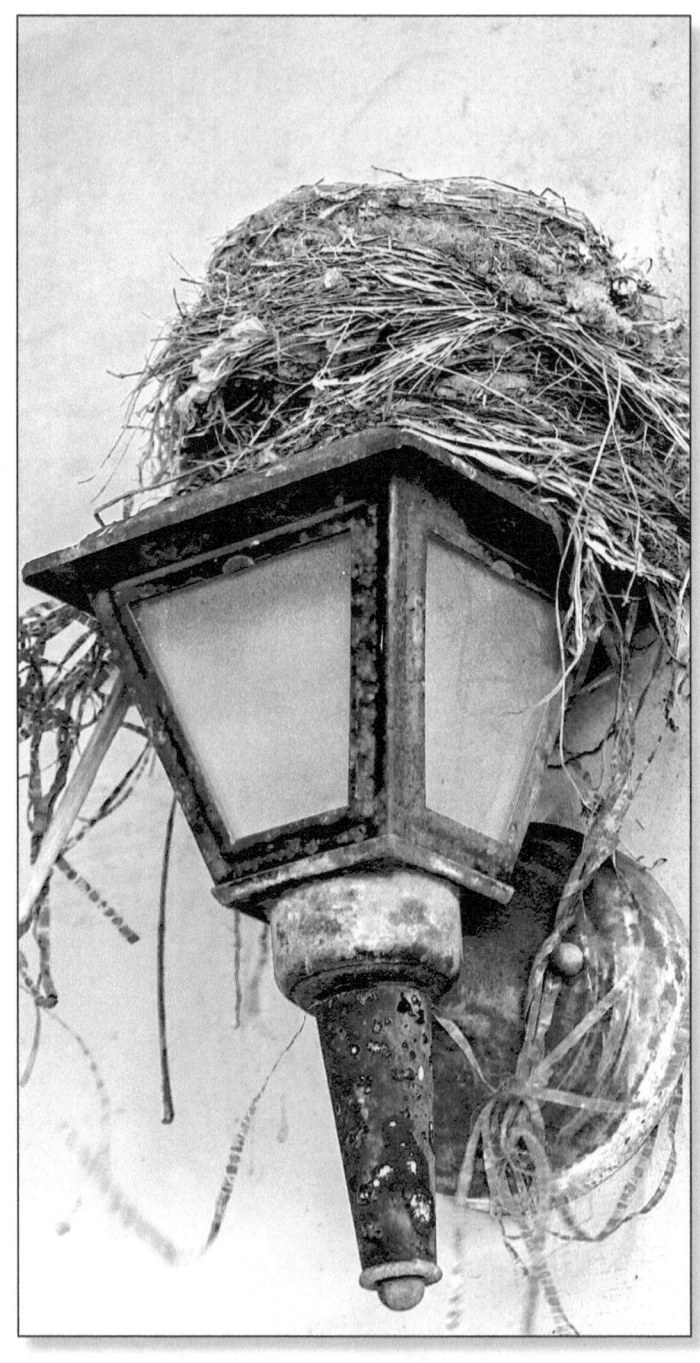

Broadalbin, NY, May 2, 2014
Nikon D1, 82mm, 1/80, f/5.6, ISO 200, A, pattern
© 2015 Shawn M. Tomlinson

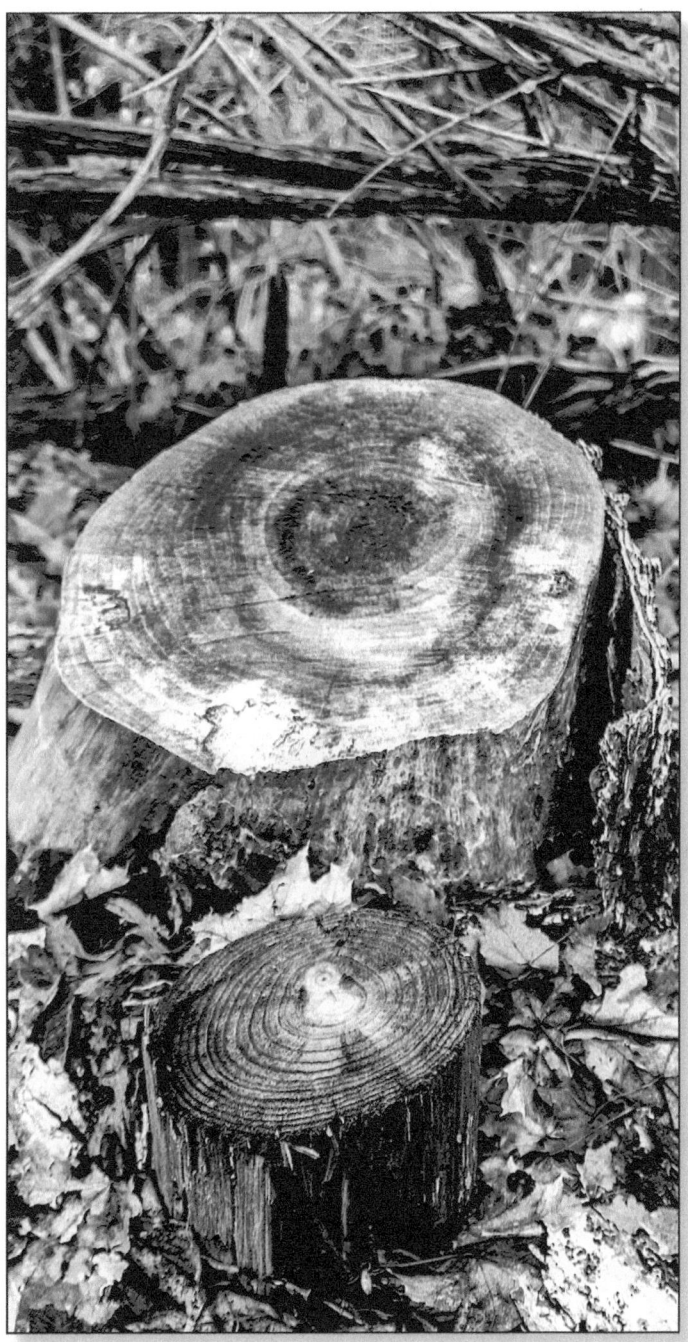

lenses — which I had been using nearly exclusively since about 1994 — each camera I put that 50mm on — and the 28mm before it, and the Nikon G 35mm f/1.8 lens, also borrowed from Gary — got much better.

The photos were crisper with

Broadalbin, NY, May 2, 2014
Nikon D1, 52mm, 1/320, f/5.6, ISO 200, A, pattern
© 2015 Shawn M. Tomlinson

more detail.

The Nikon D1 does have a very low resolution — 2.65 megapixels — by today's standards, but you can put those megapixels to work for you more effectively with a prime lens.

Later in the year, I bought a Nikon AF-S 105mm f/2.8 VR Micro lens, another prime, to get the most

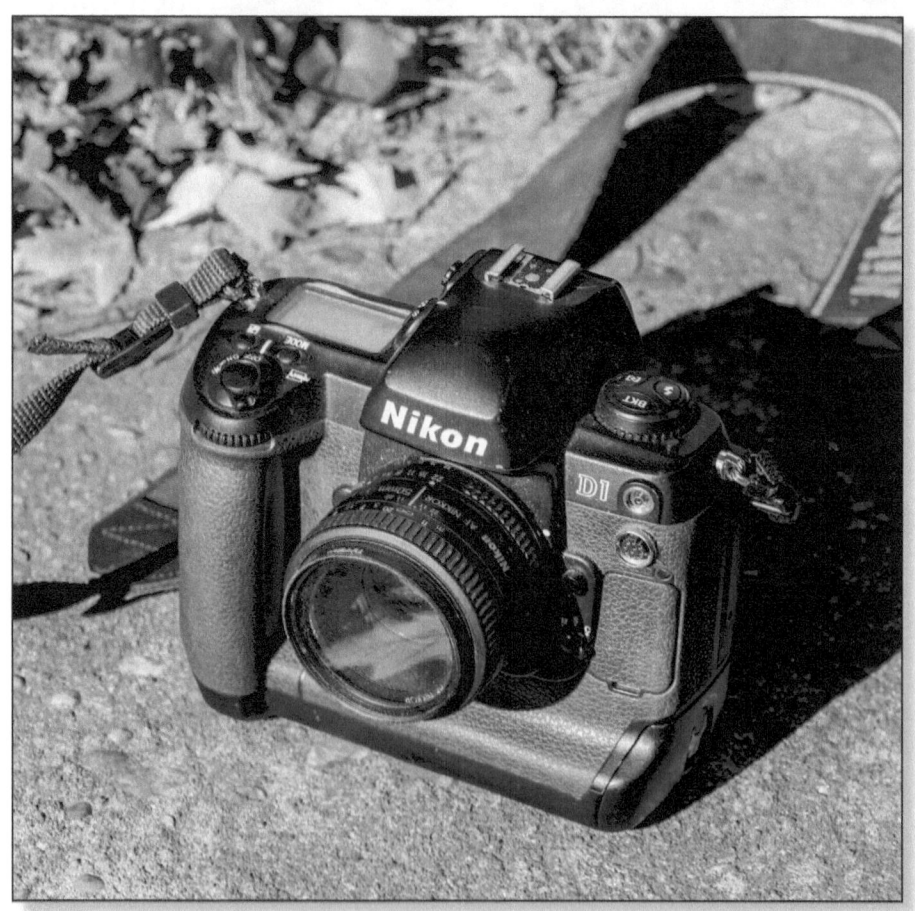

The Nikon D1 is shown with a Nikon AF D 50mm f/1.8 prime lens
Oct. 19, 2015 in Ballston Lake, NY.

out of those 36 megapixels in the Nikon D800e.

Again, I started trying it on all the other Nikon DSLRs, and again, the results were fantastic.

The Nikon D1 — and virtually every other DSLR — benefits wonderfully from prime lenses.

Many photographers go on and on about the advantages of "good glass," the best lenses you can

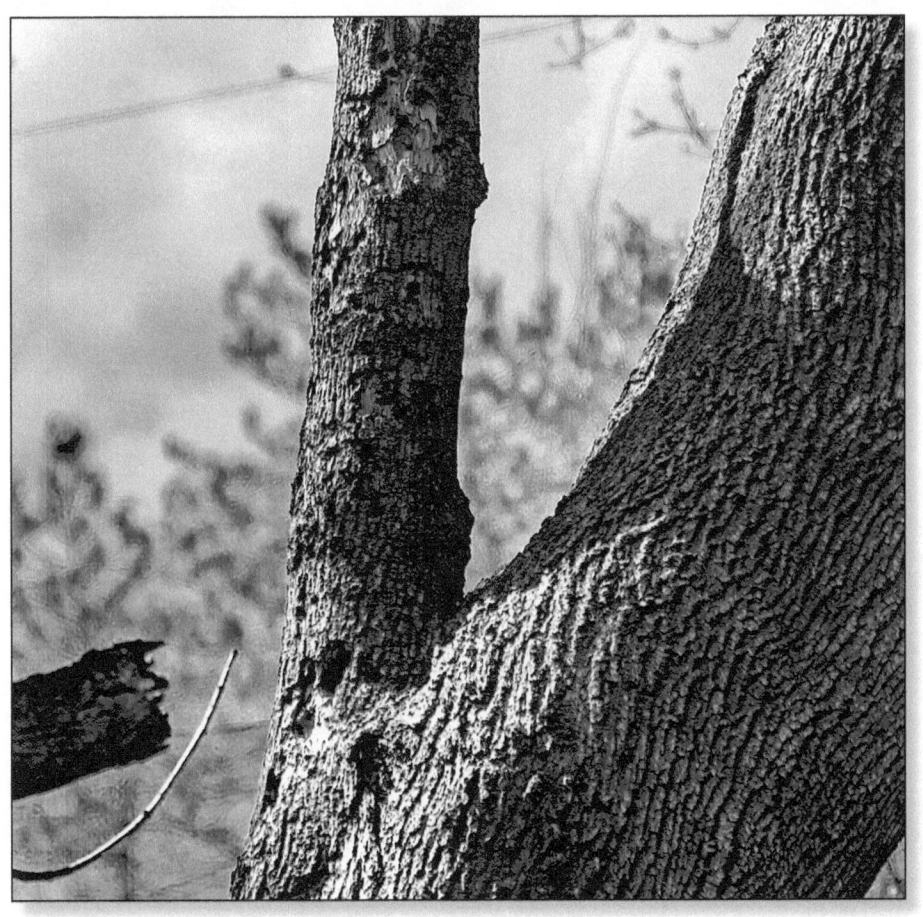

Broadalbin, NY, May 2, 2014
Nikon D1, 82mm, 1/1250, f/5.6, ISO 200, A, pattern
© 2015 Shawn M. Tomlinson

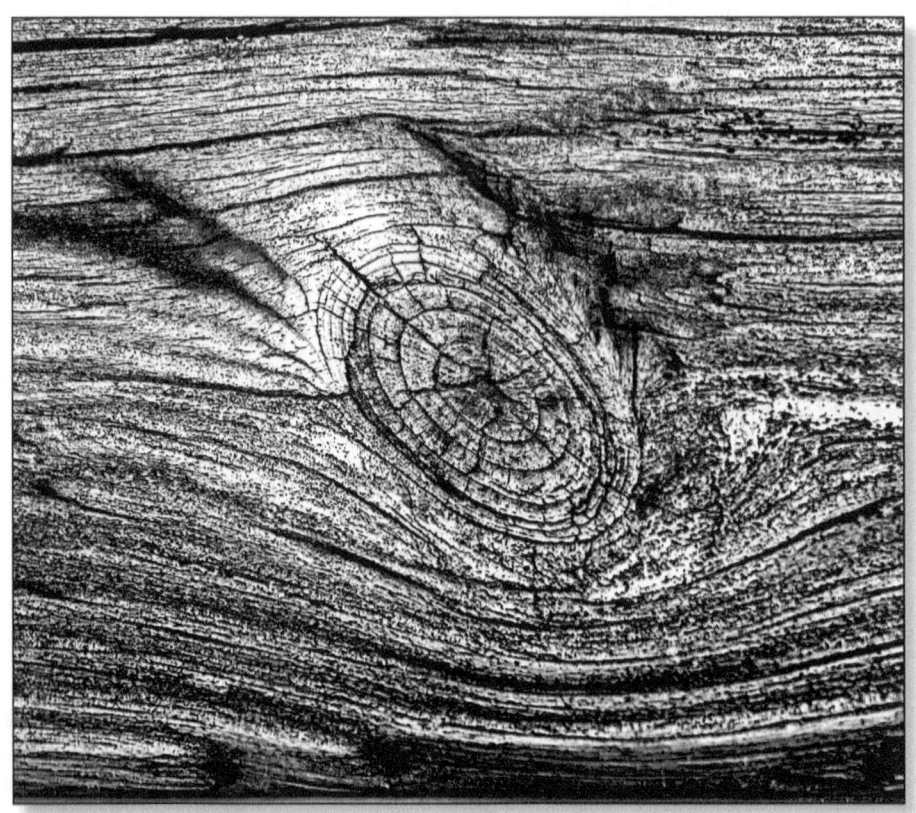

Ballston Lake, NY, May 4, 2014
Nikon D1, 82mm, 1/320, f/5.6, ISO 200, A, pattern
© 2015 Shawn M. Tomlinson

get.

I do, too.

Zoom lenses are much more convenient than primes, but the trade-off most of the time is a decrease in sharpness in your images.

You probably don't even notice this if you've never shot with prime lenses. I didn't notice it, and I had shot with manual-focus primes many years previously.

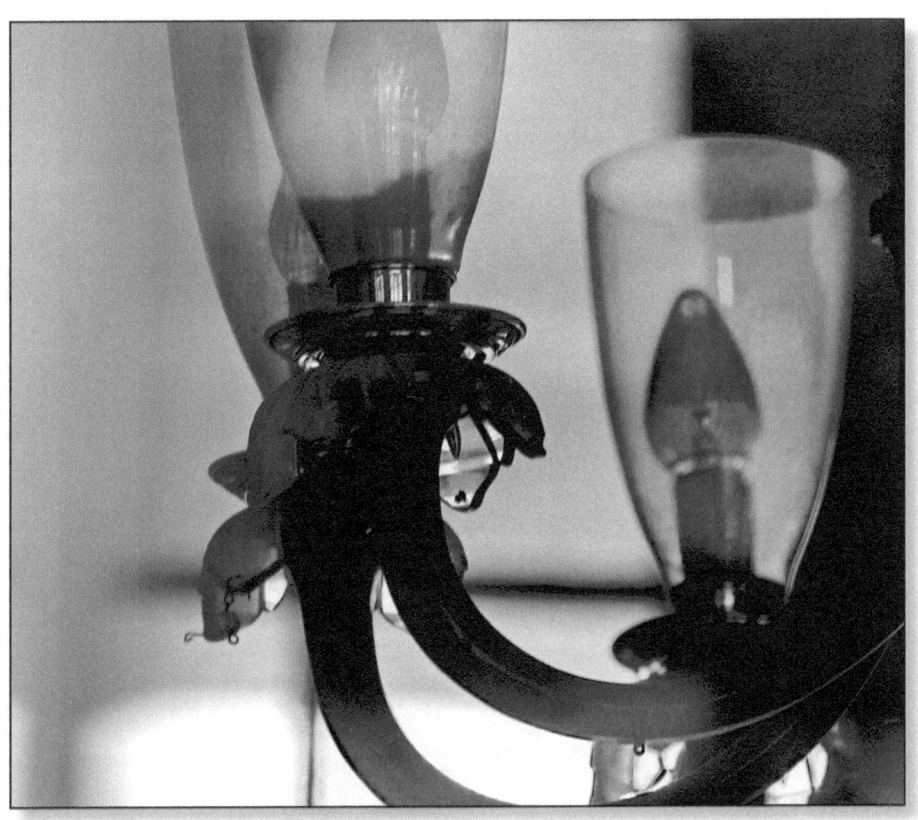

Roosevelt Baths, Saratoga Springs, NY, Aug. 2, 2014
Nikon D1, 300mm, 1/160, f/5.6, ISO 200, A, pattern
© 2015 Shawn M. Tomlinson

Once you see the results, though, my guess is that you may shun your zoom lenses much of the time.

I used to use a Nikon AF 28-80mm f/3.5-5.6 lens most of the time on the D1. Then I used the Tamron D LD 70-300mm f/4-5.6 super zoom a lot.

As an aside, if you like to shoot macro flower images, that Tamron lens does work well on the D1.

It is not the sharpest of lenses, far from it. I only

paid $29 for it.

What it gives you, especially on the Nikon D1, is softer images.

Most of the time, you probably won't want softer images, but in the case of close-up macro shots of flowers, it really adds to the effect.

Anyway, now I generally put the 50mm lens

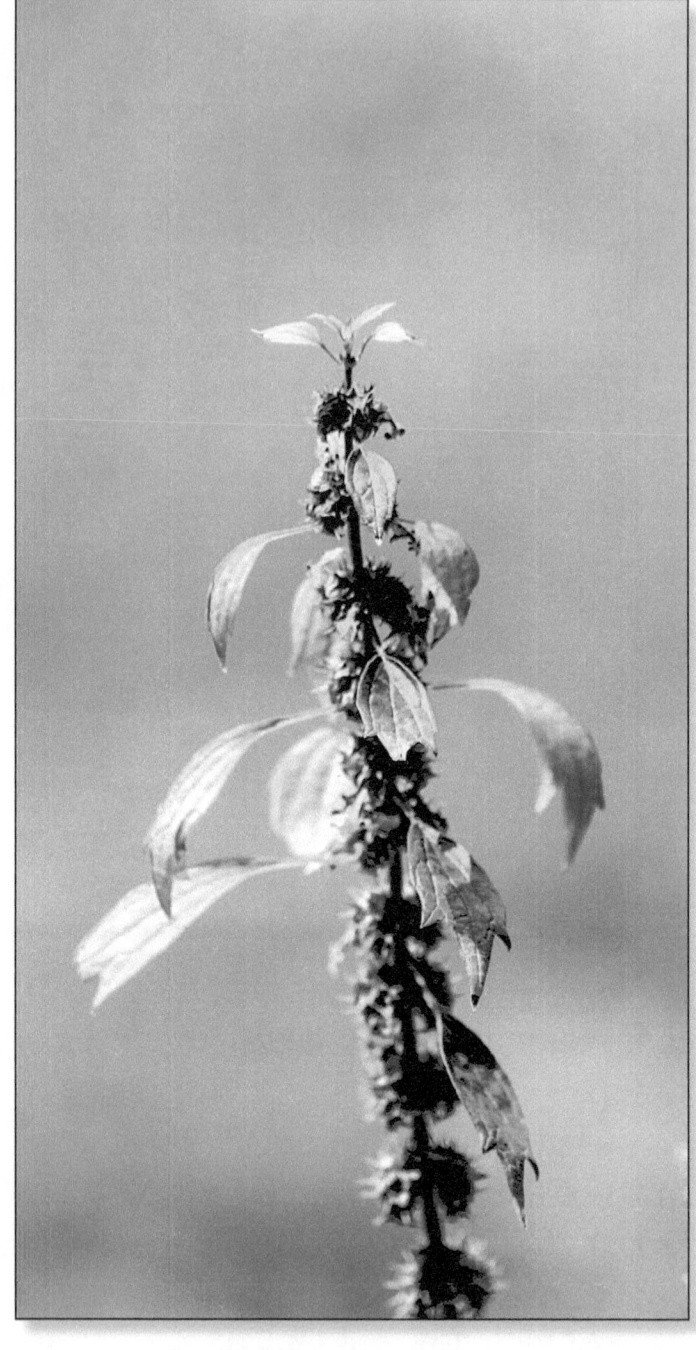

Saratoga Springs, NY, Aug. 2, 2014
Nikon D1, 300mm, 1/500, f/5.6, ISO 200, A, pattern
© 2015 Shawn M. Tomlinson

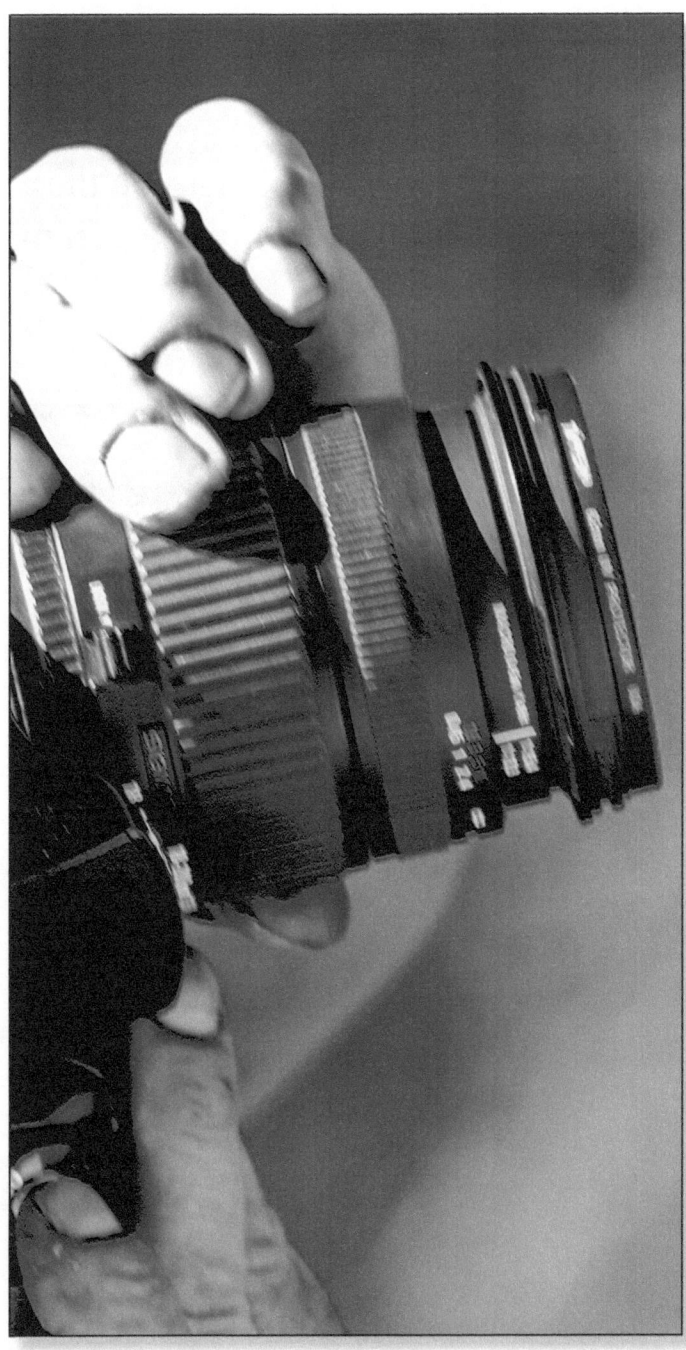

Gary Ziroli, Roosevelt Baths, Saratoga Springs, NY, Aug. 2, 2014
Nikon D1, 300mm, 1/125, f/5.6, ISO 200, A, pattern
© 2015 Shawn M. Tomlinson

on the D1 when I take it out to shoot. That is, unless as indicated above, I'm photo-graphing flowers.

There are many prime lenses in a variety of focal lengths.

I happen to like that 50mm best because on the D1's APS-C sensor, it gives me an equiv-alent focal length of 75mm (1.5 x 50 = 75), which is considered a portrait lens. It produces great bokeh and just looks *right* to me.

If you want a "normal" lens focal length on the D1 — or any APS-C DSLR — you'll need a 35mm (1.5 x 35 = 52.5) to get there.

However, you can get a wider-angle with other

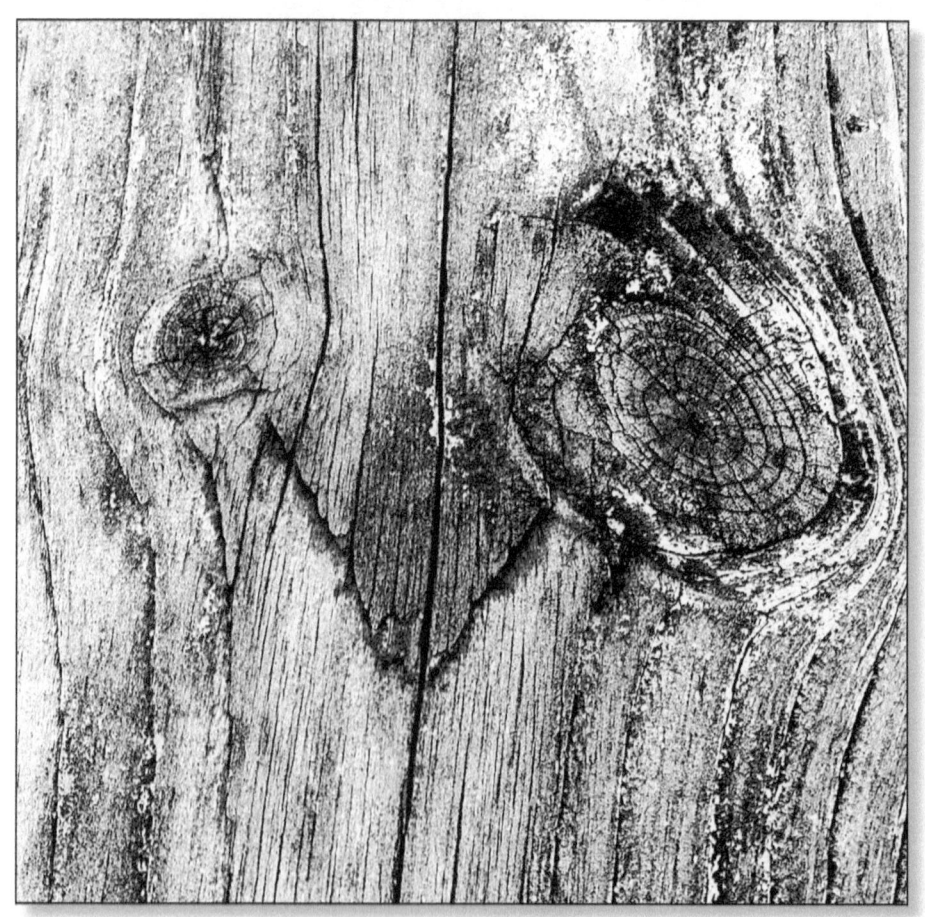

Ballston Lake, NY, May 4, 2014
Nikon D1, 60mm, 1/250, f/5.6, ISO 200, A, pattern
© 2015 Shawn M. Tomlinson

primes such as the Nikon AF D 20mm (1.5 x 20 = 30), a 24mm (1.5 x 24 = 36) or that 28mm (1.5 x 28 = 42) I mentioned.

The same thing with telephoto lenses.

My two favorite focal lengths of telephoto primes are that 105mm (1.5 x 105 = 157.5) I mentioned and 300mm (1.5 x 300 = 450). I have yet to

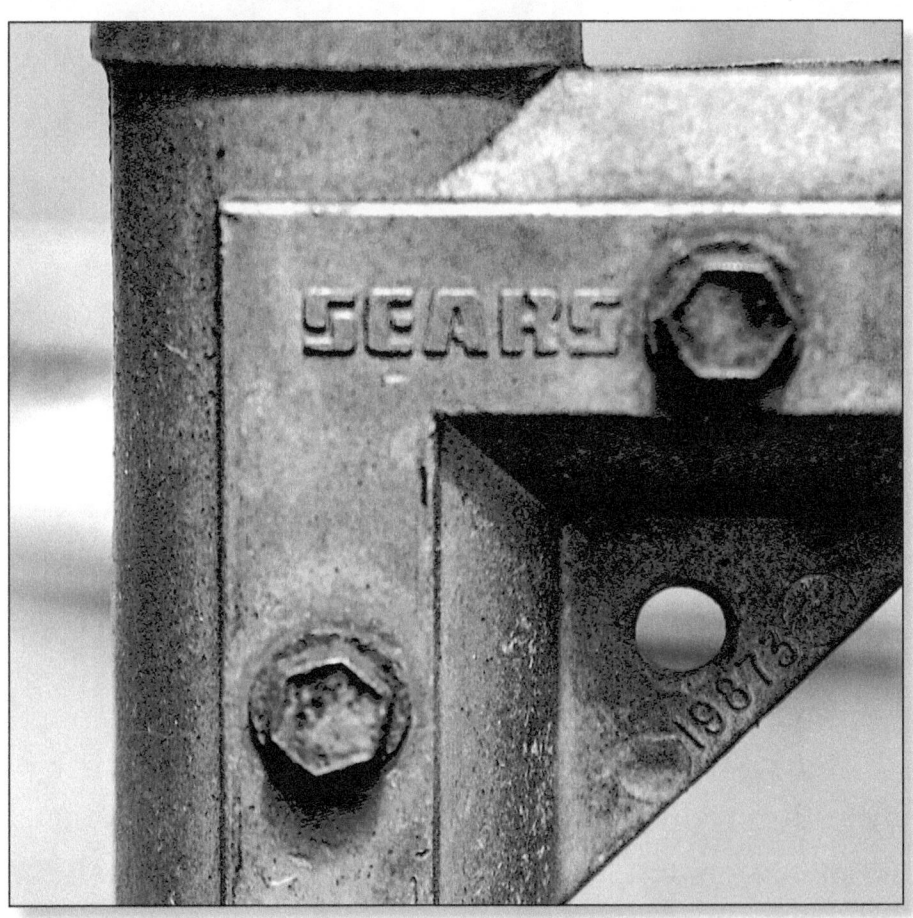

Ballston Lake, NY, May 5, 2014
Nikon D1, 82mm, 1/250, f/5.6, ISO 200, A, pattern
© 2015 Shawn M. Tomlinson

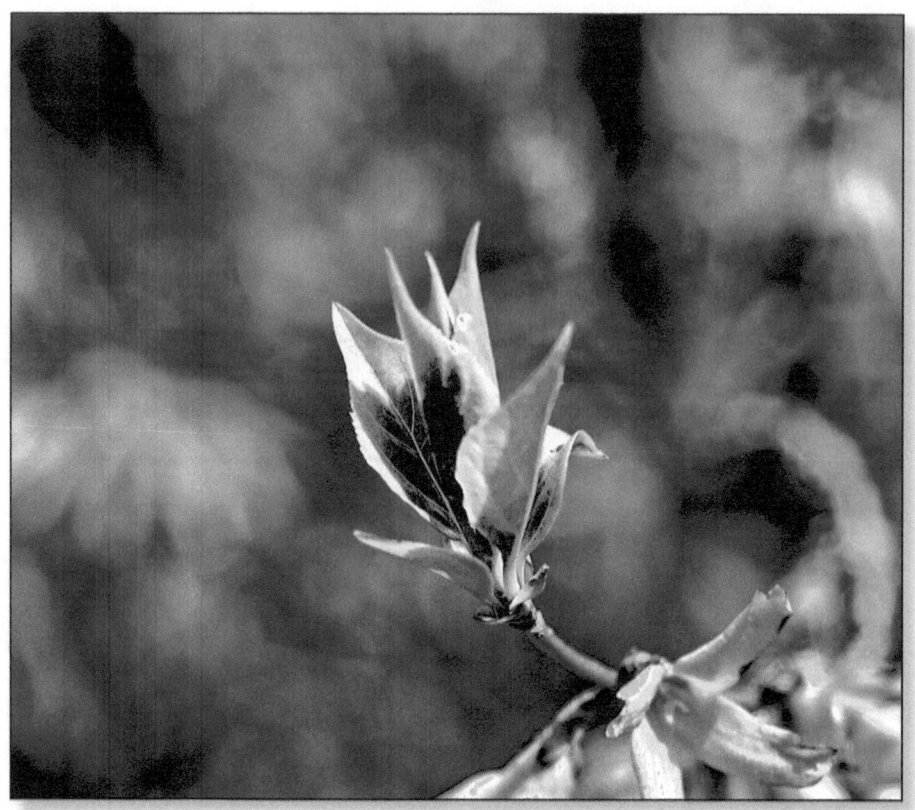

Ballston Lake, NY, May 5, 2014
Nikon D1, 82mm, 1/400, f/5.6, ISO 200, A, pattern
© 2015 Shawn M. Tomlinson

acquire a 300mm prime because of the price, but that Nikon AF-S 105mm f/2.8 VR Micro lens is the best I've ever used, even better than my beloved 50mm.

Because of that lens' image stabilization (VR = vibration reduction), you can shoot at slower shutter speeds when necessary, and get amazingly sharp images.

The best lens in the world, however, will not

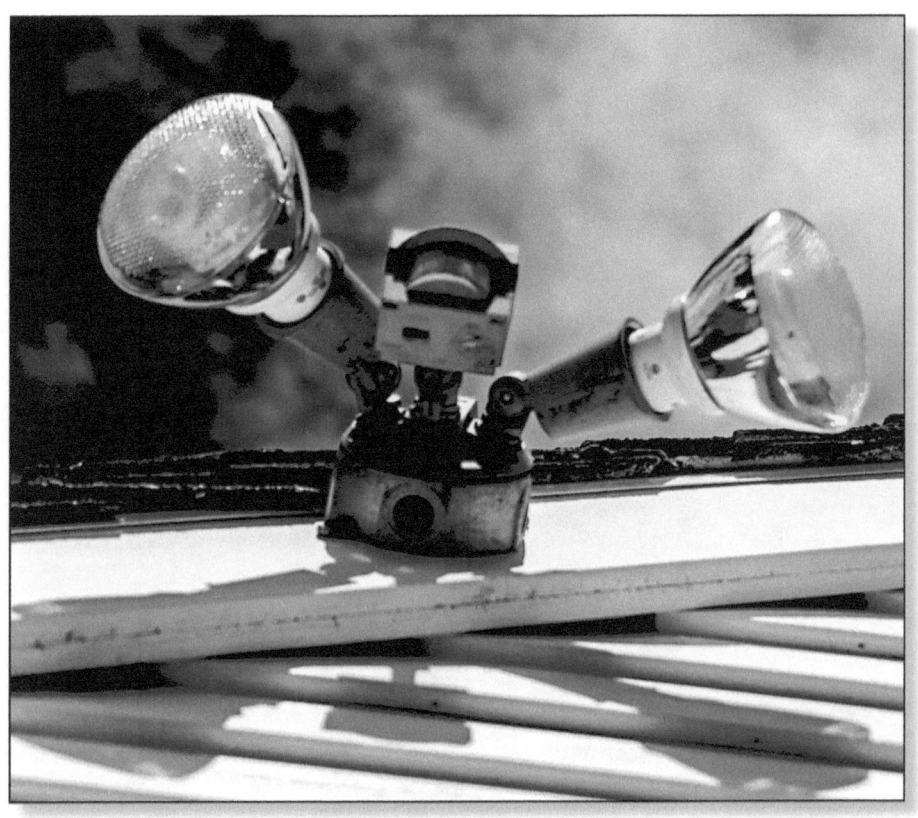

Ballston Lake, NY, May 5, 2014
Nikon D1, 62mm, 1/1250, f/5.6, ISO 200, A, pattern
© 2015 Shawn M. Tomlinson

solve the one image problem I have seen in the
Nikon D1: white washout.

If you shoot a scene that has very bright light
and shadows, the D1 tends to washout anything in
the brightest areas.

So, for example, if you see a shaft of light in a
forest illuminating a single flower when all else
around it is the dark of the underside of many trees
bunched together, you may think, hmmm, that

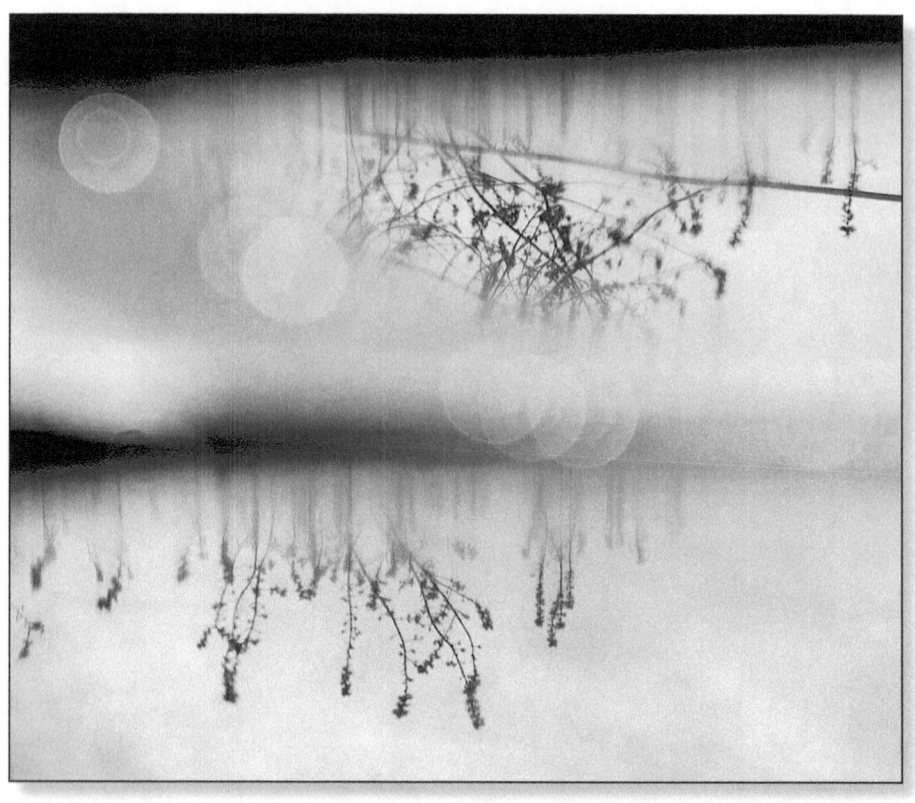

Ballston Lake, NY, May 5, 2014
Nikon D1, 82mm, 1/400, f/5.6, ISO 200, A, pattern
© 2015 Shawn M. Tomlinson

would make an interesting photo.

The problem is that if you shoot it in Program Mode on the D1 or if you stick strictly to the settings made by the camera in Shutter-Priority Mode or Aperture-Priority Mode, chances are, the single flower will be washed out.

You can switch to manual, take the shutter speed up a few notches above what the D1 tells you is optimal. This will cut down the light so there will be more detail in the flower, but you will lose detail in the shadows.

An evenly lit bright scene isn't usually a problem for the D1 because it meters it better and shoots more accurately.

Still, this is something to keep in mind when

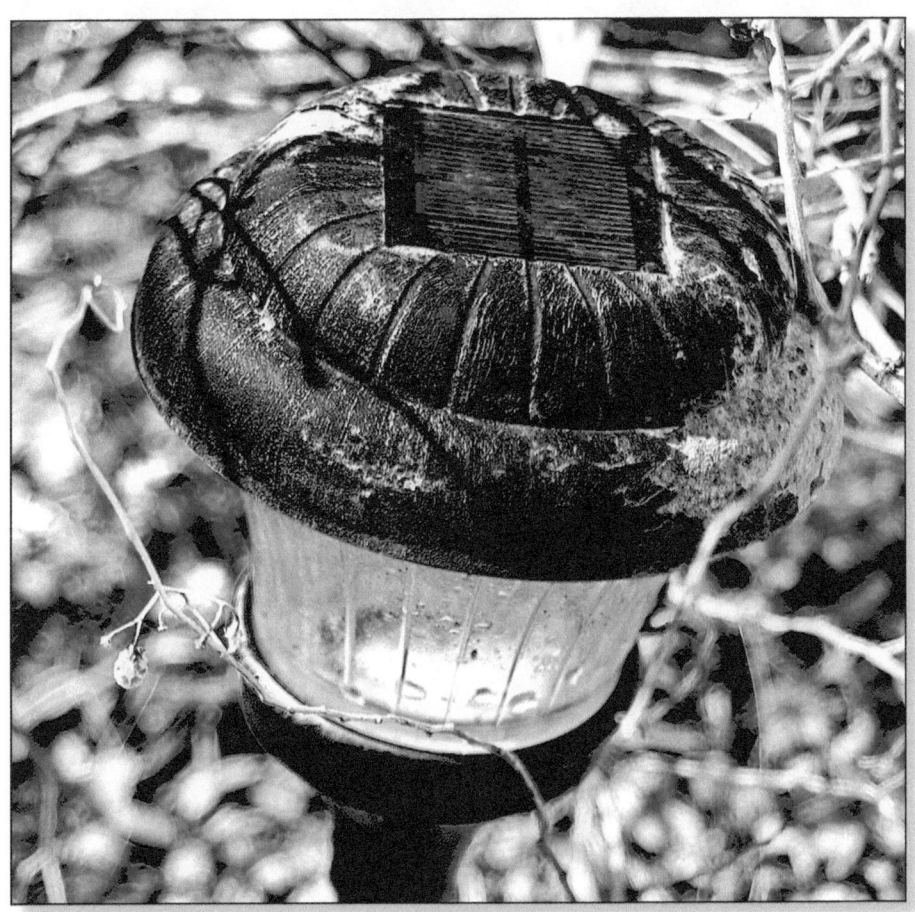

Ballston Lake, NY, May 5, 2014
Nikon D1, 62mm, 1/640, f/5.6, ISO 200, A, pattern
© 2015 Shawn M. Tomlinson

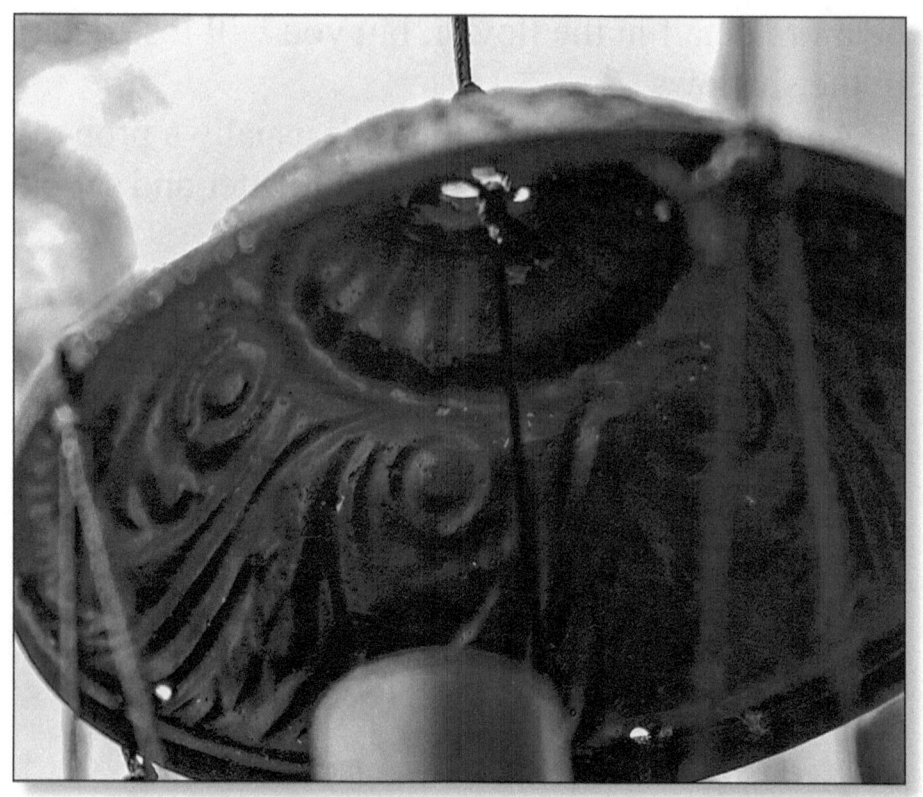

Ballston Lake, NY, May 5, 2014
Nikon D1, 62mm, 1/640, f/5.6, ISO 200, A, pattern
© 2015 Shawn M. Tomlinson

shooting with the D1.

Of course, the assumption here is that you are buying a D1 to have fun with, not to replace your more modern DSLR.

As long as you keep that in mind, you will have fun with the Nikon D1.

Just try not to mix extremes of lighting in the same photograph.

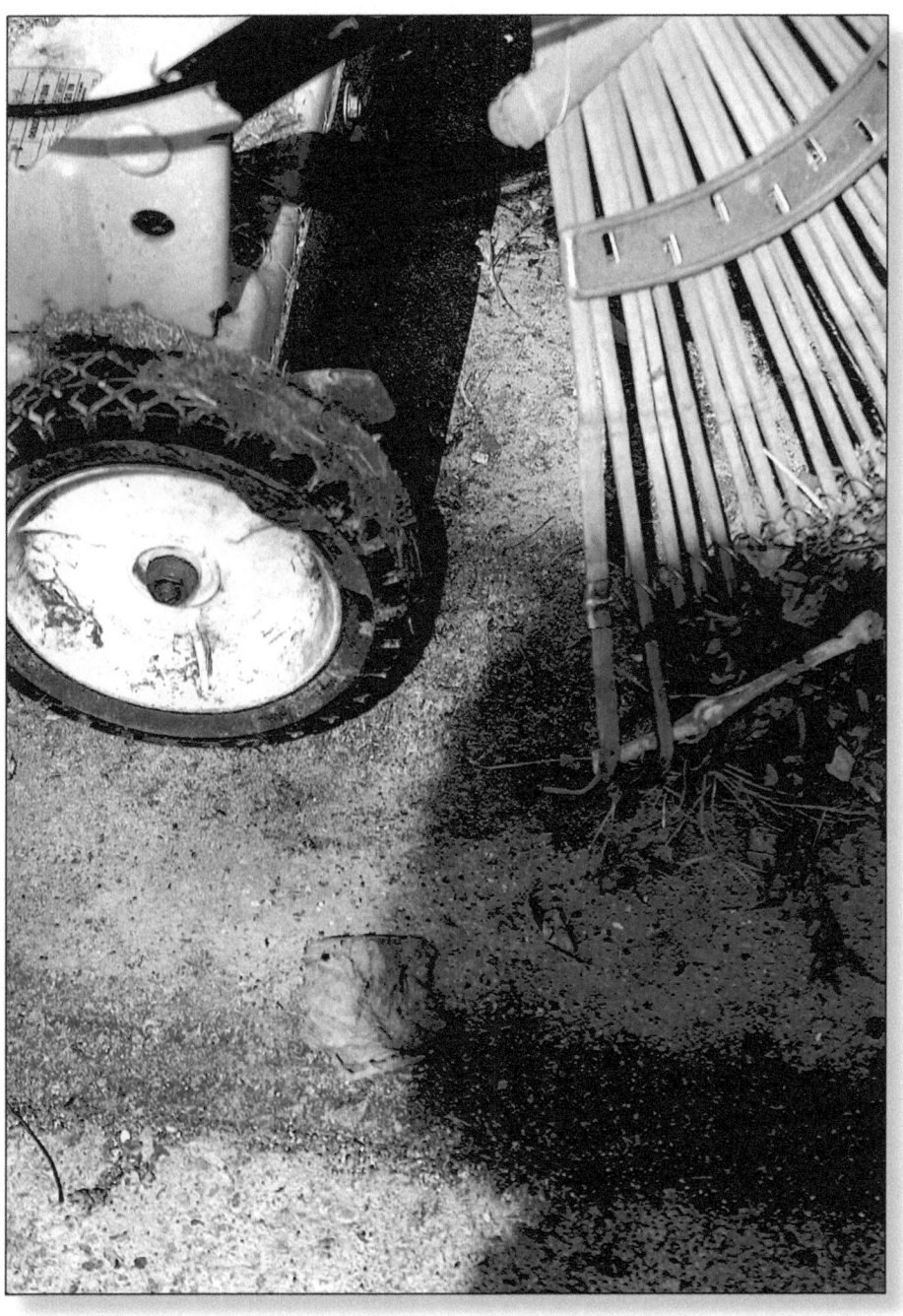

Ballston Lake, NY, May 5, 2014
Nikon D1, 82mm, 1/500, f/5.6, ISO 200, A, pattern
© 2015 Shawn M. Tomlinson

Going Pro for $200 • Page 83

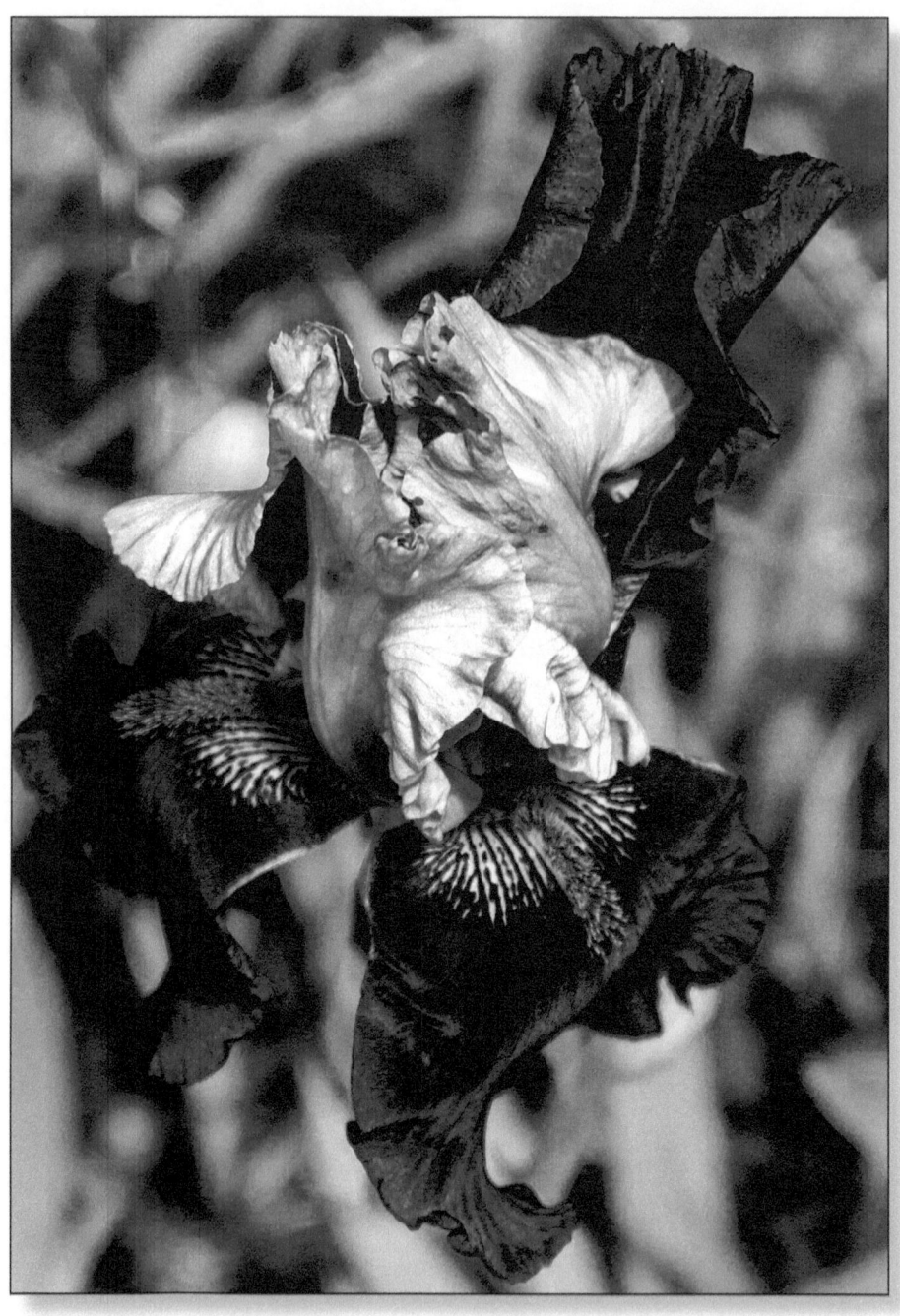

Saratoga Springs, NY, May 31, 2014
Nikon D1x, 82mm, 1/250, f/7.6, ISO 200, P, pattern
© 2015 Shawn M. Tomlinson

# Part 4
# The Sequels:
# The D1x & D1H

When I originally wrote this guide, I left out the Nikon D1x and D1H, the successors to the Nikon D1, because they still were relatively expensive.

It would have been hard to buy either of these pro DSLRs and a lens for less than $200.

In the time since this guide originally appeared, prices have come down a bit on both of these cam-

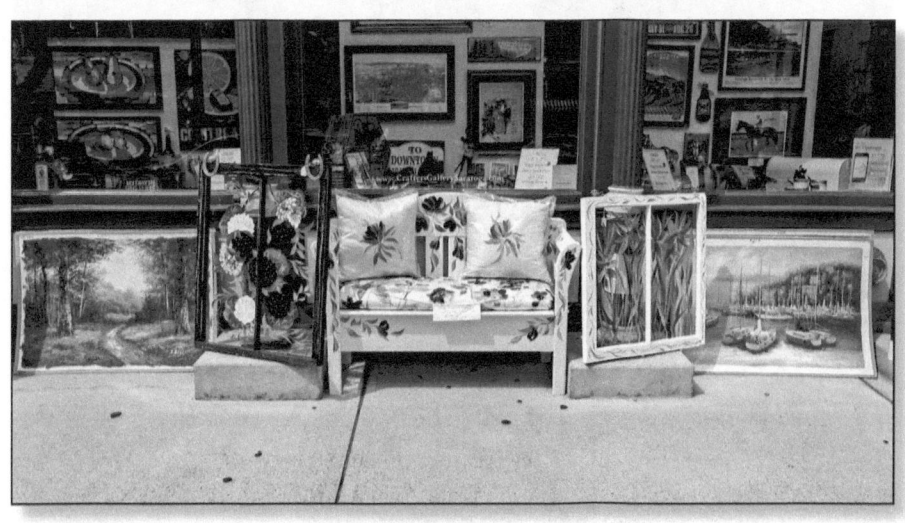

Saratoga Springs, NY, Aug. 23, 2014
Nikon D1x, 18mm, 1/640, f/12, ISO 400, P, pattern
© 2015 Shawn M. Tomlinson

eras.

If you find the right deal, you can get either one for about $100, leaving you with $100 for a lens.

Even if you pay $120 or $130, you still can come in under budget by buying a Nikon "kit" lens.

The Nikon D1x and D1H cameras also are only

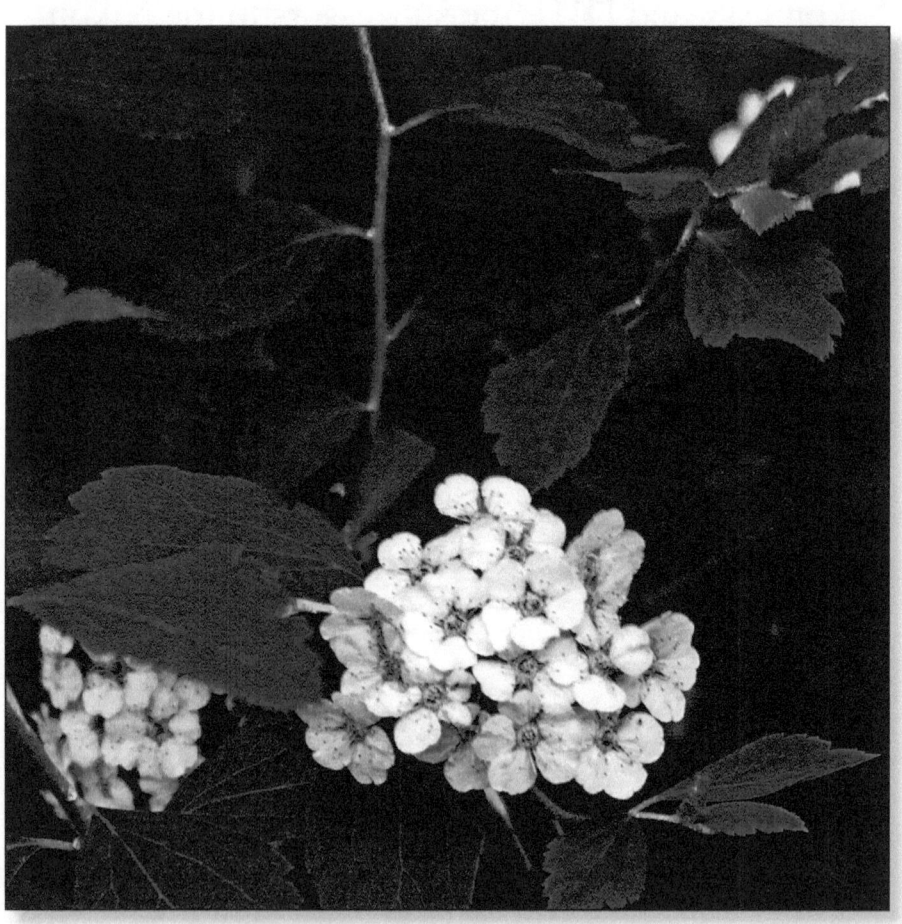

Saratoga Springs, NY, May 31, 2014
Nikon D1x, 82mm, 1/350, f/10, ISO 200, P, pattern
© 2015 Shawn M. Tomlinson

evolutionary and relatively slight improvements over the D1, so they do fit the idea. They also use the same batteries as the D1 and have the 2gb CF card limit.

The main if minor differences, however, are significant because they make the D1x and D1H a bit

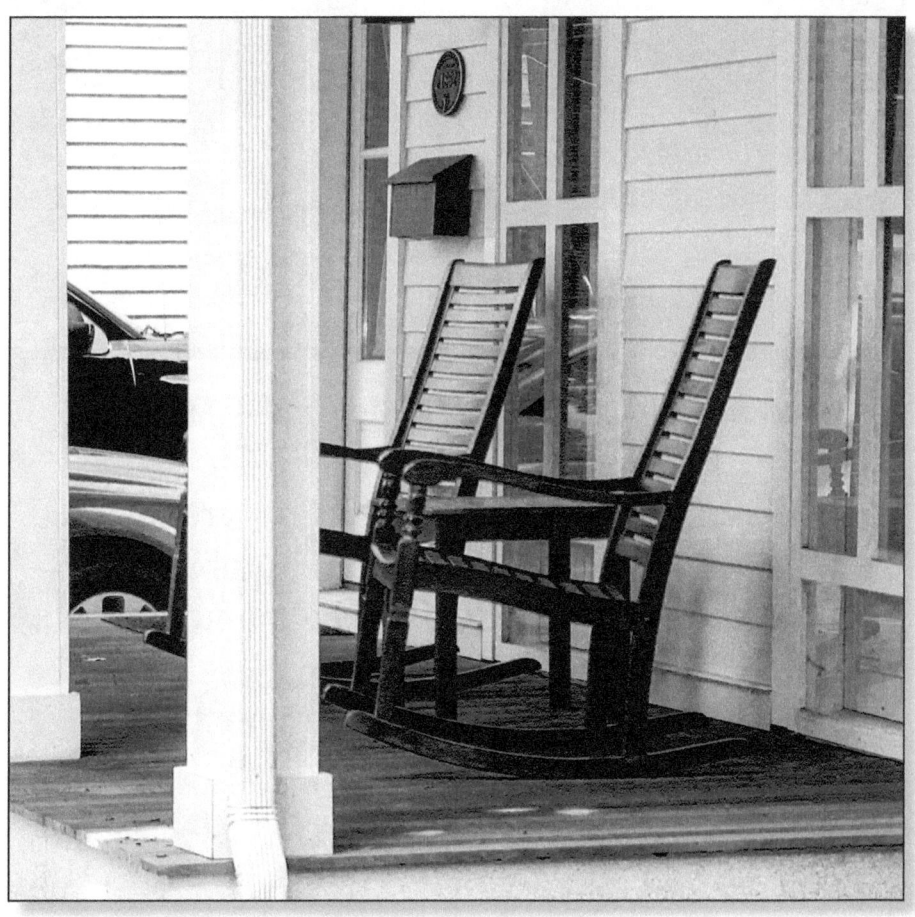

Saratoga Springs, NY, May 31, 2014
Nikon D1x, 82mm, 1/250, f/7.6, ISO 200, P, pattern
© 2015 Shawn M. Tomlinson

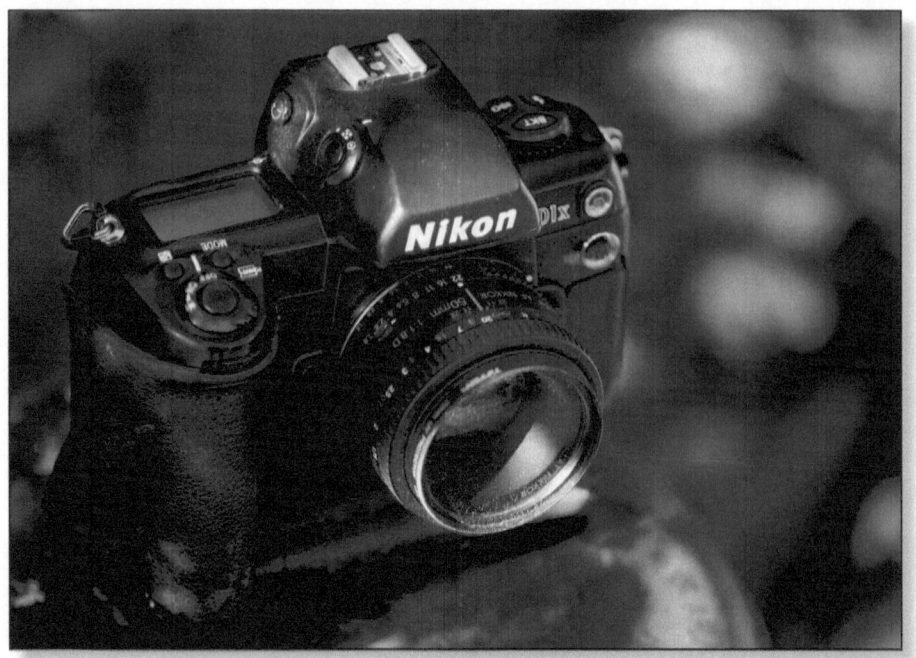

The Nikon D1x is shown with the Nikon AF D 50mm f/1.8 prime lens
Oct. 19, 2015 in Ballston Lake, NY.

easier to use — especially in the field — than the D1.

By the time these two pro DSLRs were released, the folks at Nikon had learned a lot, probably through feedback from professional photographers who used the D1.

OK, so, let's talk about why there are two of them and what each can do.

The D1x at 5.3 megapixels was designed specifically to have a little more resolution than the D1's 2.65 megapixels. In order to get that higher resolution at the time, the shooting speed was kept relatively low.

This concept still is true, for both Nikon and Canon.

The top Nikon DSLR, the D4s, has 16 megapixels but shoot at 10 frames per second.

Canon's top DSLR, the 1Dx, has 18.1 megapixels and shoots at 11 fps.

However, Nikon's highest resolution DSLR is the D810 at 36 megapixels. Canon has introduced two 50-megapixels DSLRs as of this writing, the 5Ds and 5Ds R.

None of these cameras, however, can match the

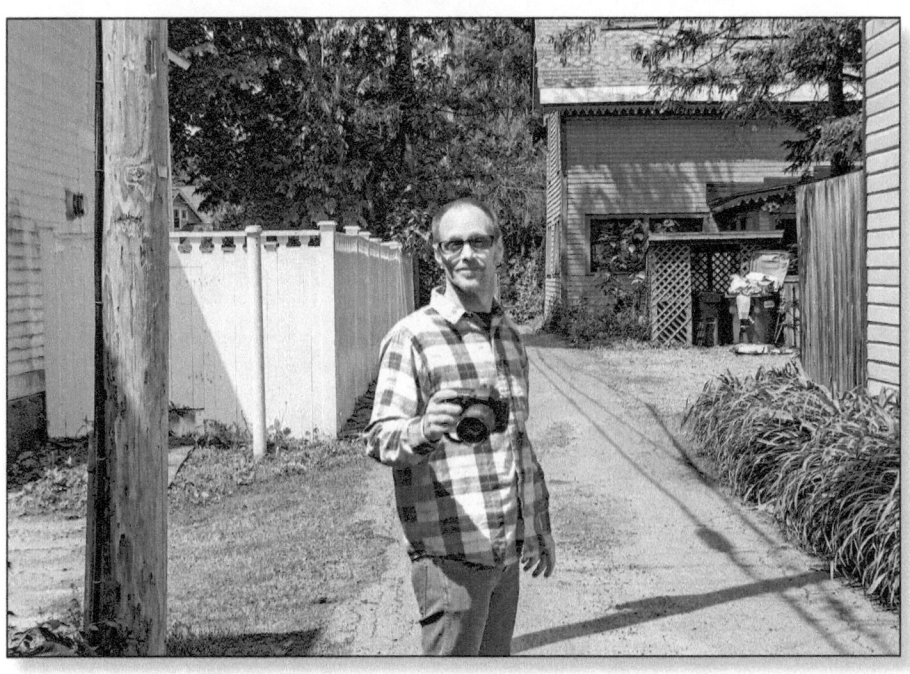

Gary Ziroli, Saratoga Springs, NY, May 31, 2014
Nikon D1x, 46mm, 1/350, f/10, ISO 200, P, pattern
© 2015 Shawn M. Tomlinson

shooting speed of the D4s or 1Dx. The Nikon D810 and the two Canons all shoot at 5 fps.

Both the D4s and 1Dx are expected to be replaced soon, but to keep the speed, they probably will not have much of a resolution boost.

The D1H has about the same resolution as the D1 — a little lower, actually, at 2.47 megapixels — but was designed to shoot faster. This was something the pros at the time — 2001 — needed.

By then, digital cameras had begun the slow road to replace film cameras at newspapers and magazines, so the folks at Nikon listened to what

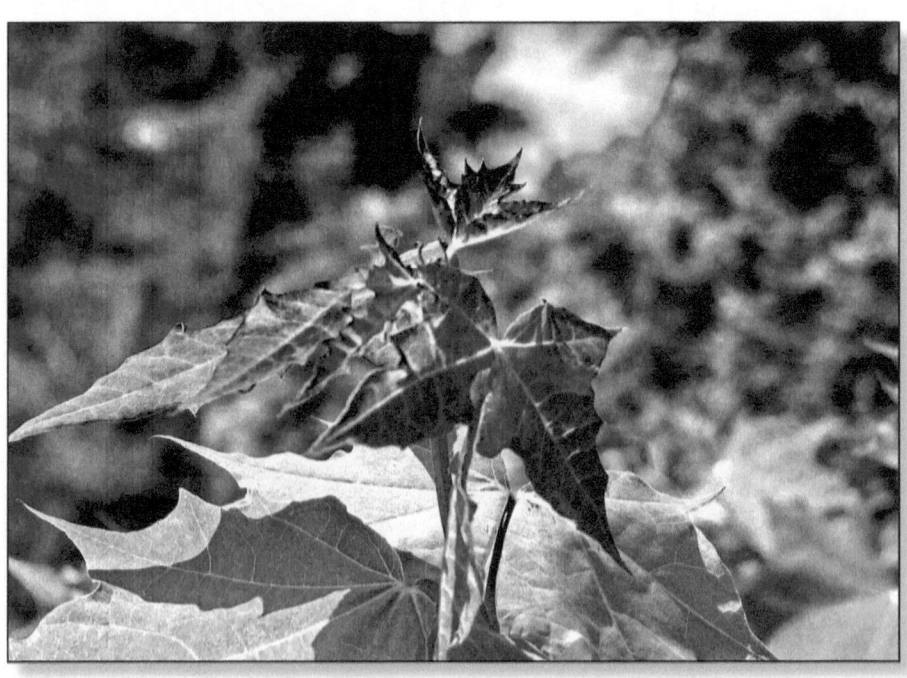

Saratoga Springs, NY, May 31, 2014
Nikon D1x, 82mm, 1/500, f/11, ISO 200, P, pattern
© 2015 Shawn M. Tomlinson

the pros needed and wanted.

The D1x and D1H look nearly identical to the D1 on the outside. If you didn't see the designation, it would be difficult to distinguish any of them from one another.

Once you look at the menus, however, you will notice a major improvement.

The esoteric codes are gone for the most part, replaced with more intuitive menus in actual English.

It is much easier to set the D1x and D1H to do what you want them to do than it is on the D1.

The image quality, at least on the D1x, is better,

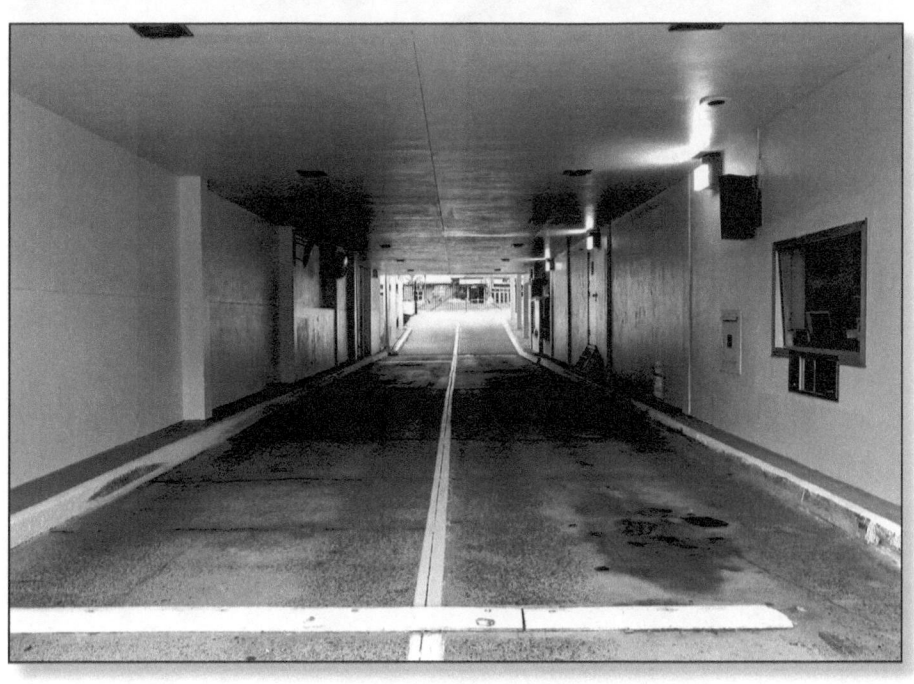

Saratoga Springs, NY, Aug. 23, 2014
Nikon D1x, 18mm, 1/250, f/7.1, ISO 400, P, pattern
© 2015 Shawn M. Tomlinson

too, in that the washout of bright areas is less pronounced. Not much less, but a little.

It wasn't until the D3 and D300 that Nikon's Active-D Lighting function was installed. This ADL saves the details in shadows and highlights, but, of course, pushes the price of cameras with it much

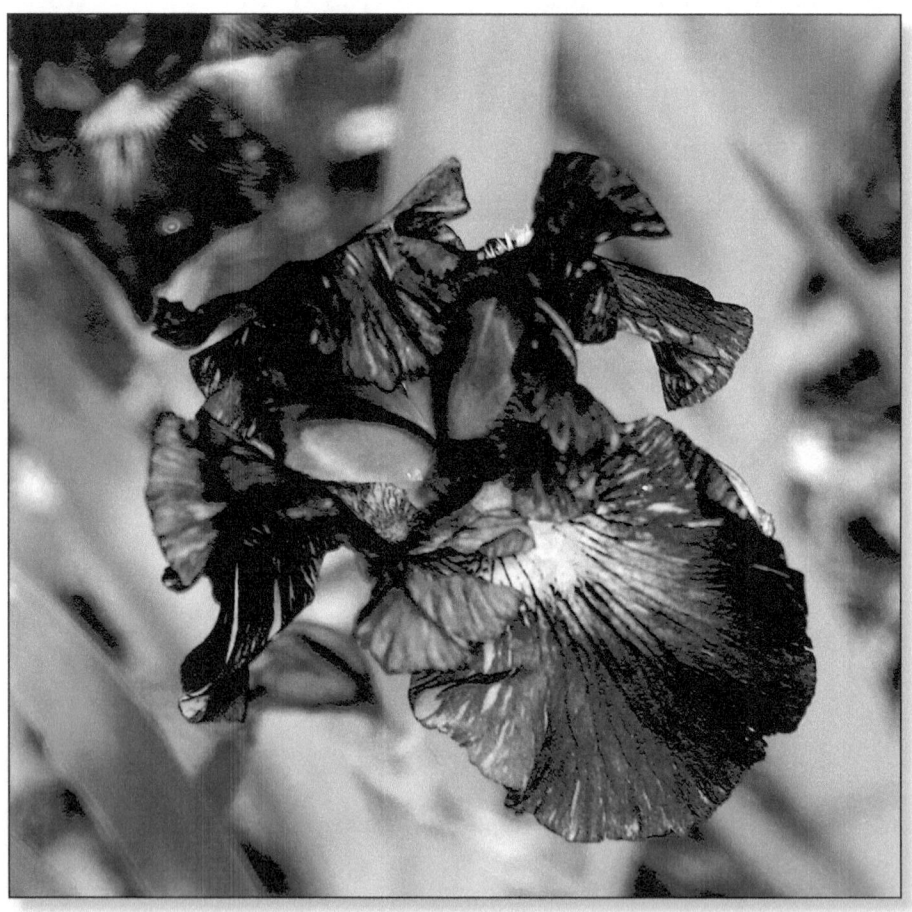

Saratoga Springs, NY, May 31, 2014
Nikon D1x, 82mm, 1/160, f/6.3, ISO 200, P, pattern
© 2015 Shawn M. Tomlinson

higher than the earlier models without it.

Anyway, the D1x and D1H do offer some small advantages over the D1. Apart from the better menu system, the improvements I like best is better file handling and a bigger buffer. It cuts the lag time between shots. This is important if you like to shoot

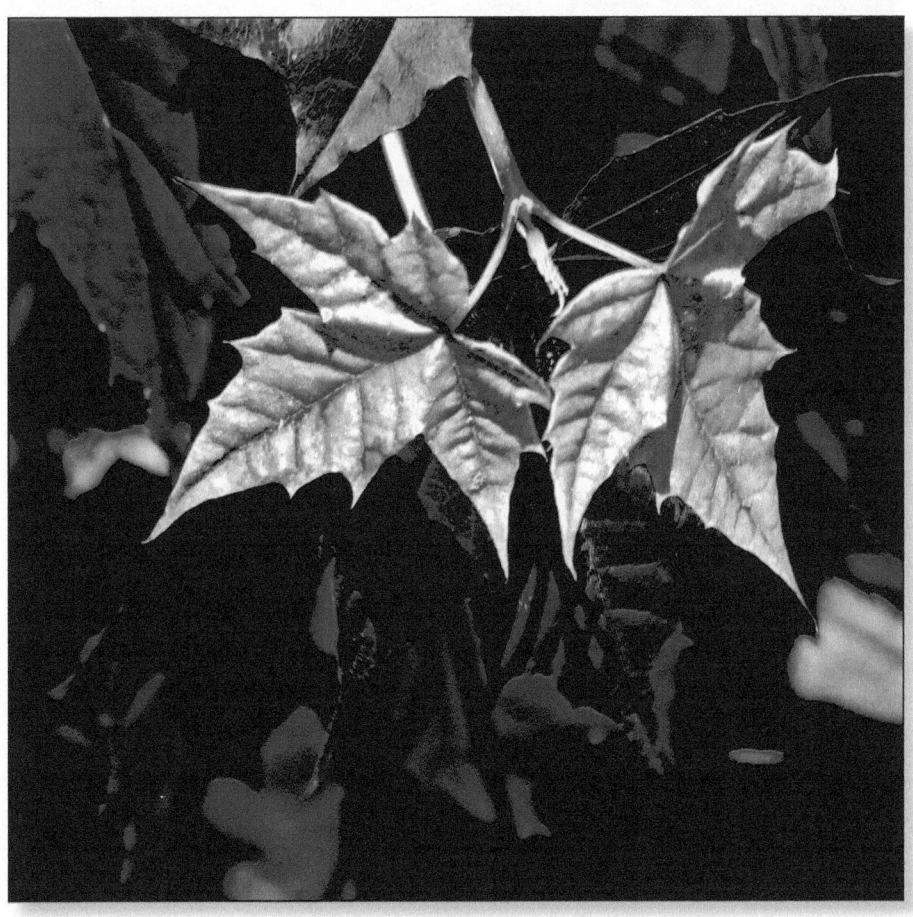

Saratoga Springs, NY, May 31, 2014
Nikon D1x, 82mm, 1/250, f/7.6, ISO 200, P, pattern
© 2015 Shawn M. Tomlinson

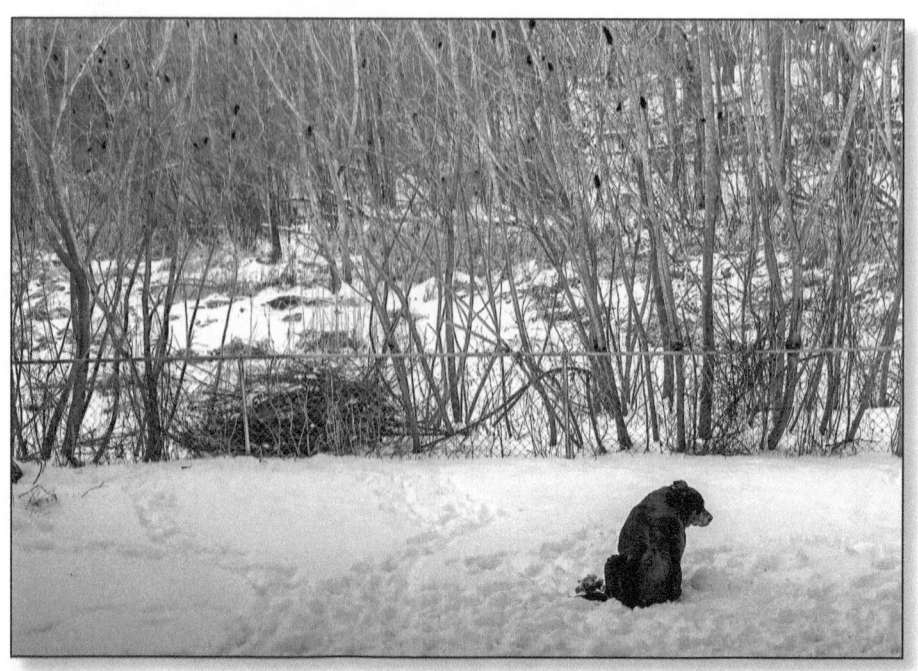

Baby, Ballston Lake, NY, Jan. 17, 2015
Nikon D1x, 22mm, 1/160, f/3.5, ISO 200, M, pattern
© 2015 Shawn M. Tomlinson

fast.

So, should you bypass the Nikon D1 and go straight to a D1x or D1H?

Probably.

Especially if you like the more intuitive menus.

The thing is, though, that the D1 holds a place in history that neither of the other two do.

It was the first designed nearly from scratch DSLR, and for me that means something.

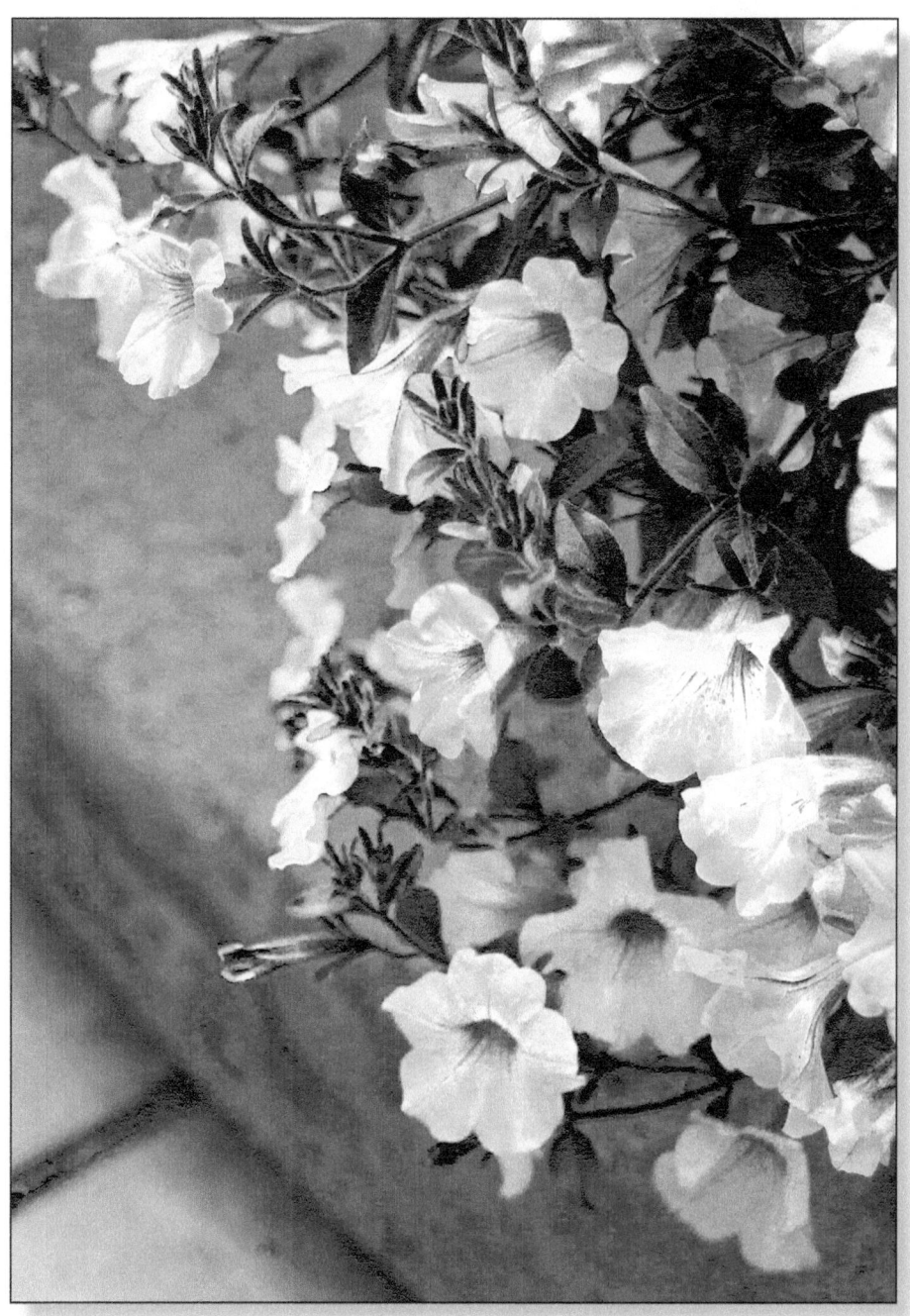

Saratoga Springs, NY, May 31, 2014
Nikon D1x, 62mm, 1/640, f/5.3, ISO 200, A, pattern
© 2015 Shawn M. Tomlinson

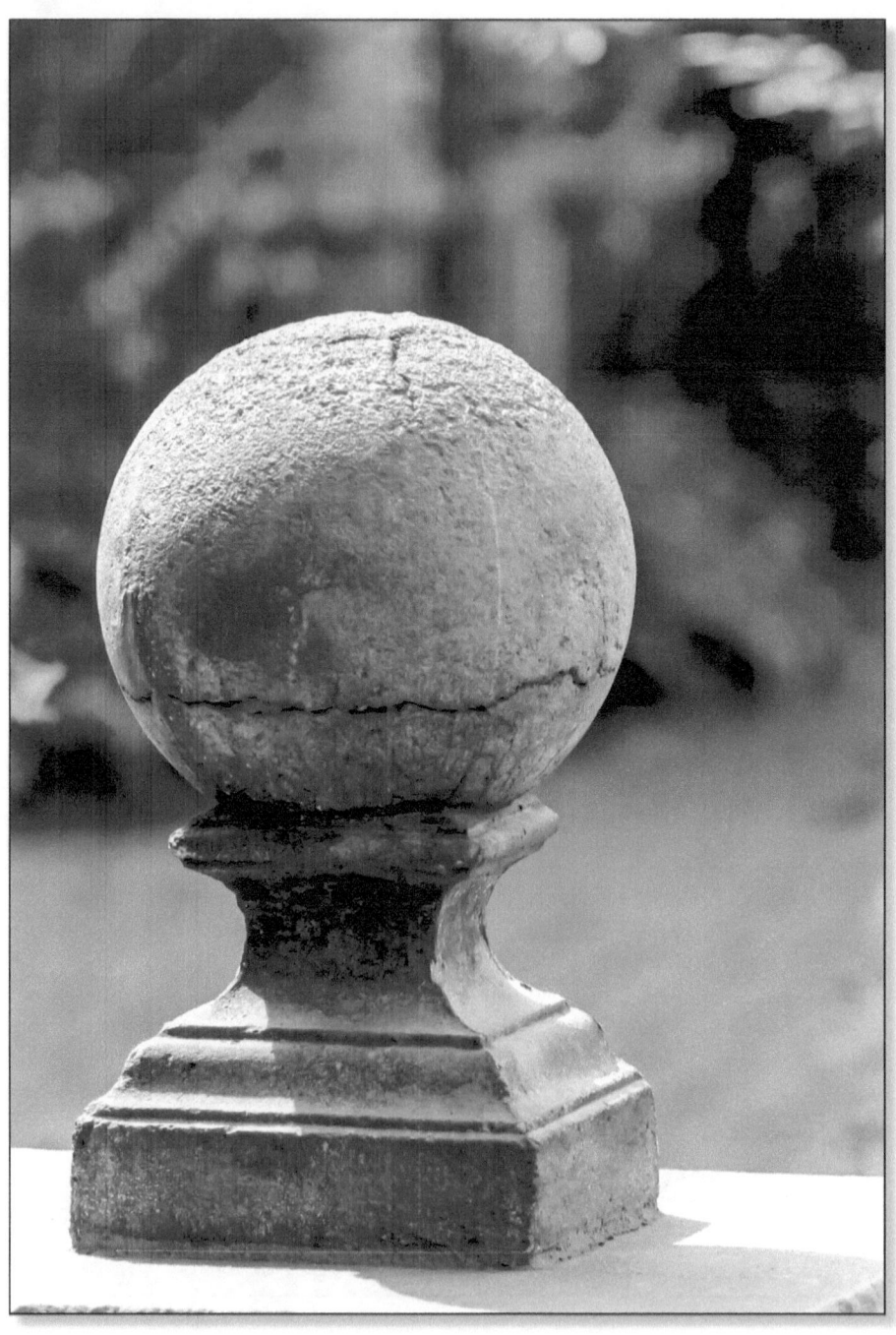

Saratoga Springs, NY, Aug. 5, 2014
Nikon D1, 180mm, 1/1250, f/4.8, ISO 200, S, pattern metering
© 2014, 2015 by Shawn M. Tomlinson

# Part 5
# The Last Details

So, OK, you're ready to turn pro with the Nikon D1.

There are a few details to consider before jumping onto eBay.

1) The Nikon D1 is old. If you get a good one, you will not be disappointed.

But they are old cameras now, so some of them have quit working or have problems.

I have two of them and neither is in perfect shape.

My first one, for example, has a problem on the sensor with a white line over to the left side of the images where pixels are dead or "hot."

This annoys me, but never stops me using the camera.

Unless the left side of the image is dark, it isn't visible, and if it is, it's close enough to the left edge to just crop it out.

This is the only problem I have with the camera, but it is annoying.

The second one, I was promised, worked wonderfully.

And it does… on rare occasion.

The shutter is going and so it will take a few photos, then it will click the shutter twice and freeze.

Turning it off and then back on clears this briefly.

You are buying a used DSLR from the last century, so if you buy on eBay, you're taking a risk.

I certainly did and had problems with both.

The first one, though, the one I use, had one problem that was my fault.

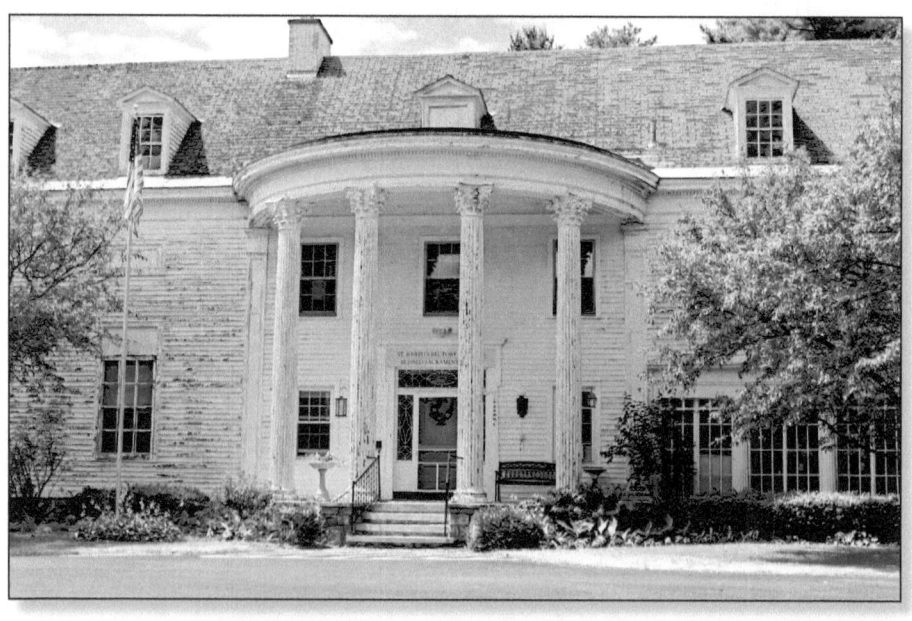

Broadalbin House, Broadalbin, NY, July 18, 2014
Nikon D1, 34mm, 1/1250, f/3.8, ISO 200, Av, pattern metering
© 2014, 2015 by Shawn M. Tomlinson

I did not read the eBay description carefully enough and so, no charger came with it.

More on that later.

The point is, no matter how camera-savvy you are, buying on eBay is a roll of the dice.

If you buy from a reputable dealer such as KEH. com, you can rest assured the seller has tested and graded appropriately the camera.

And, if there is a problem with it they did not discover, they will replace or repair it, or refund your money.

Yes, this will cost a bit more than eBay, but from my own experience, it is worth it.

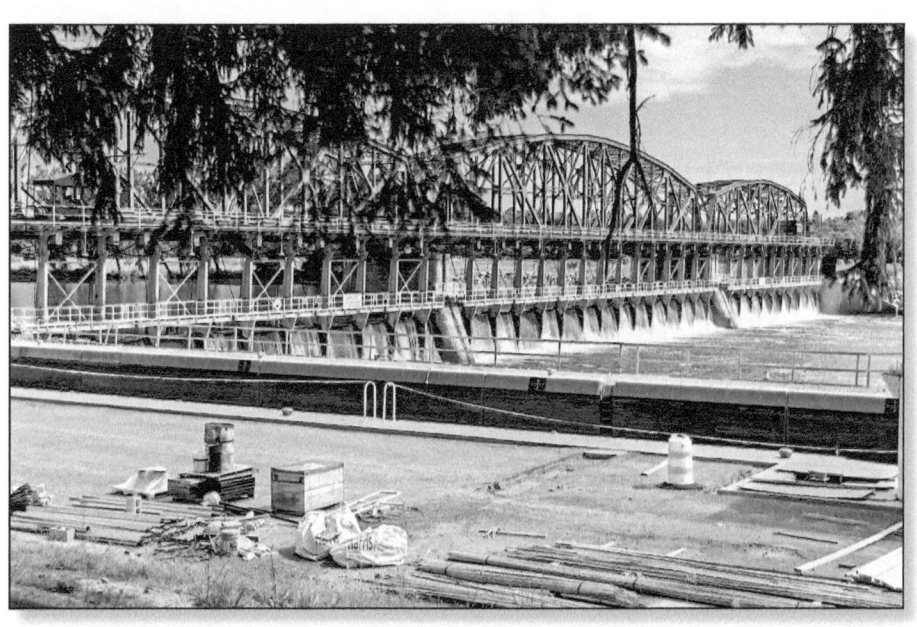

Lock 8, Rotterdam, NY, July 20, 2014
Nikon D1, 31mm, 1/1600, f/3.5, ISO 200, Av, pattern metering
© 2014, 2015 by Shawn M. Tomlinson

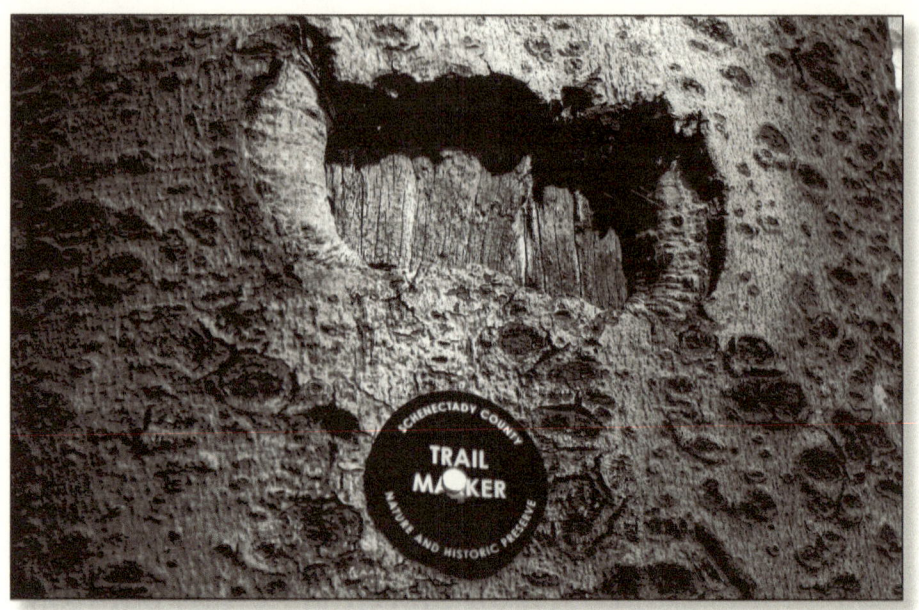

Indian Kill Nature Preserve, Glenville, NY, July 21, 2014
Nikon D1, 60mm, 1/90, f/5, ISO 200, Av, pattern metering
© 2014, 2015 by Shawn M. Tomlinson

I knew about KEH and had bought equipment from the company previously, but I was stupid and bid upon a D1 on eBay.

I got it cheap, too: $57!

However, it turned out to have the sensor pixel problem, and the real problem, which is it did not come with a charger.

Again, I was stupid.

I assumed it did have a charger because usually eBayers say when a DSLR doesn't have one.

Besides, I thought, how much could a charger be?

The answer: A lot.

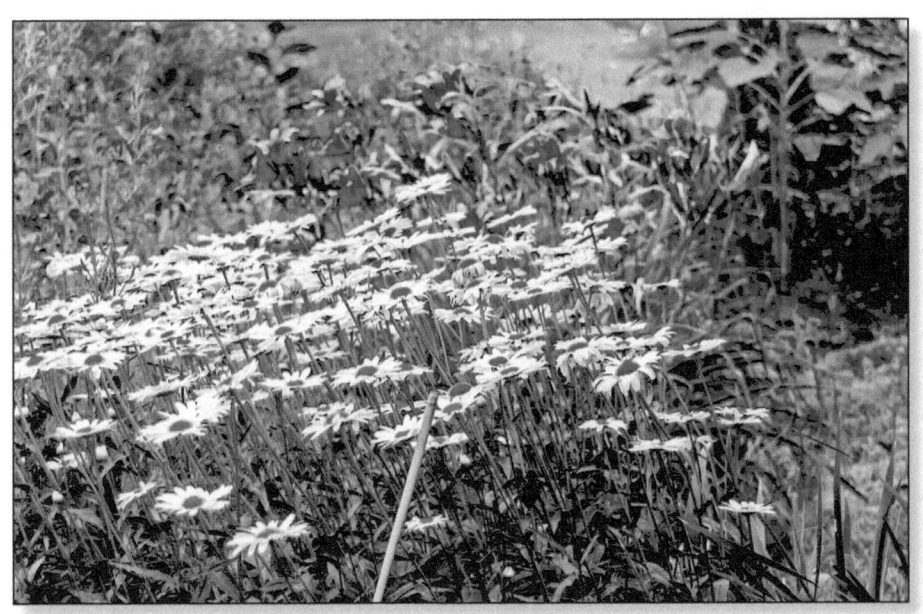

Riverside Park, the Stockade, Schenectady, NY, July 23, 2014
Nikon D1, 70mm, 1/500, f/5.3, ISO 200, Av, pattern metering
© 2014, 2015 by Shawn M. Tomlinson

2) The battery and charger thing, along with a warranty, are the things to consider when buying a D1.

That's why my cautionary tale should tell you that you need to buy from a dealer, not an eBay seller.

KEH — the best photographic equipment dealer — generally supplies a battery and charger with used cameras.

For this, of course, they charge a bit more.

When the company doesn't supply these things, it states it clearly and discounts the price.

Typically, KEH charged about $110 for a Nikon

D1 with a used but working battery and the charger.

Sounds like a lot more than my $57 deal, right?

The charger alone, when you can find one, usually costs about $100.

The battery, again when you can find one, usually costs at least $30.

So, suddenly my $57 deal

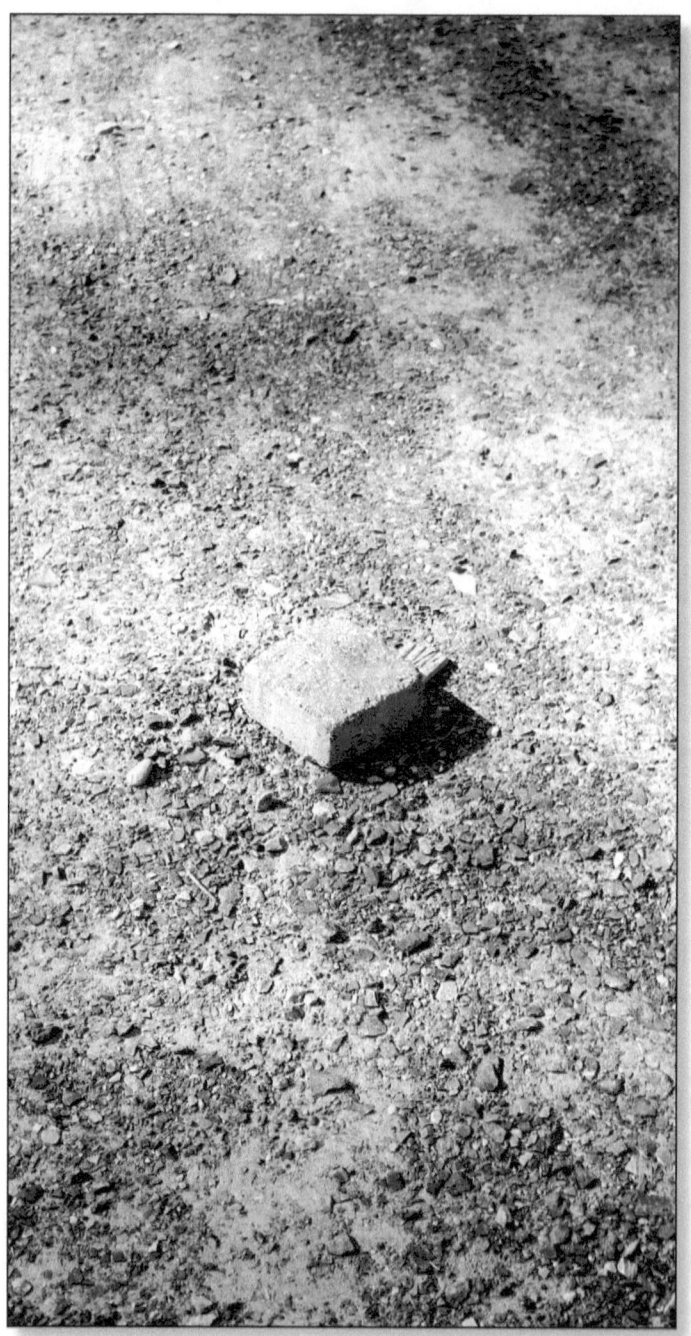

Indian Kill Nature Preserve, Glenville, NY, July 21, 2014
Nikon D1, 38mm, 1/1250, f/4, ISO 200, Av, pattern metering
© 2014, 2015 by Shawn M. Tomlinson

costs $187, $77 more than if I bought the D1 from KEH.

I didn't do it quite that way.

I bid — again stupidly — on a Nikon D1H with five batteries and a charger that I won for $125 plus $25 shipping.

Which would have solved all my problems with the D1 and given me

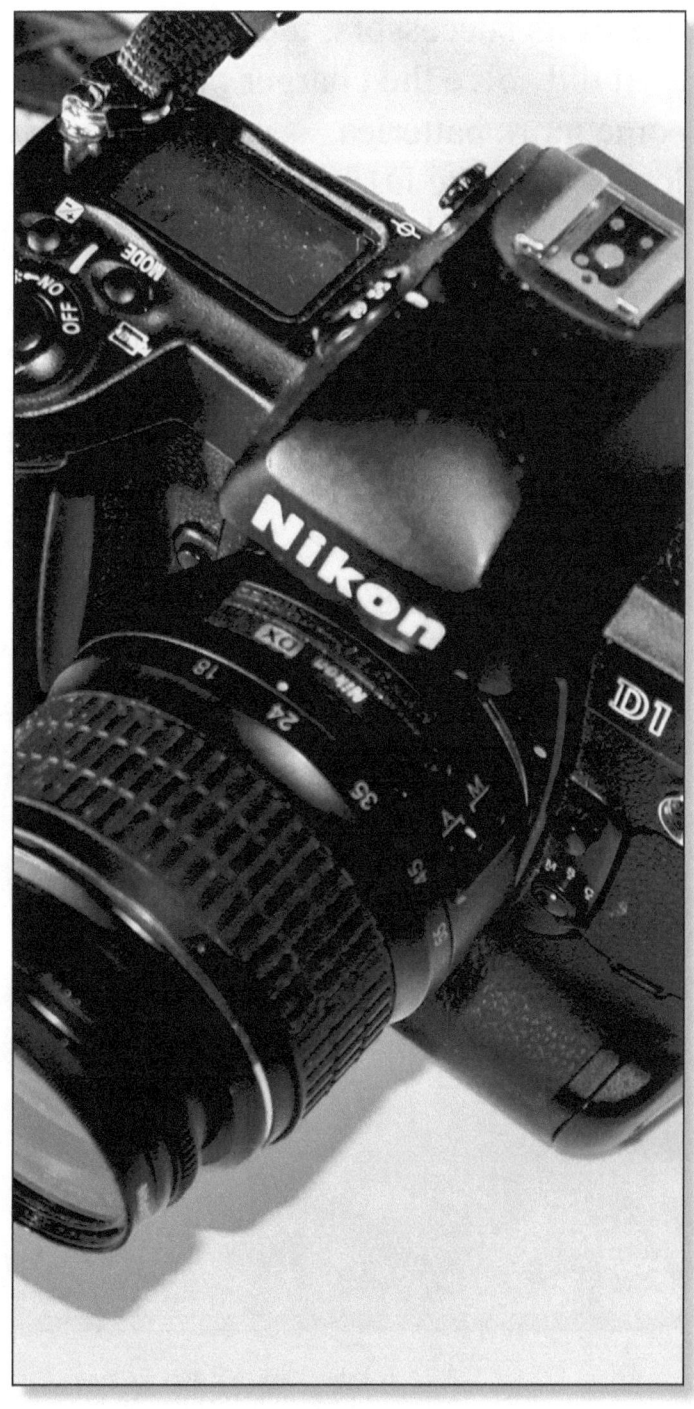

one of its successors, the D1H, to use.

It did solve the charger problem and gave me some more batteries — none of which last very long — but the D1H did not work.

Well, it works fine as a camera, but just will not write to or read from a memory card.

The only fix for that, apparently, is getting a different D1H, and that's not worth it.

Anyway, my $57 deal cost $207 in the end.

Much more than I should have or would have paid.

So, if you are going to look on eBay for a D1, make sure it comes with a working battery and

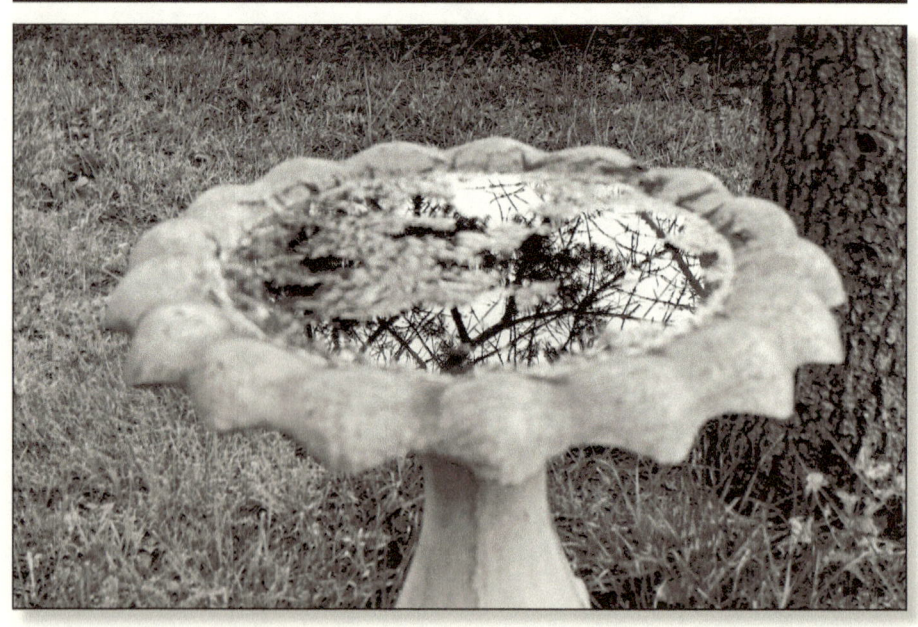

Ballston Lake, NY, July 29, 2014
Nikon D1, 50mm, 1/125, f/5.6, ISO 400, Av, pattern metering
© 2014, 2015 by Shawn M. Tomlinson

charger.

Or be smarter than me and buy from KEH or another actual store, be it online or real.

3) SecureDigital (SD) memory cards pretty much have become the standard in cameras, smartphones and other devices.

They didn't even exist when the D1 was made, so it takes the older, better CompactFlash (CF) memory cards.

You can't find those in big box stores anymore, only usually online, or perhaps, if you are lucky enough to have an actual, physical camera store near you, there.

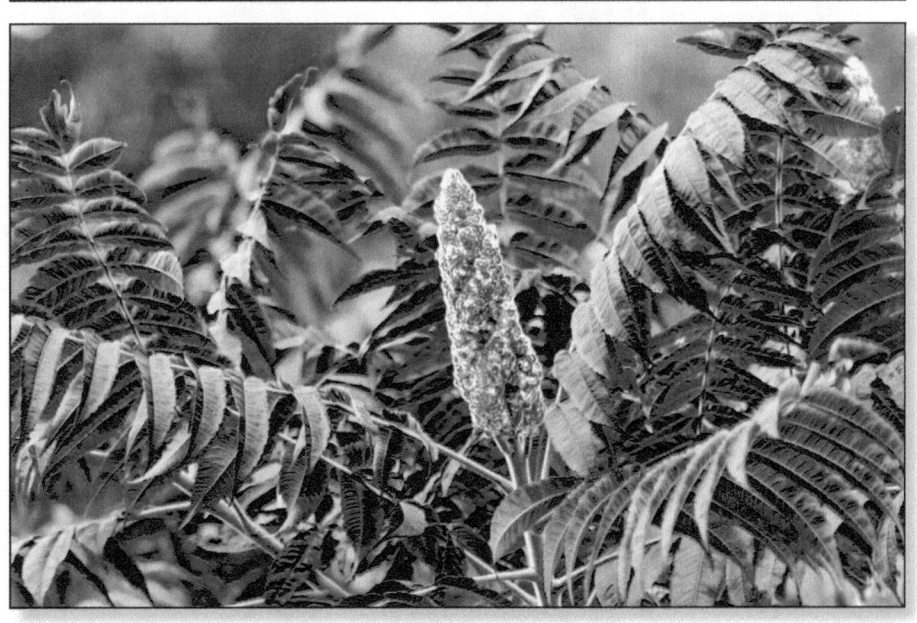

Ballston Lake, NY, July 30, 2014
Nikon D1, 270mm, 1/200, f/5.3, ISO 200, Av, pattern metering
© 2014, 2015 by Shawn M. Tomlinson

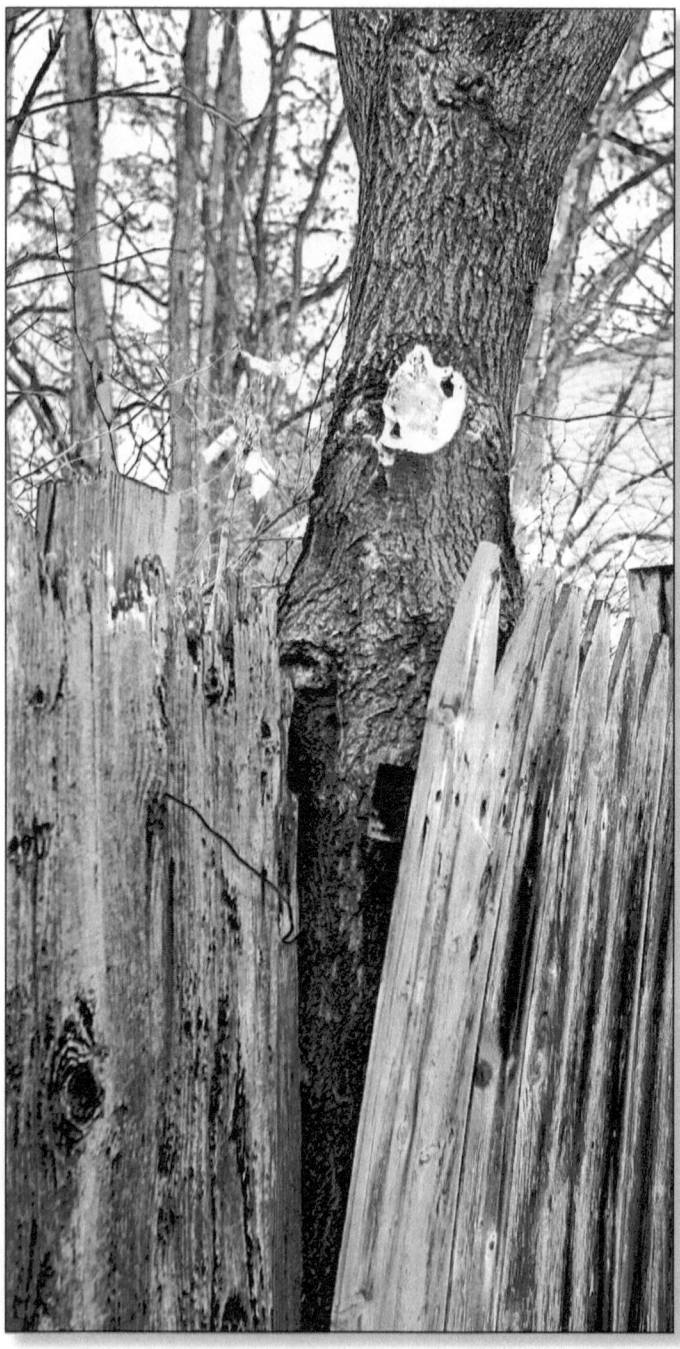

Saratoga Springs, NY, Dec. 13, 2014
Nikon D1, 28mm (prime), 1/160, f/5.6, ISO 200, Av, pattern metering
© 2014, 2015 by Shawn M. Tomlinson

But wait, there's less!

CF cards still were new in 1999 when the D1 came out.

They didn't have the kind of capacity they do now.

They had 64mb or 128mb capacities.

That is tiny by today's standards, but they were comparable to what photographers were getting with film in 1999 and the D1 was the transition camera from film to digital.

Yes, you can use larger capacity CF cards than those with the D1, but not by much.

The maximum CF capacity card for the D1 is 2gb.

If you put a 4gb or larger card in, the D1 either

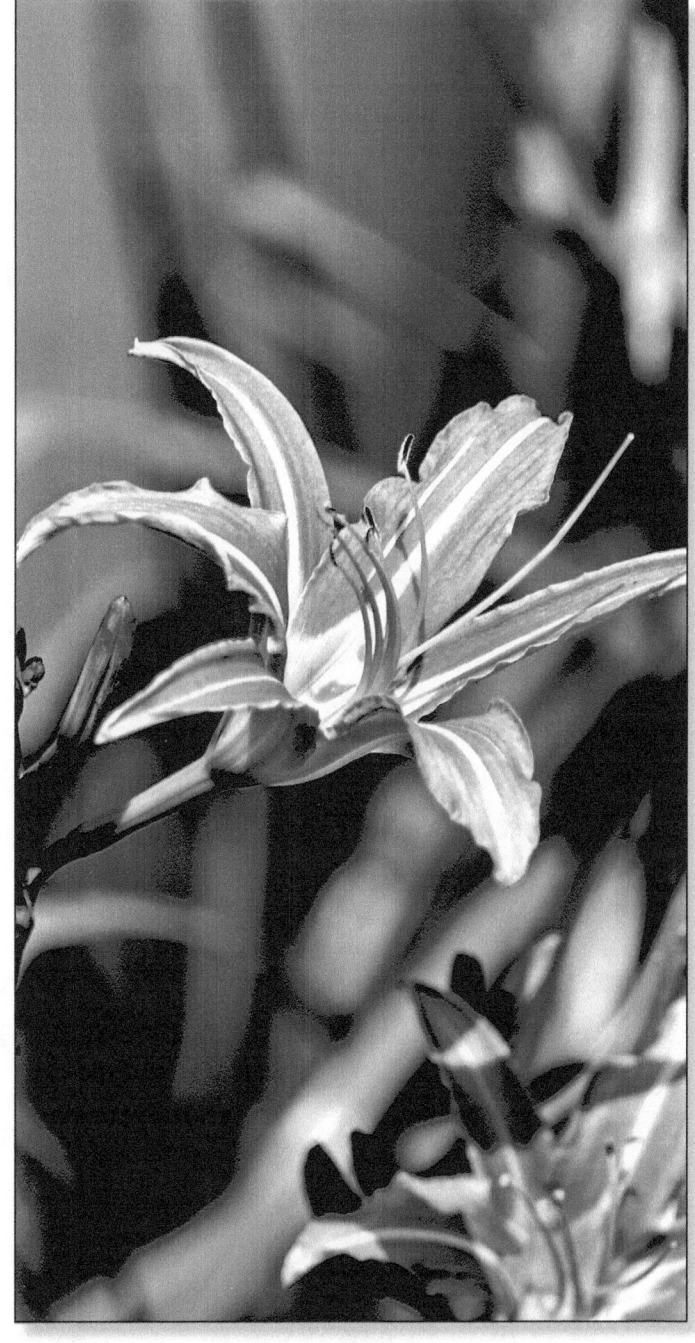

Ballston Lake, NY, July 30, 2014
Nikon D1, 300mm, 1/800, f/5.6, ISO 200, Av, pattern metering
© 2014, 2015 by Shawn M. Tomlinson

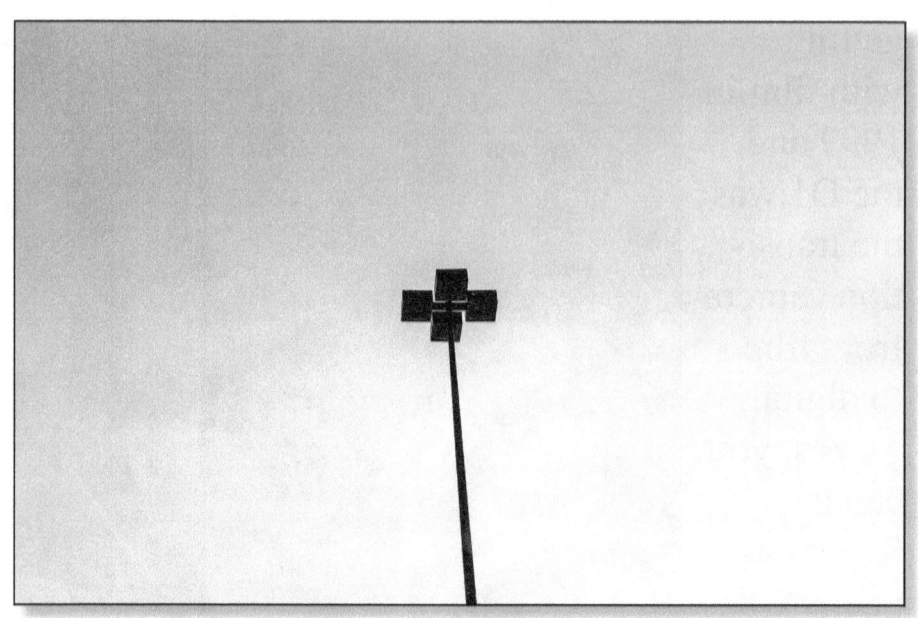

Glenville, NY, Feb. 28, 2014
Nikon D1, 28mm, 1/500, f/11, ISO 320, P, pattern metering
© 2014, 2015 by Shawn M. Tomlinson

won't read it at all or will use 2gb and not the rest.

It will tell you the card is full when you know it is not, but there's no reasoning with it.

The D1 knows best.

Still, RAW images at 2.65 megapixels are only about 4mb, so you get quite a few on a 2gb card. I get about 249.

Obviously, shooting in JPEG will get you more, but why have a pro DSLR and shoot in JPEG?

That's like driving your Ferrari only back and forth to drop the kids off at school.

You can use virtually any capacity CF card up to 2gb, and 2gb CF cards still are reasonably cheap.

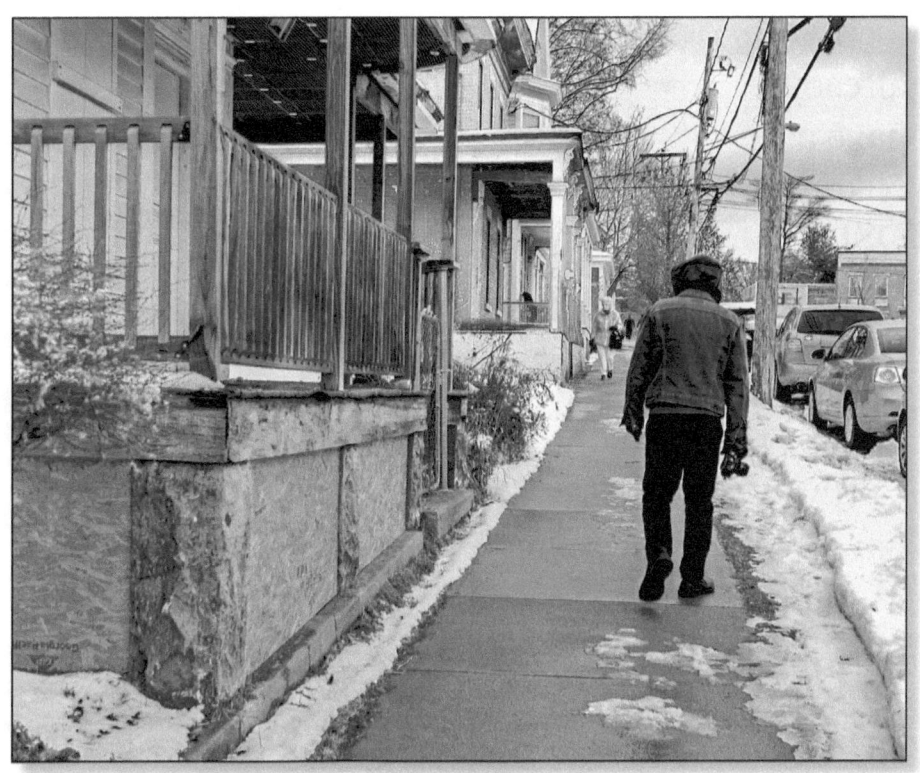

Gary W. Ziroli, Saratoga Springs, NY, Dec. 13, 2014
Nikon D1, 28mm, 1/160, f/5.6, ISO 200, Av, pattern metering
© 2014, 2015 by Shawn M. Tomlinson

You can find them online at places such as Amazon and eBay, as well as at camera dealer websites.

Note that CF cards have one Achilles heel, which is that they have many tiny holes that accept the pins in the camera and the card reader.

It is relatively easy to bend these pins, especially in card readers, if you aren't careful.

4) The lens. Chances are you will not get a lens with your Nikon D1, unless you spend more for a package deal on eBay.

If you already have a Nikon DSLR, your lenses from that will work on the D1.

If you have lenses for an old Nikon film SLR, chances are those lenses will work as well.

The only lenses that do not work that Nikon made are the "invasive" fisheye lenses

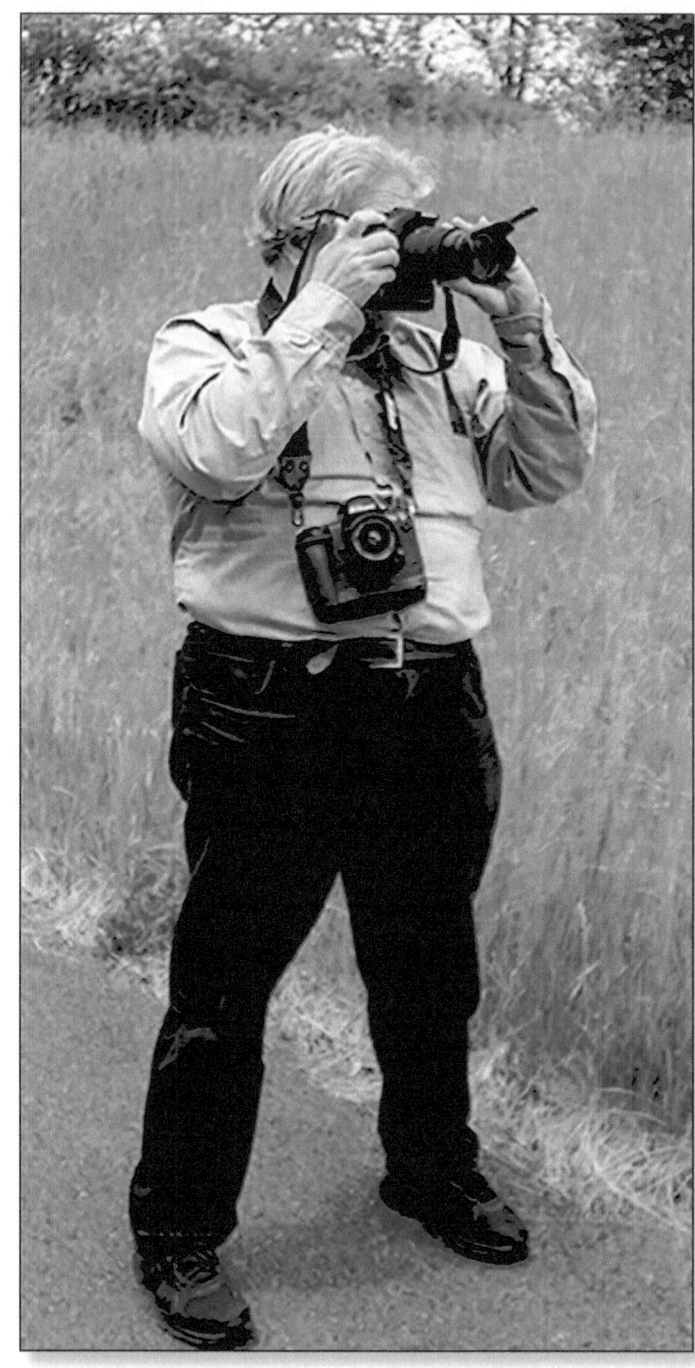

Shawn M. Tomlinson, Rotterdam, NY, May 31, 2014
Canon EOS 10D, 28mm, 1/1000, f/4, ISO 200, S, spot metering
© 2014 by Gary W. Ziroli

— the back of the lens sticks into the camera body and would break the mirror — and what are termed non-AI Nikon lenses.

These are the early lenses built from 1959 to the early 1970s. They have strange-looking prong acceptors on the aperture ring and only one

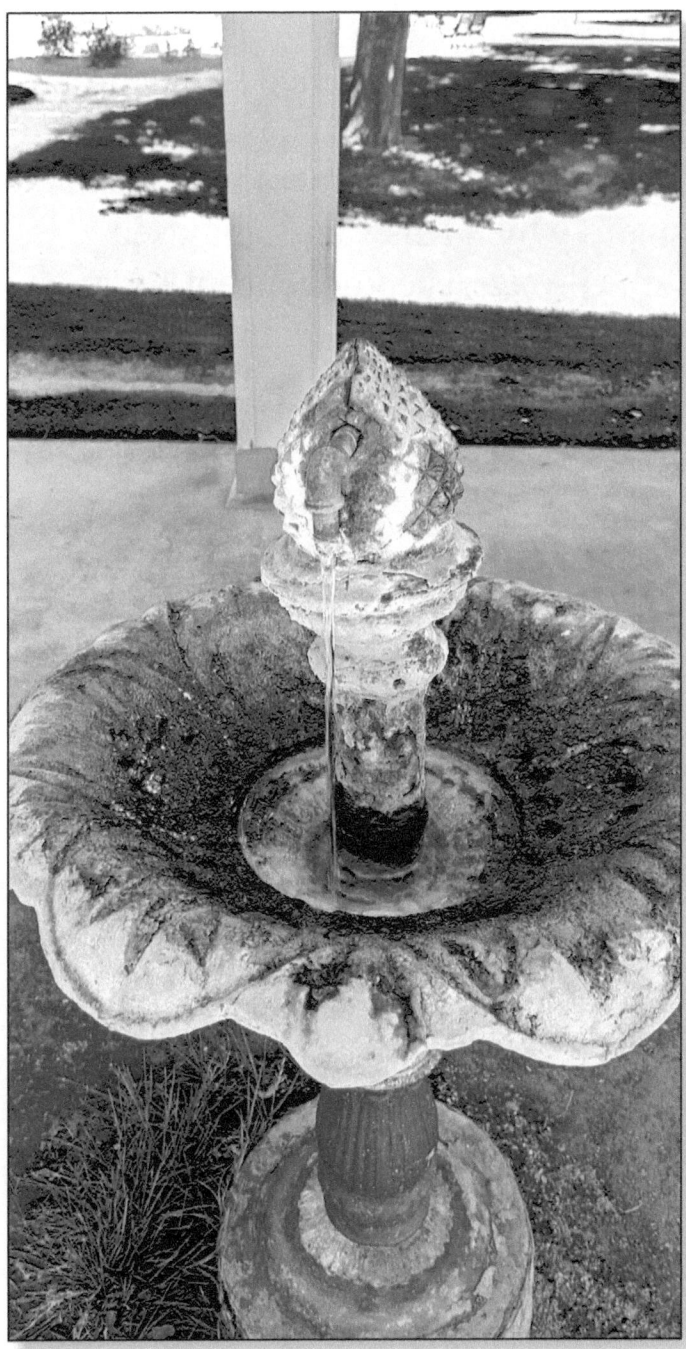

Saratoga Springs, NY, Aug. 19, 2014
Nikon D1, 18mm, 1/80, f/5.6, ISO 200, Av, pattern metering
© 2014 by Shawn M. Tomlinson

set of aperture numbers.

The metal acceptor thingy coupled with a prong sticking out of older, manual Nikon, Nikkormat and Nikomat cameras allowed the camera to adjust its meter according to which lens was being used.

Nikon kept the prong-acceptor concept for a while, but started making auto-indexing (AI) lens-

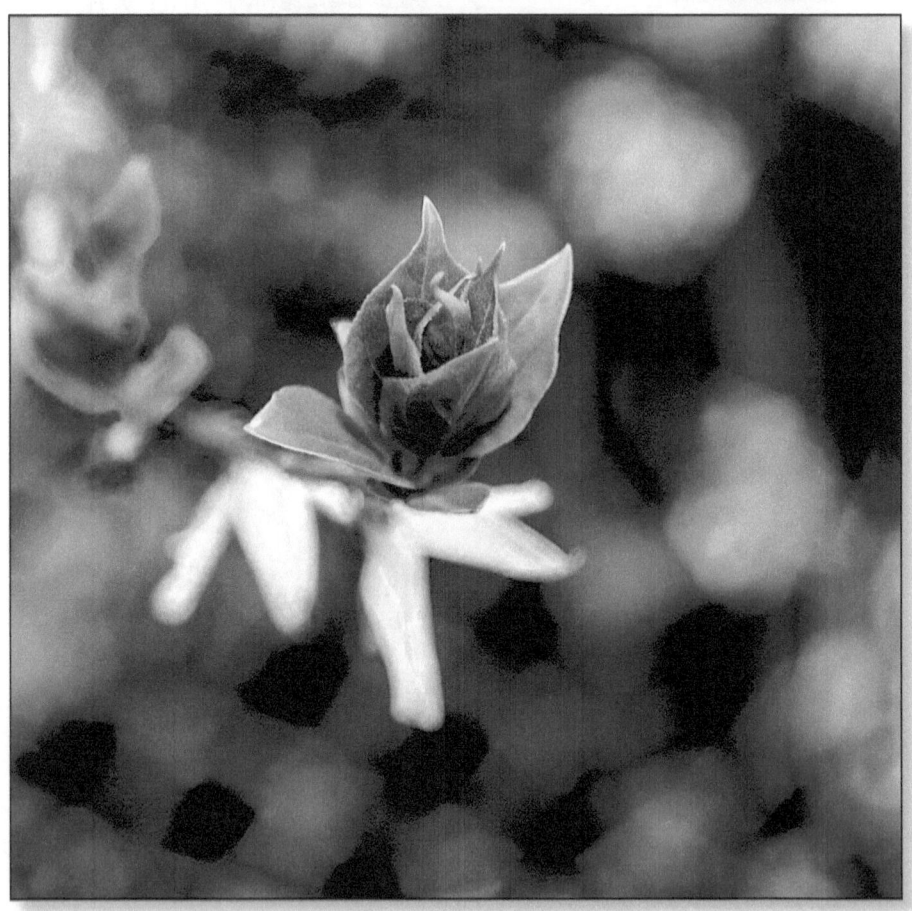

Ballston Lake, NY, May 5, 2014
Nikon D1, 82mm, 1/200, f/5.6, ISO 200, A, pattern
© 2015 Shawn M. Tomlinson

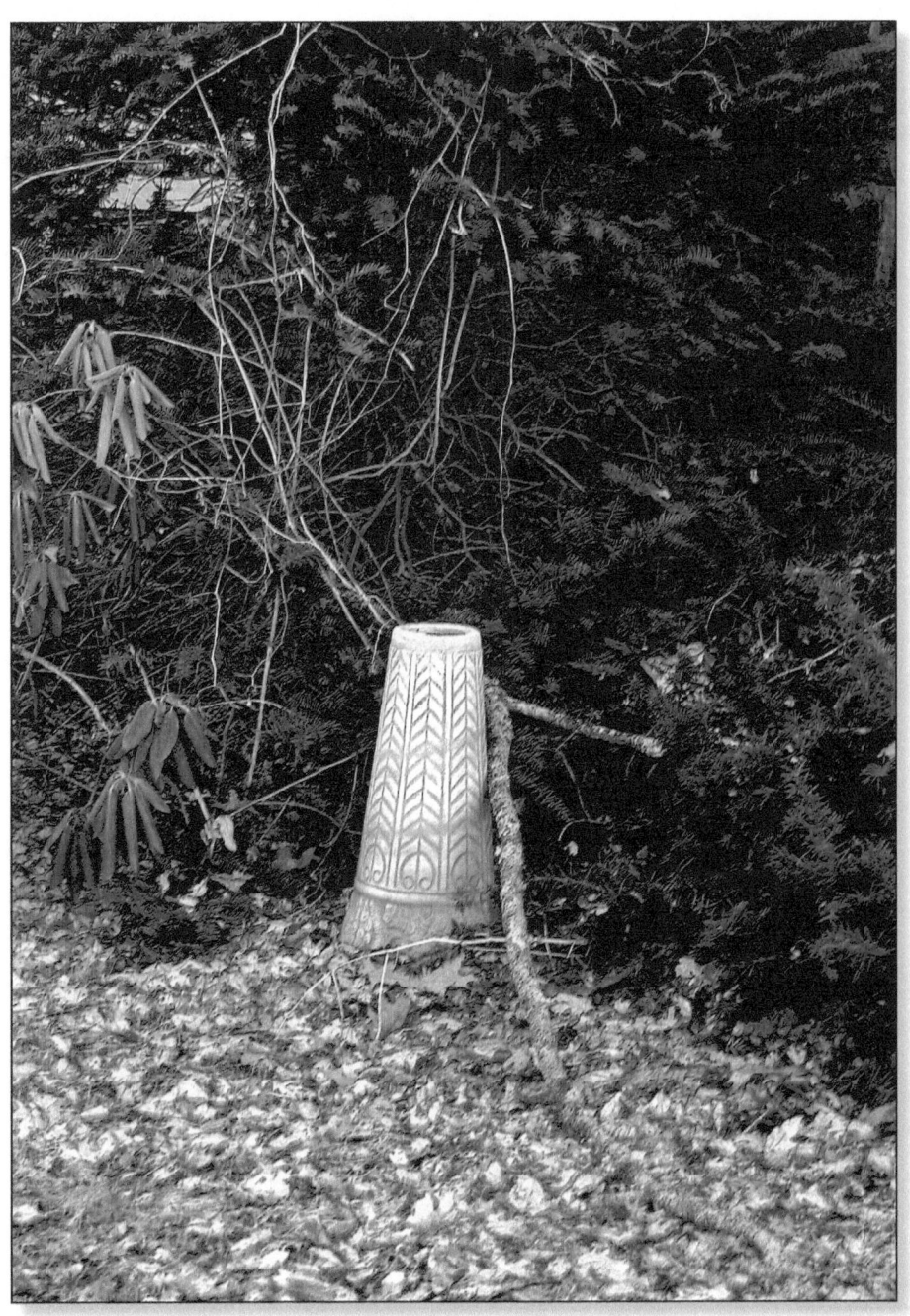

Ballston Lake, NY, April 2, 2014
Nikon D1, 66mm, 1/30, f/5.3, ISO 200, P, pattern metering
© 2014, 2015 by Shawn M. Tomlinson

es.

You can tell the difference between non-AI and AI lenses because close to the lens mount, the AI lenses have a second, identical set of aperture numbers and the non-AI lenses don't.

As long as that second set of aperture numbers is there, the lens will work on the D1.

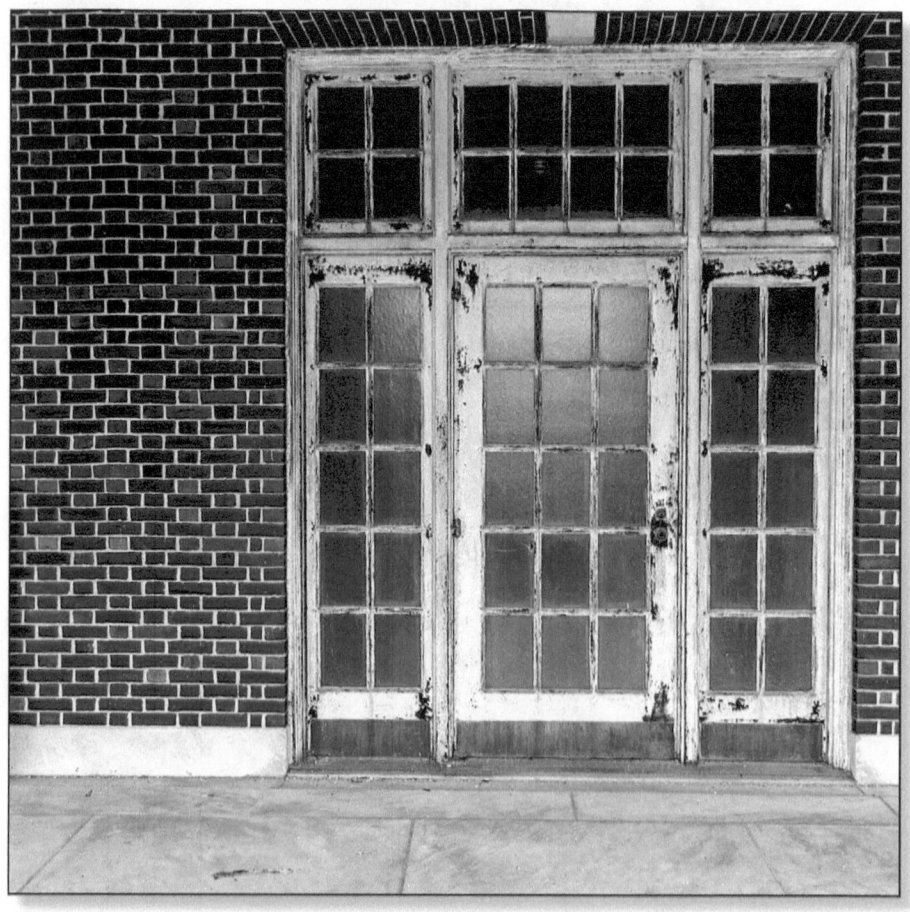

Roosevelt Baths, Saratoga Springs, NY, Aug. 2, 2014
Nikon D1, 18mm, 1/160, f/3.5, ISO 200, A, pattern
© 2015 Shawn M. Tomlinson

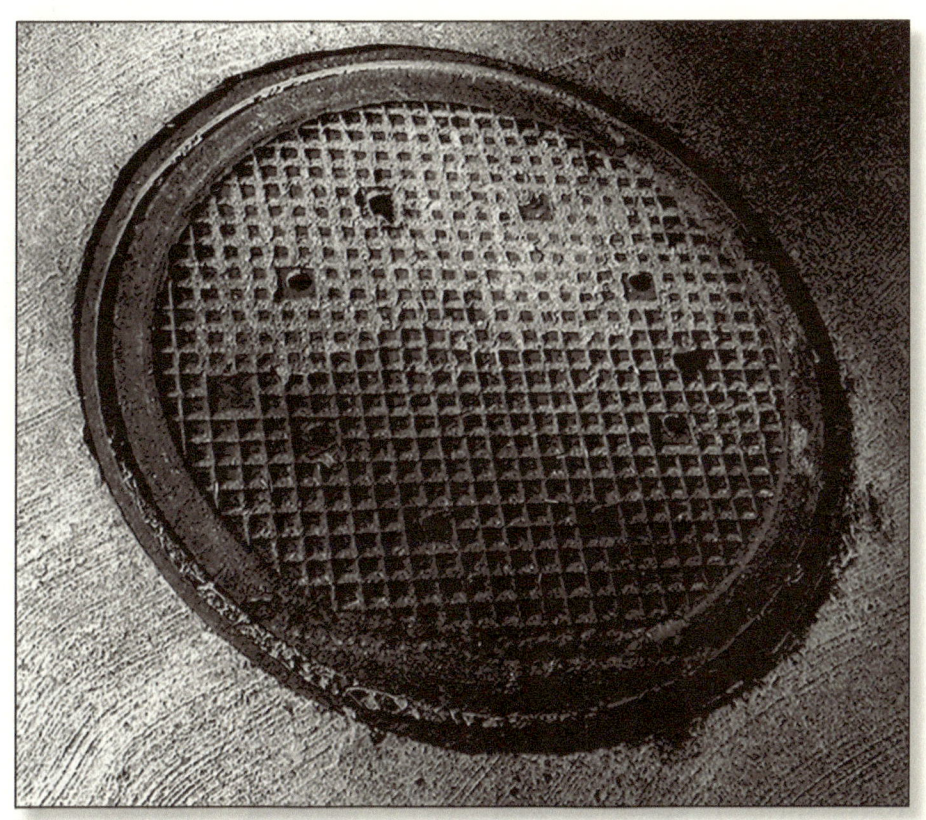

Saratoga Springs, NY, Sept. 24, 2015
Nikon D1x, 28mm (prime), 1/160, f/8, ISO 200, P, pattern
© 2015 Gary W. Ziroli

And, naturally, any Nikon lens without the odd apparatus as long as it is for the "F" mount, also will work, such as Series E and later lenses.

Oh, not lenses labeled Pronea, though. This was an oddball camera from Nikon and the lenses work on nothing except Pronea cameras.

You will have to focus manual lenses manually, of course, and it is best to use aperture-priority (A) mode on the D1.

This
allows you
to man-
ually set
the aper-
ture on the
ring on the
lens and
the cam-
era sets
the shutter
speed ac-
cordingly.
   You also
can go to
full manual
(M) mode
on the D1
and set the
aperture
and shut-
ter speed
yourself.
   If you
do not al-
ready have
a Nikon
lens, prob-

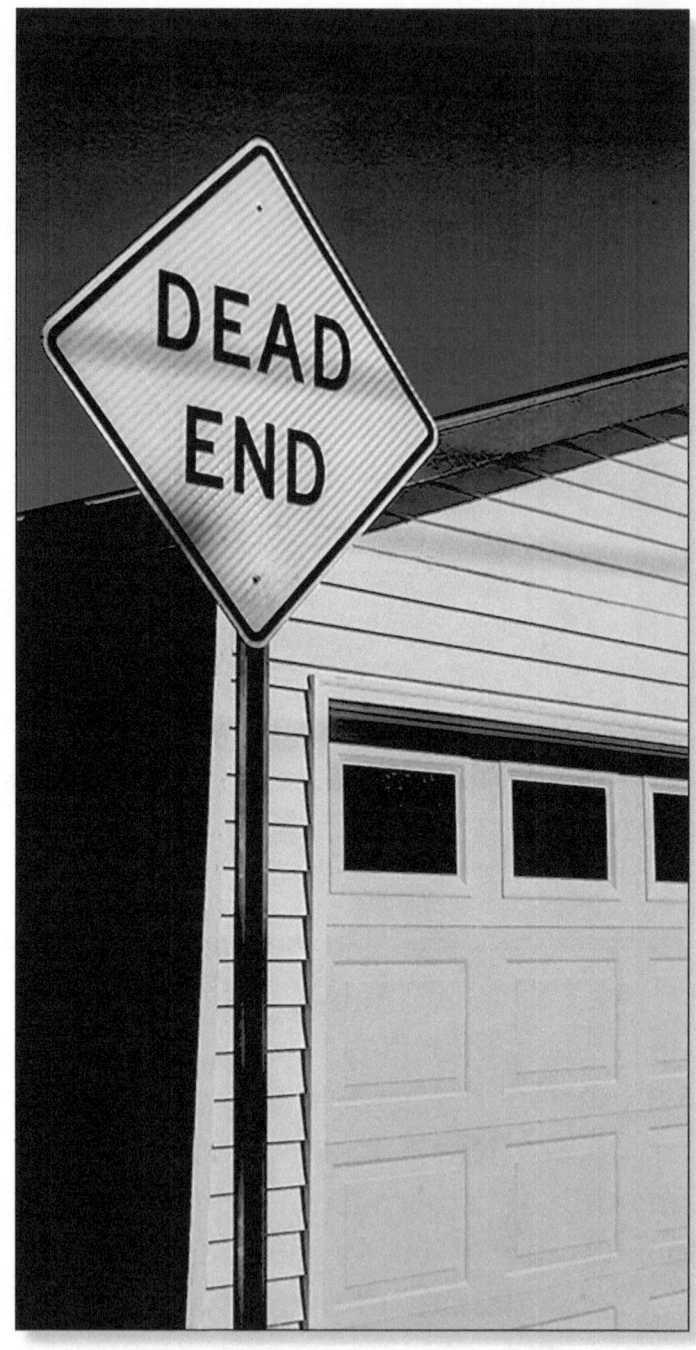

Saratoga Springs, NY, Sept. 24, 2015
Nikon D1x, 28mm (prime), 1/400, f/13, ISO 200, P, pattern
© 2015 Gary W. Ziroli

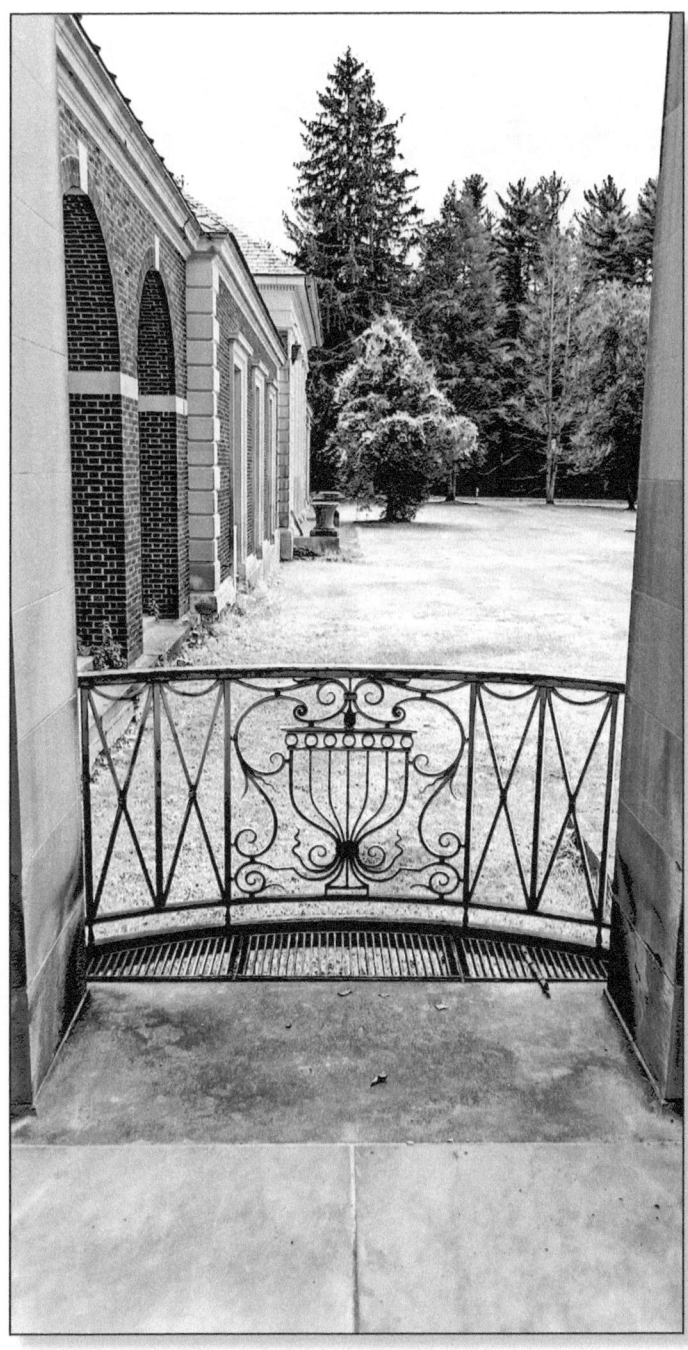

ably the two least expensive lenses to get for it — one or the other — are the Nikon G DX 18-55mm f/3.5-5.6 or the Nikon AF D 50mm f/1.8.

The 18-55mm is known as a "kit" lens because it often is sold with entry-level DSLRs. It is a good all-around and versa-

Roosevelt Baths, Saratoga Springs, NY, Aug. 2, 2014
Nikon D1, 18mm, 1/800, f/3.5, ISO 200, A, pattern
© 2015 Shawn M. Tomlinson

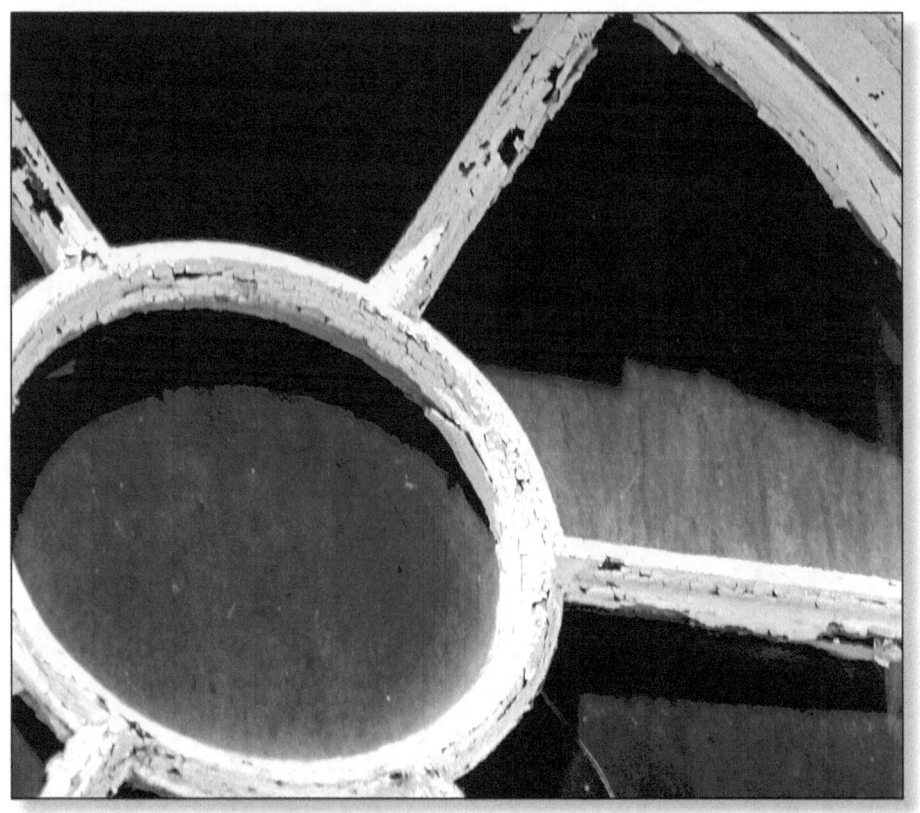

tile lens, but not the sharpest.

The 50mm lens, a prime, will give you quite sharp images and has the bonus of a bright maximum aperture.

Since you really won't be able to use the D1 at anything higher than ISO 400 — and you are most likely to get the best images at ISO 200 — a bright lens is great.

It allows higher shutter speeds when needed.

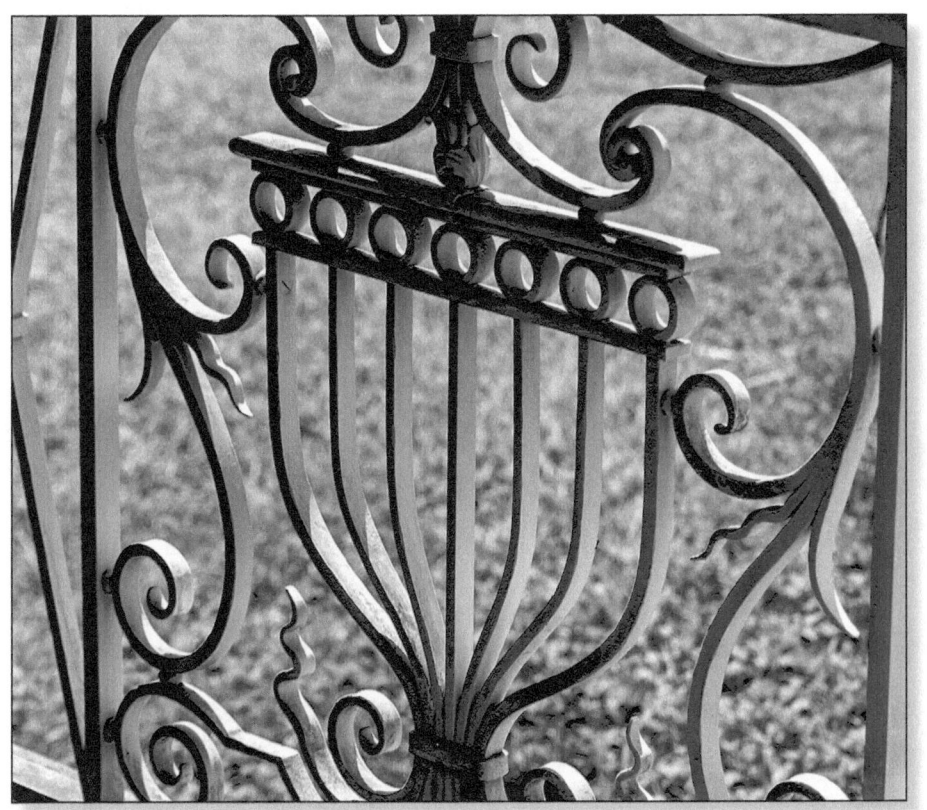

Roosevelt Baths, Saratoga Springs, NY, Aug. 2, 2014
Nikon D1, 70mm, 1/1500, f/4, ISO 200, A, center-weighted
© 2015 Shawn M. Tomlinson

If you want to be able to have the versatility of a zoom lens, than the 18-55mm definitely is your lens.

If you don't mind physically moving yourself, the 50mm is much better.

I'm suggesting these lenses because they keep the budget for the D1 down.

If you want to spend more, it's almost impossible to spend too much on a good lens.

The better then lens, the better the images.

But because both of these lenses are relatively cheap — about $60 for the 18-55mm and about $100 for the 50mm — they keep the cost of the whole package to around $200.

And that is a great bargain, an unbeatable bargain, when it comes to pro DSLRs.

There is no other pro DSLR that sells as cheaply.

The other early pro DSLR, the Canon EOS 1D — which followed the Nikon D1 two years later in 2001 — has slightly better resolution and a better

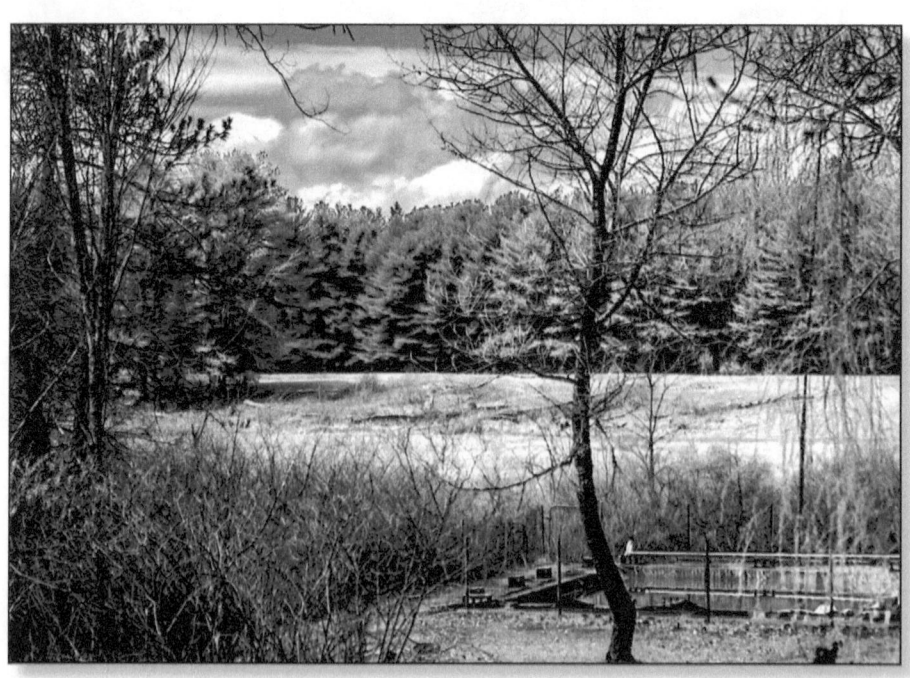

Broadalbin, NY, May 2, 2014
Nikon D1, 82mm, 1/640, f/5.6, ISO 200, A, pattern
© 2015 Shawn M. Tomlinson

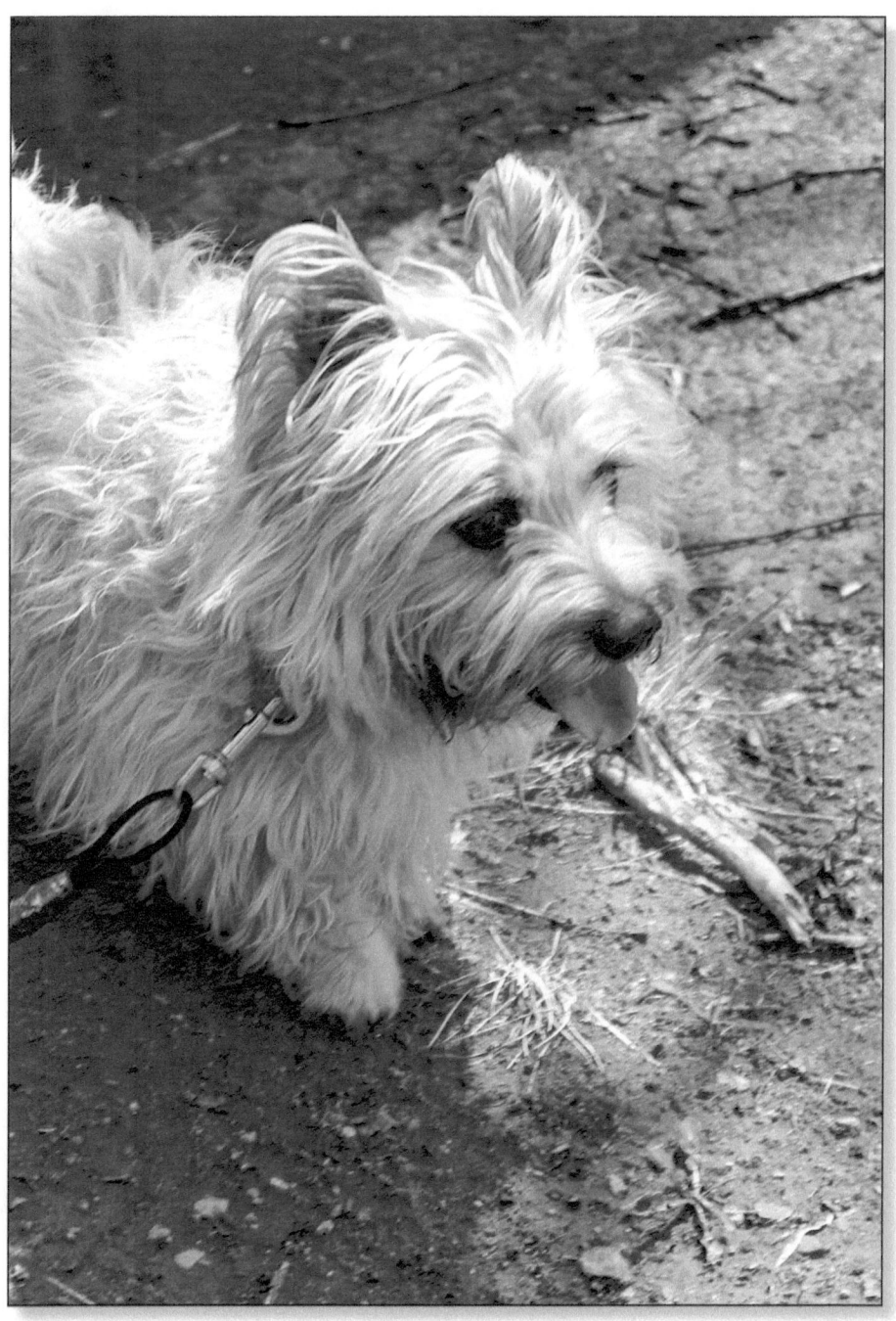

Jake MacDougal, Broadalbin, NY, May 2, 2014
Nikon D1, 82mm, 1/320, f/5.6, ISO 200, A, pattern
© 2015 Shawn M. Tomlinson

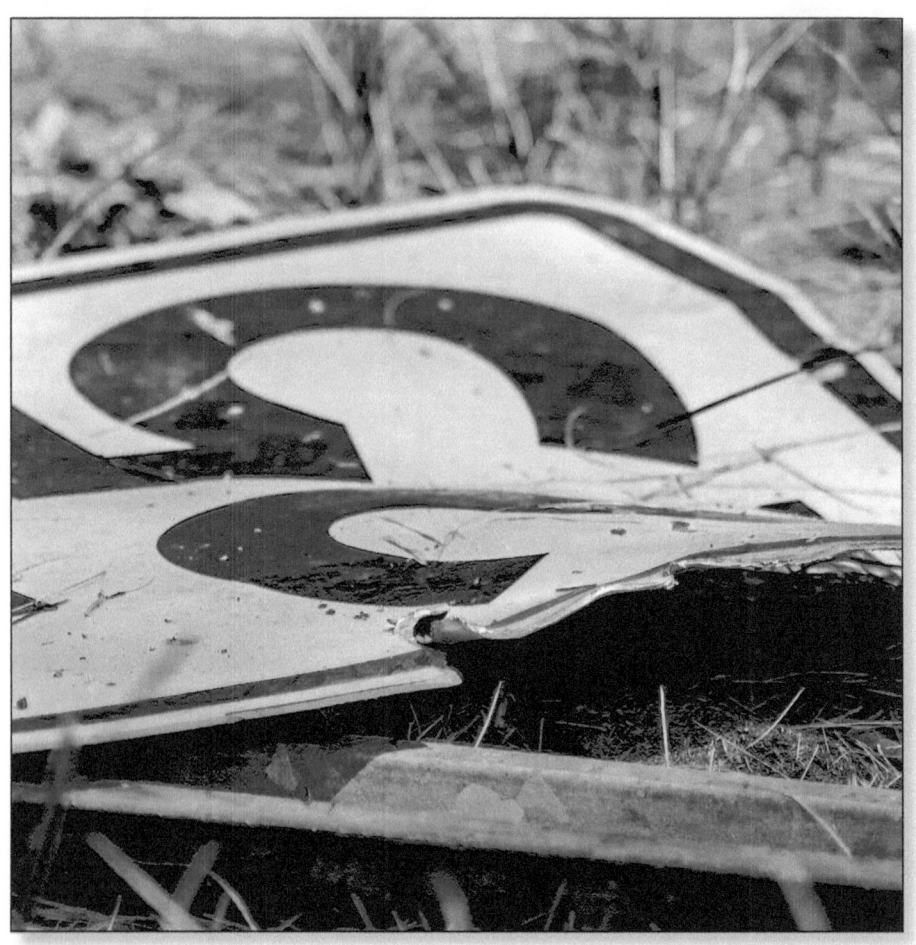

Roosevelt Baths, Saratoga Springs, NY, Aug. 2, 2014
Nikon D1, 300mm, 1/320, f/5.6, ISO 200, A, pattern
© 2015 Shawn M. Tomlinson

APS-C crop factor (1.3x for the Canon, 1.5x for Nikon) usually costs between $150 and $250.

The Nikon D1 simply is the least expensive pro DSLR available.

If nothing else, it is a significant piece of history, but it also is a great camera.

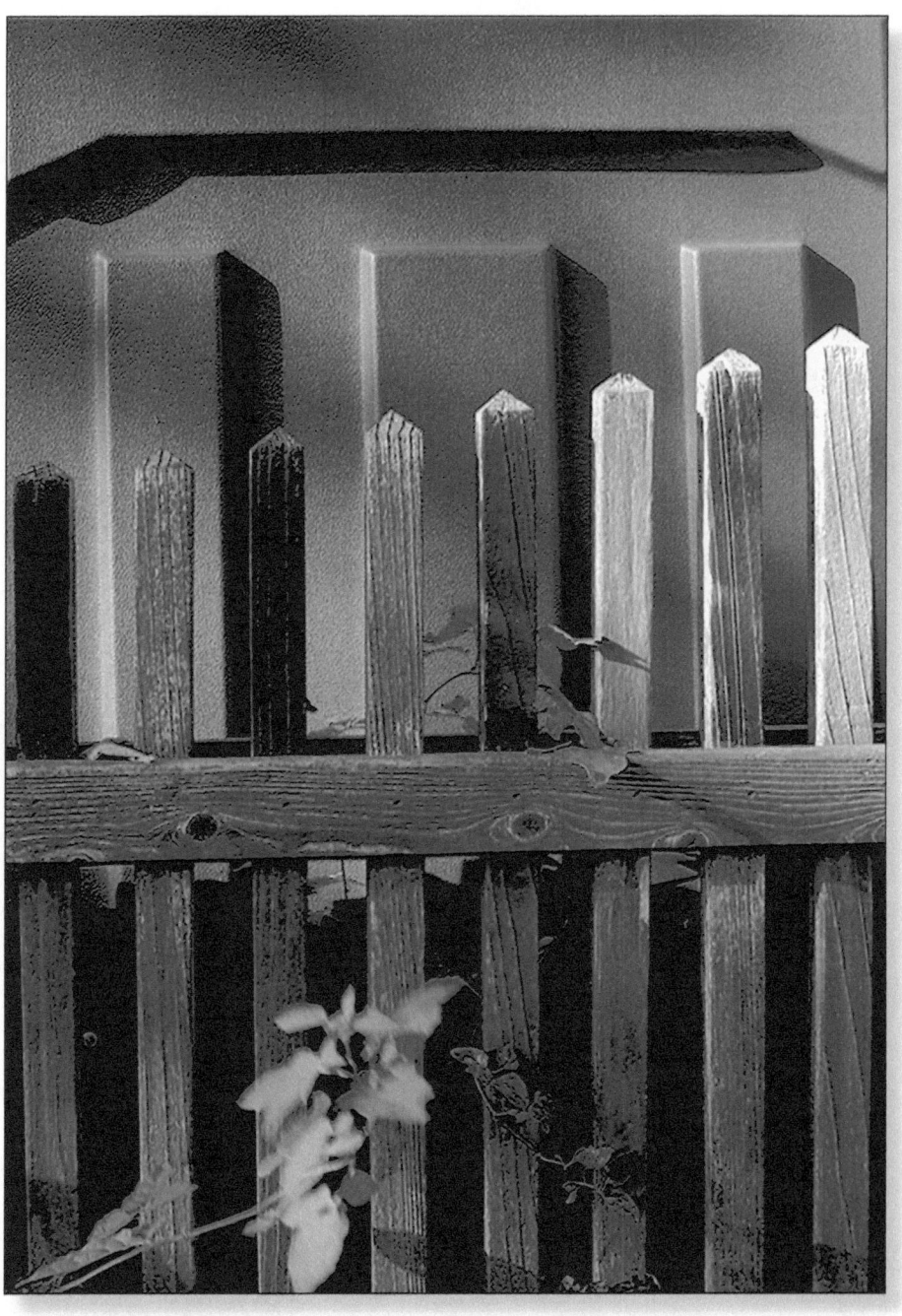

Saratoga Springs, NY, Sept. 24, 2015
Nikon D1x, 28mm (prime), 1/80, f/4.5, ISO 200, P, pattern
© 2015 Gary W. Ziroli

Going Pro for $200 • Page 123

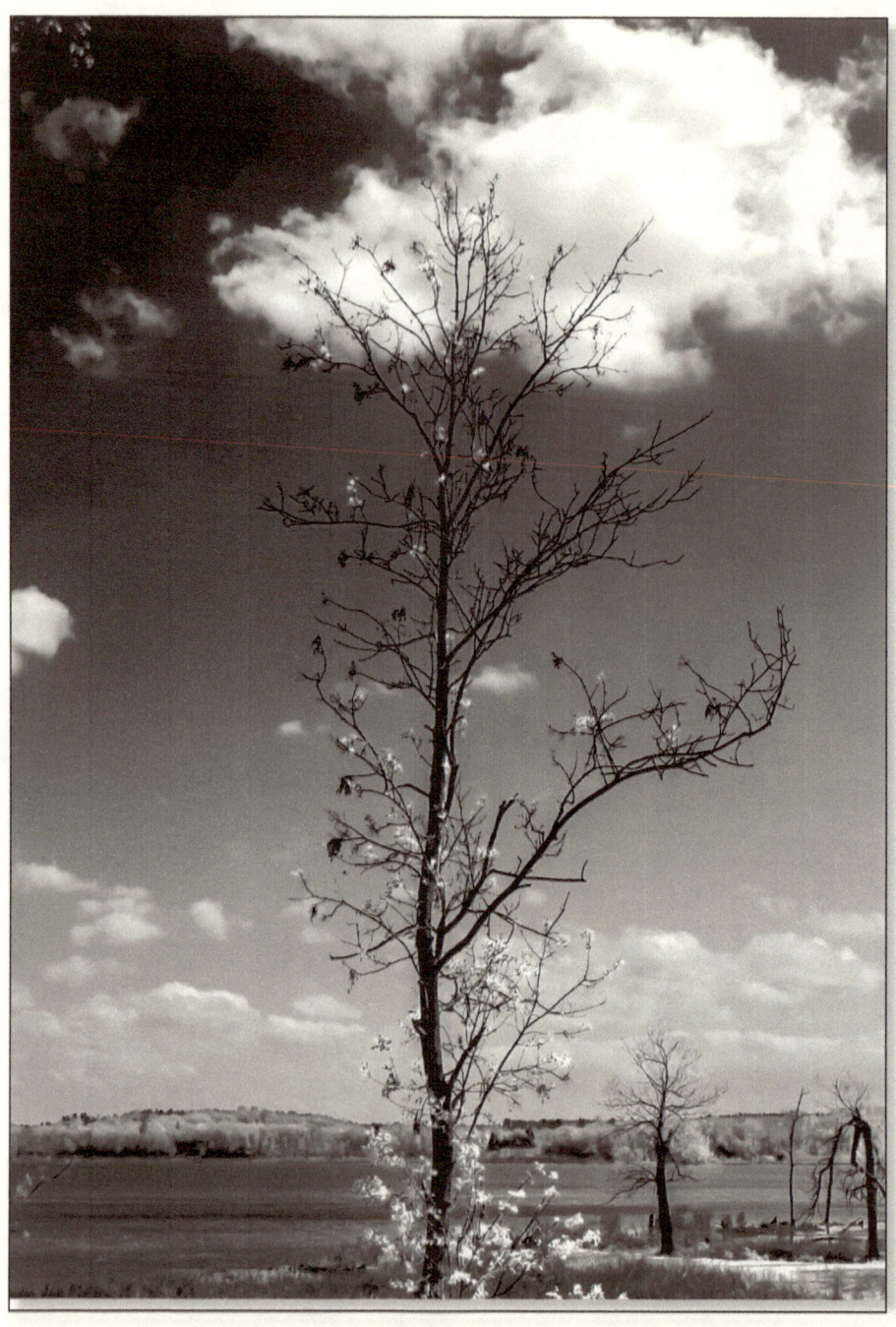

Round Lake, NY, May 17, 2014
Nikon D1, 38mm, 1/1500, f/5.6, ISO 200, Av, pattern metering
© 2014, 2015 by Shawn M. Tomlinson

# *Last Words*

An ancient professional DSLR such as the Nikon D1 isn't for everyone.

The average person who wants to take photos of their pets and post them on Instagram, for example, will find it annoying.

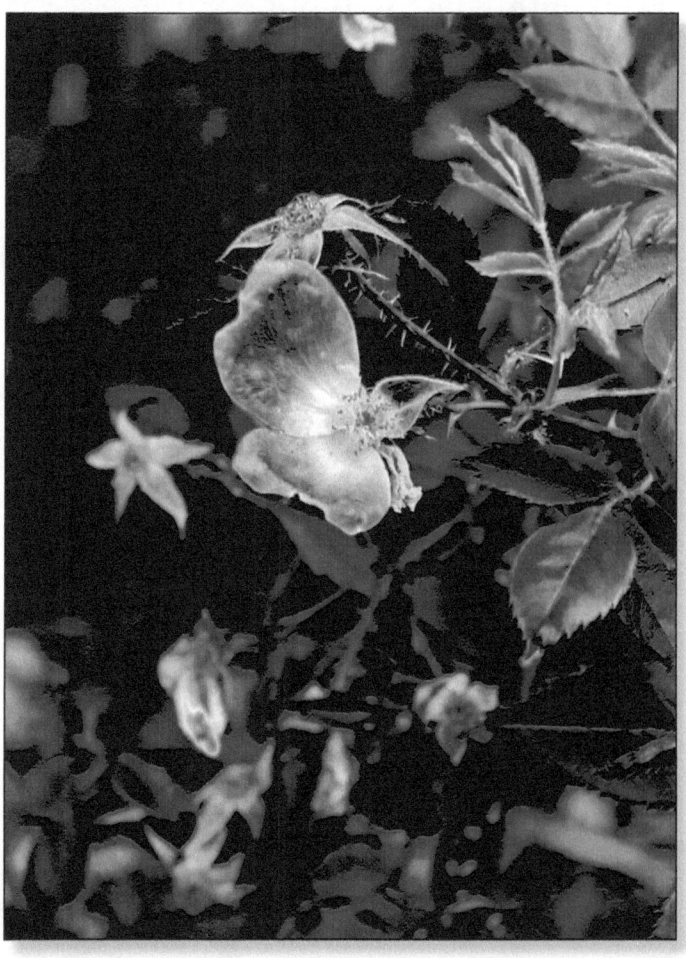

Saratoga Springs, NY, Dec. 13, 2014
Nikon D1, 55mm, 1/60, f/5.6, ISO 200, Av, pattern metering
© 2014 by Shawn M. Tomlinson

It really is for the photographer enthusiast who wants to know what its like to shoot with a pro DSLR but does not want to or cannot afford to pay the thousands of dollars required for a modern one.

The D1 these days is a quirky, fun, experimental DSLR camera that will give you lots of enjoyment as an enthusiast without costing a lot.

And there's nothing wrong with that.

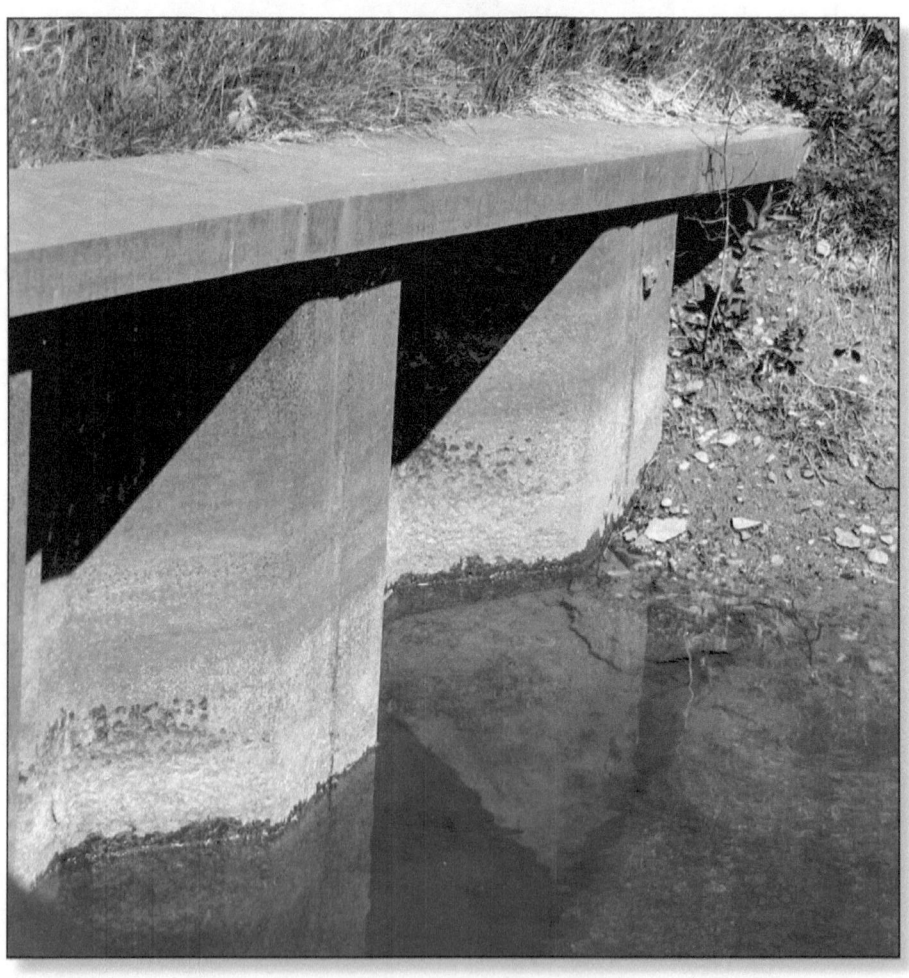

Round Lake, NY, May 17, 2014
Nikon D1, 80mm, 1/500, f/5.6, ISO 200, Av, pattern metering
© 2014, 2015 by Shawn M. Tomlinson

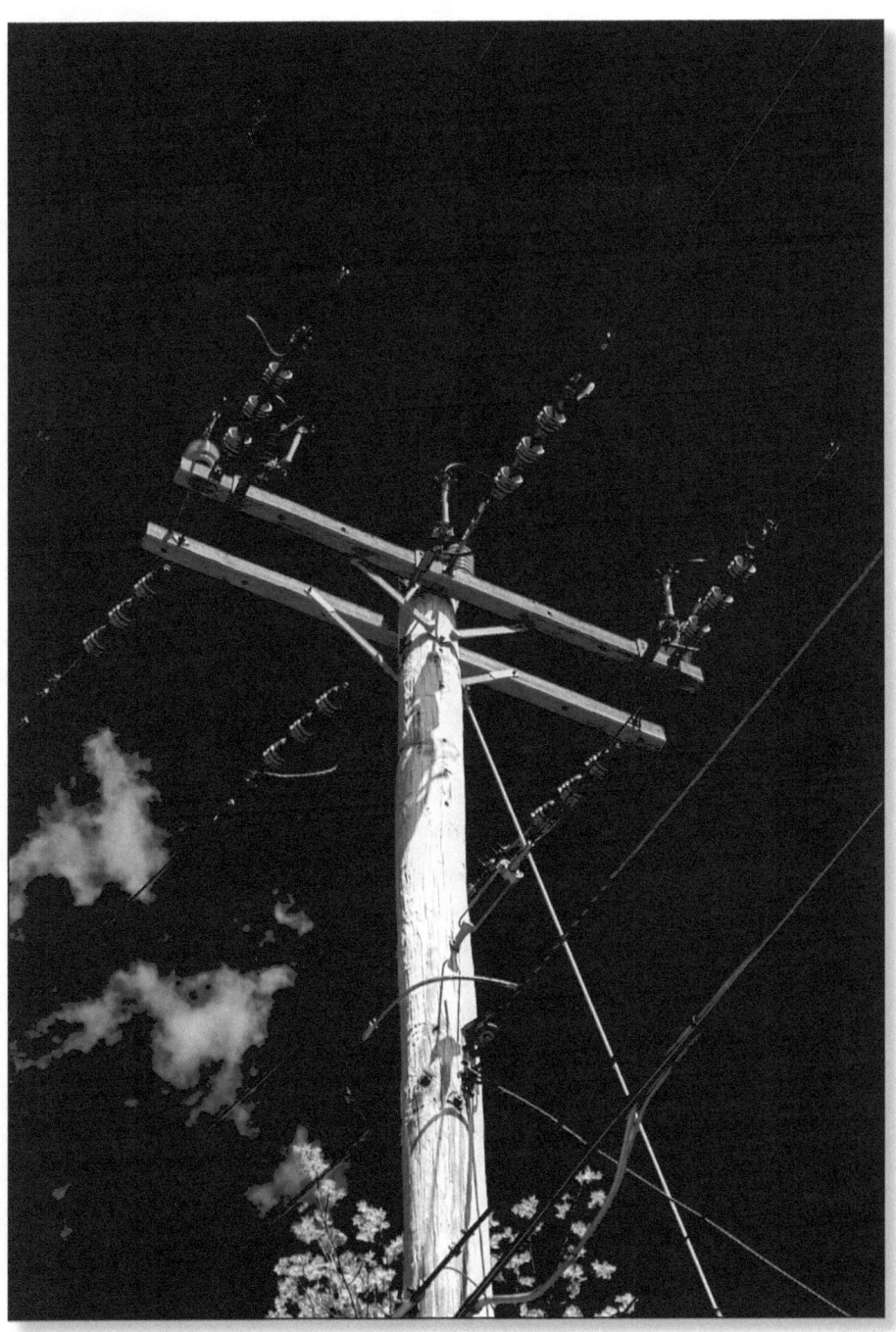

Round Lake, NY, May 17, 2014
Nikon D1, 48mm, 1/1000, f/5.6, ISO 200, Av, pattern metering
© 2014, 2015 by Shawn M. Tomlinson

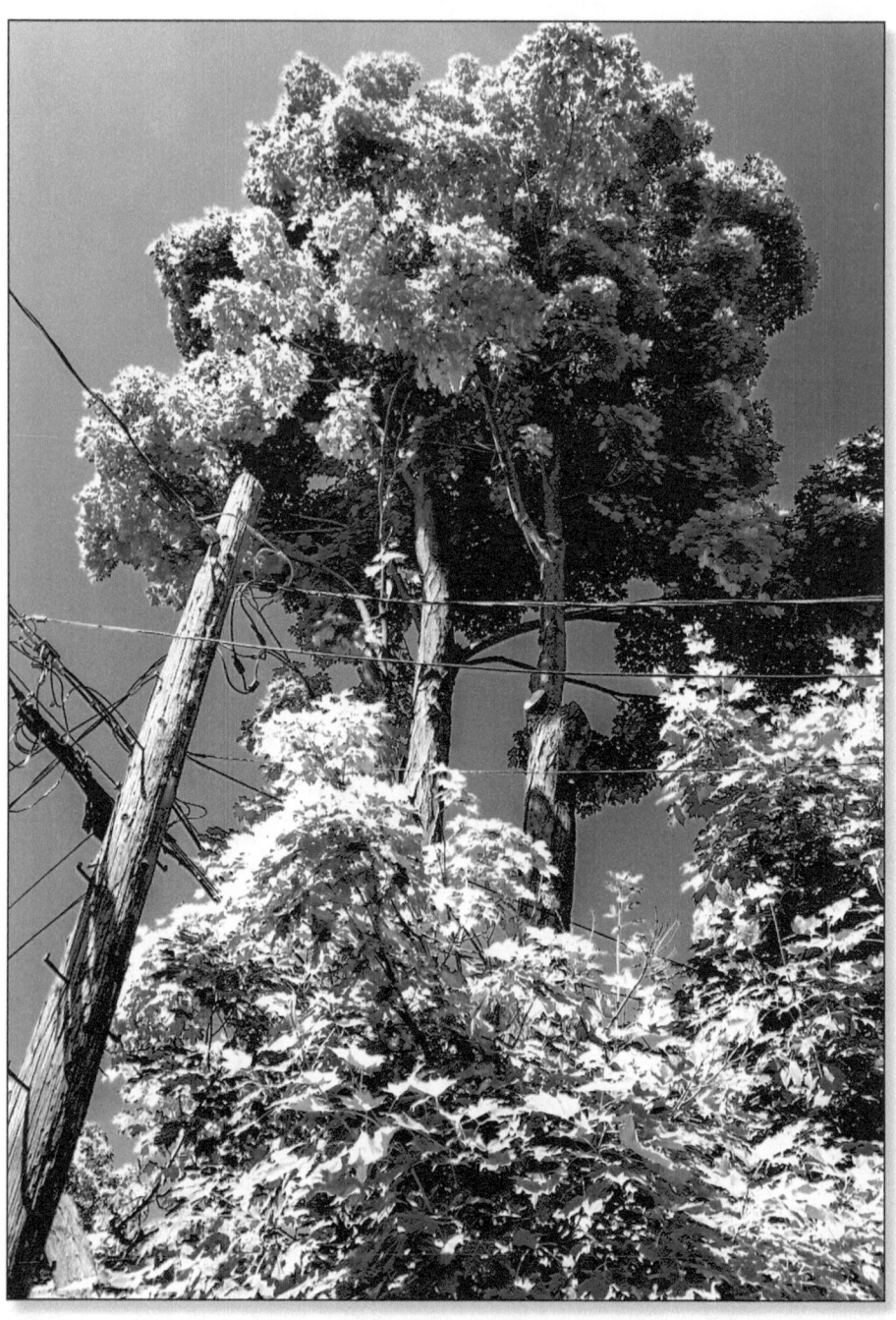

Saratoga Springs, NY, Aug. 19, 2014
Nikon D1, 18mm, 1/500, f/5.6, ISO 200, Av, pattern metering
© 2014 by Shawn M. Tomlinson

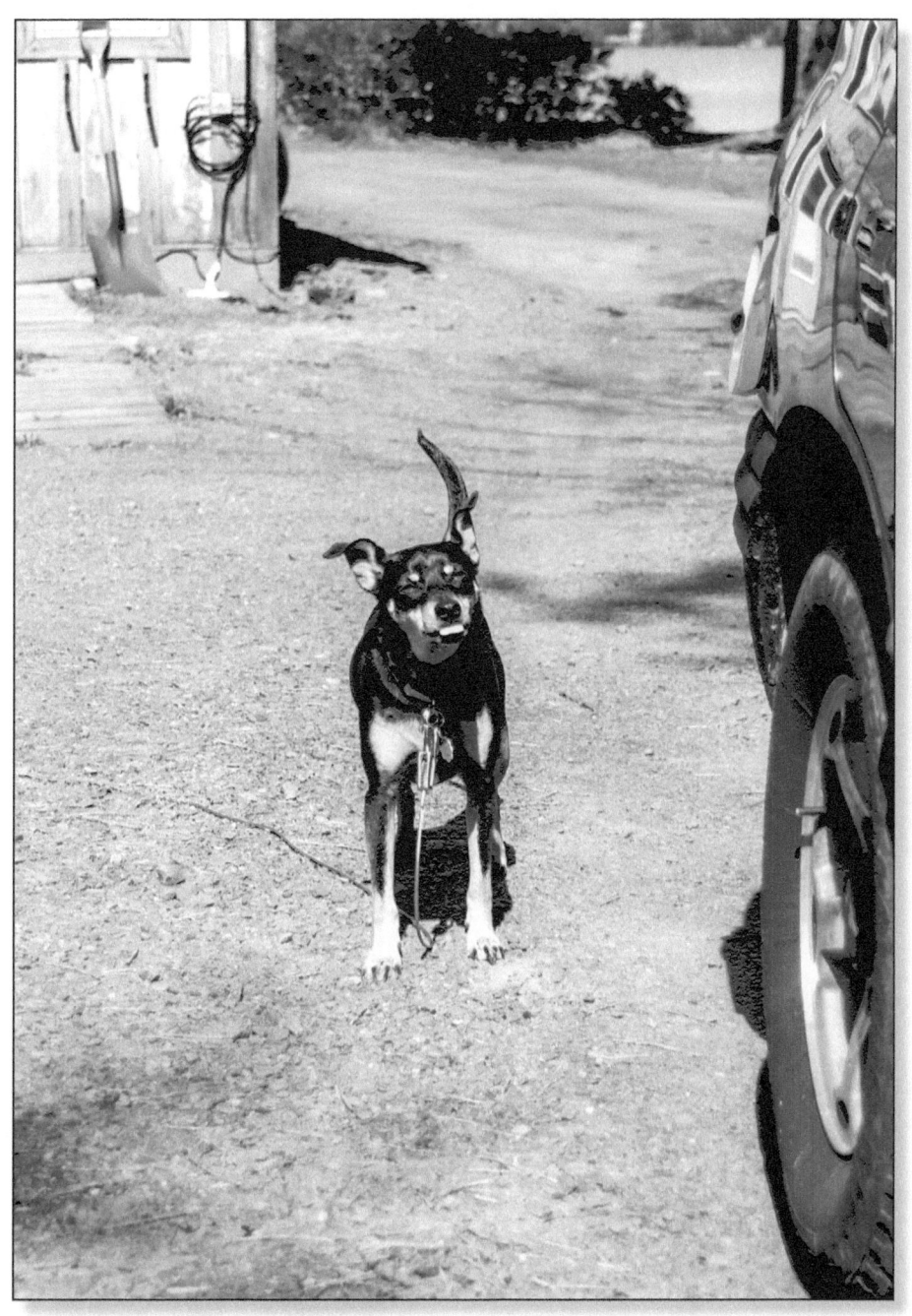

Oscar, Caroga Lake, NY, May 20, 2014
Nikon D1, 75mm, 1/1600, f/5.6, ISO 400, Av, pattern metering
© 2014, 2015 by Shawn M. Tomlinson

# Shawn M. Tomlinson's Guide to Photography Series

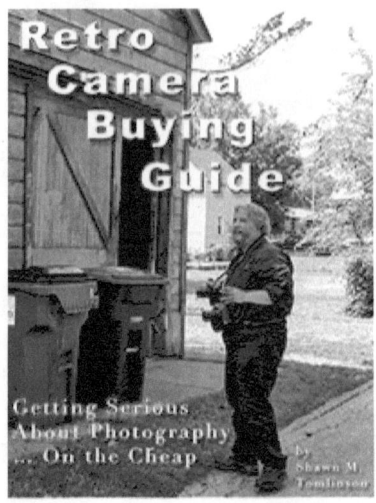

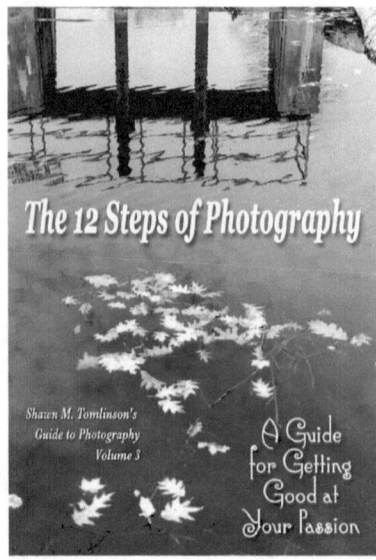

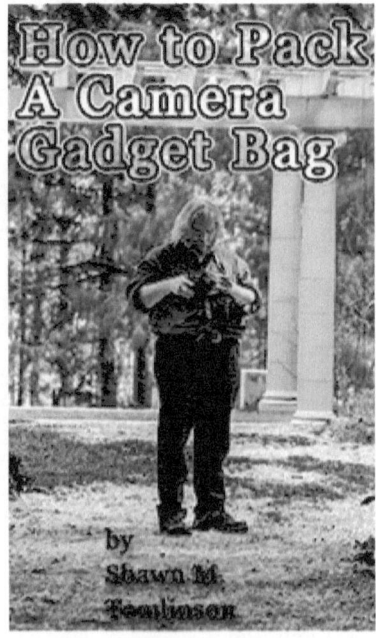

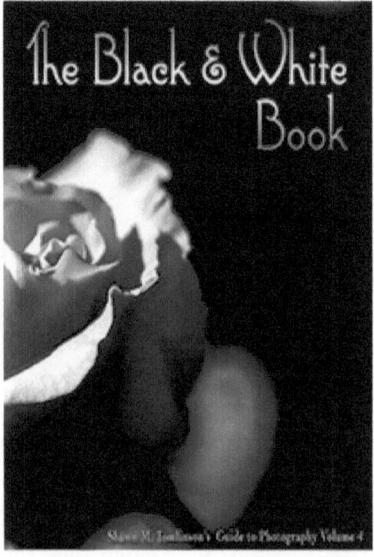

# Shawn M. Tomlinson's Guide to Photography Series

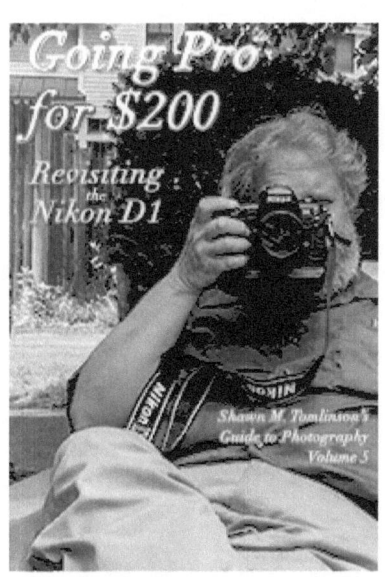

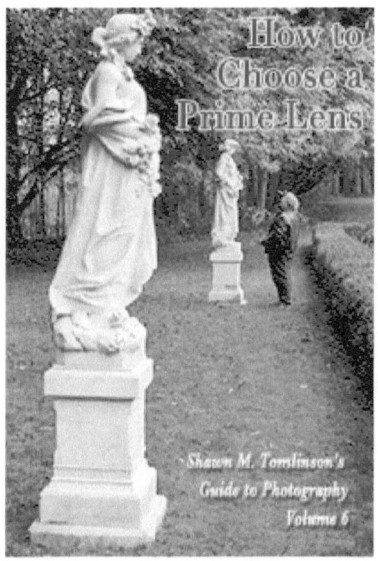

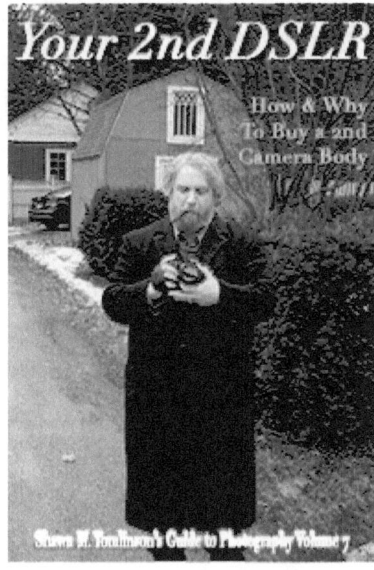

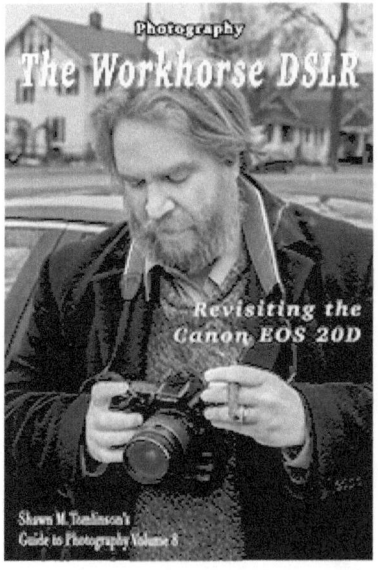

# Shawn M. Tomlinson's Guide to Photography Series

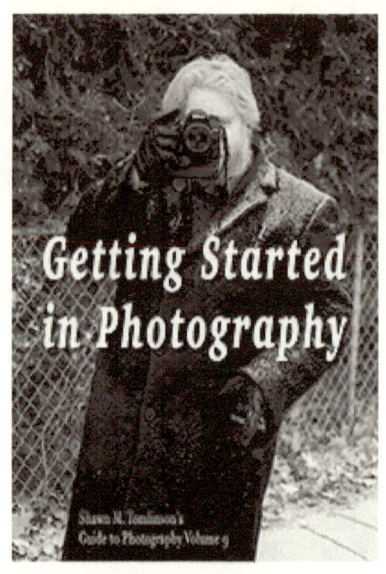

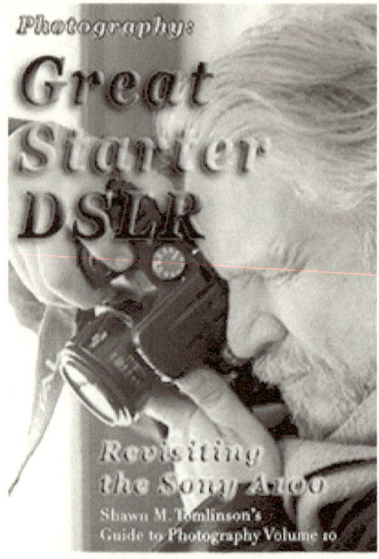

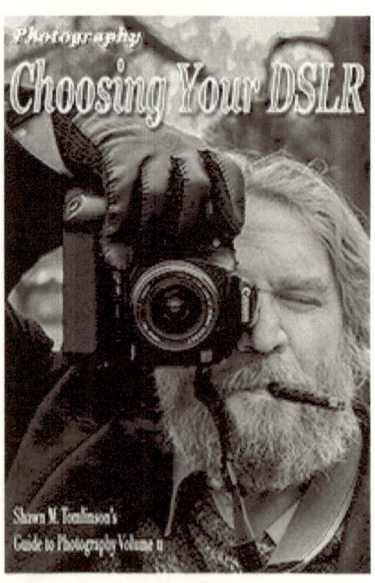

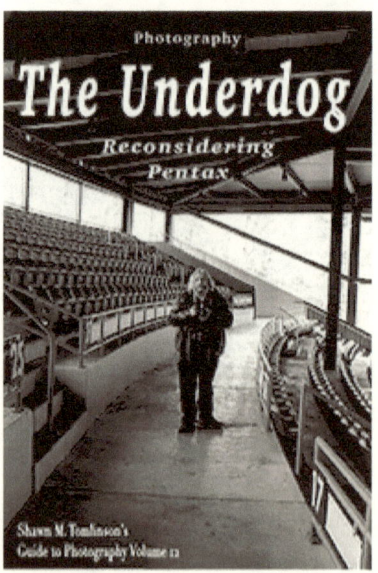

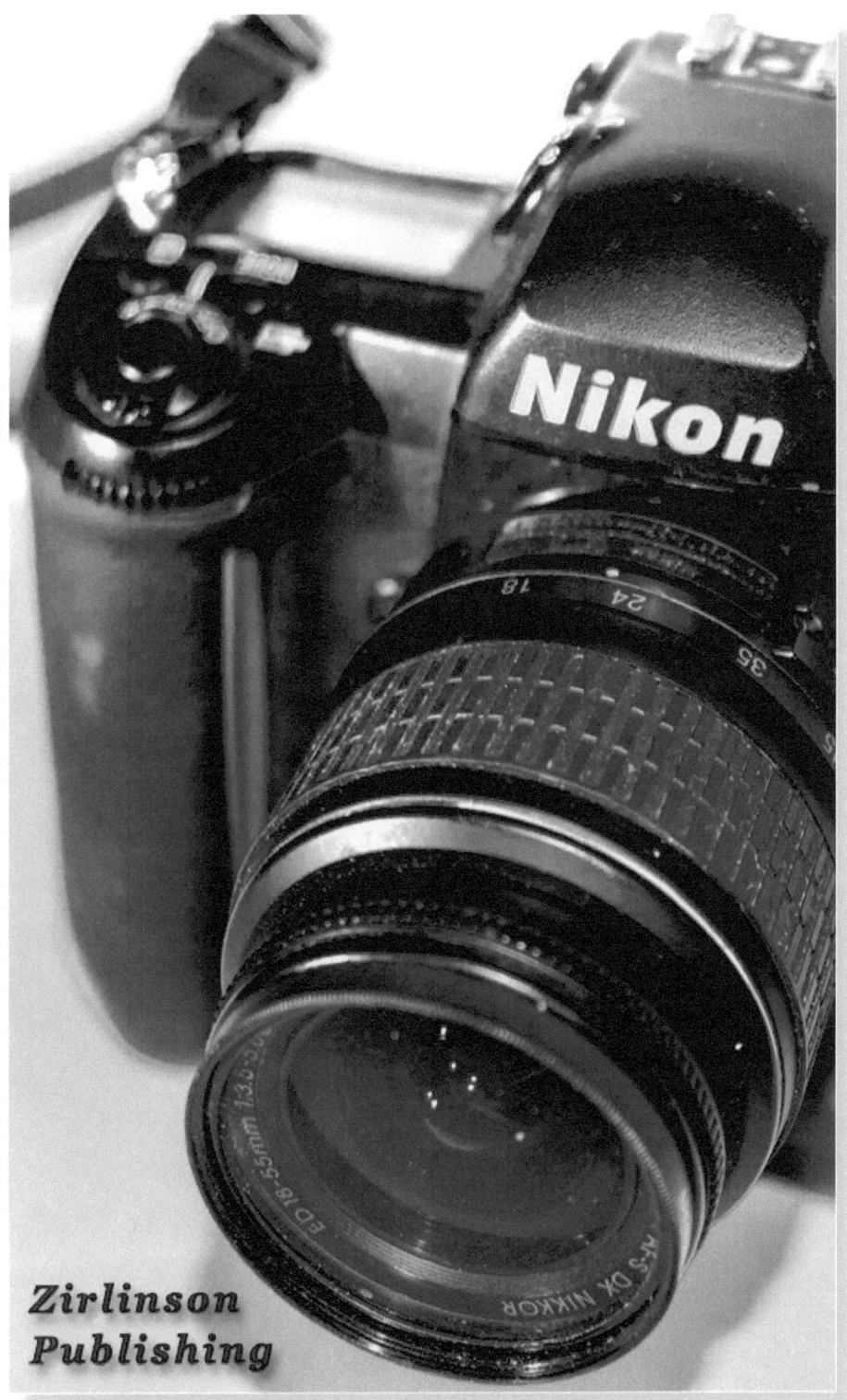

Zirlinson
Publishing